Tim Kelsey is a senior journ[illegible] his career based in Turkey, cove[illegible] as well as Turkish issues. He worked for the *I[illegible]pendent* for several years and, as a broadcaster, has made documentaries for British television. He lives in Sussex with his family.

TIM KELSEY

Dervish

The Invention of Modern Turkey

PENGUIN BOOKS

For Ali and Christopher

PENGUIN BOOKS

Published by the Penguin Group
Penguin Books Ltd, 27 Wrights Lane, London W8 5TZ, England
Penguin Books USA Inc., 375 Hudson Street, New York, New York 10014, USA
Penguin Books Australia Ltd, Ringwood, Victoria, Australia
Penguin Books Canada Ltd, 10 Alcorn Avenue, Toronto, Ontario, Canada M4V 3B2
Penguin Books (NZ) Ltd, 182–190 Wairau Road, Auckland 10, New Zealand

Penguin Books Ltd, Registered Offices: Harmondsworth, Middlesex, England

Frist published by Hamish Hamilton 1996
Published in Penguin Books 1997
1 3 5 7 9 10 8 6 4 2

Printed in England by Clays Ltd, St Ives plc

Contents

Acknowledgements

Many people have helped me complete this book. I cannot identify most of them, which is a sad reflection on the country they all love in their different ways. This book could not have happened without Ersoy Haktanir, my friend and long-suffering travelling companion; or Keith Jordan, with whom I shared some frightening (exciting) weeks in the East. It would have been a great deal more difficult had the Society of Authors not awarded me a Kay Blundell trust grant to cover some of the costs of research. I cannot thank them enough.

Dr Metin Kunt and Professor Metin And were among the many prominent academics who took the time to share with me their insights into the history of the Ottomans. David Barchard was consistently helpful. Orhan Pamuk, the novelist and historian, was among the most influential. The staff at the British Library were always helpful; and so too, in my brief encounter, were the workers at the Ottoman Archives in Istanbul.

Ahmet Ersoy, then press attaché at the embassy in London, persuaded the Turkish authorities to let me visit the prison, and helped me in countless other ways. Merih at the Ministry of Information in Ankara was unfailingly courteous and as helpful as she could be. Okay Temiz, the Moguls, Genco Erkal, Huysus Virgin, Omer Kavur and Ugur Yucel showed me what it is to be a Turkish artist; as did Metin Demirtas and Hulya Ugurlu, neither of whom will ever realize just how much I respected them. My former employers at the *Independent* kindly gave me the time to research the book. Hugh Pope put me right on many misconceptions. Brian Cathcart and Angus Mackinnon both took the time to read the draft and made some very valuable criticisms. Needless to say, what I have written and any mistakes I may have made are mine alone.

I owe a great deal to my agents Toby Eady, who had the original idea for this book, and Alexandra Pringle, who saw the book through from start to finish. I could not have wished for more brilliant publishers than Andrew Franklin or Sally Abbey.

Above all, I owe my greatest debt to my family. Ali cajoled, encouraged, and inspired much of this book. She spotted most of my mistakes and never once complained about my long absences or the ridiculous hours. I am very lucky. She is a unique and wonderful person.

Prologue

Five years ago Yusuf Tavukcu was a farmer in the north-western province of Canakkale. His name, literally, means 'chicken man'; in fact he raised pigs. There was strong demand for pork, he said, among foreigners and young Westernized Turks who bore no loyalty to the old Islamic taboos against consumption of the meat. Turkey is, in any case, constitutionally a secular state.

But his neighbours, encouraged by their local imam, or priest, denounced him as a 'devil worshipper'. During a night raid they attacked his farm and butchered most of the animals, many of which, Mr Tavukcu said later, were pregnant. 'They came and killed most of them by breaking their bellies and feet,' he said. He saved only twenty-five of his fifty-six pigs.

The local court, to which he had gone pleading assistance, ordered him not to feed the surviving animals. 'I saw the starving ones eating each other,' he said sadly. Shortly afterwards a higher court intervened to order the permanent closure of the farm. He had secretly been feeding a handful of pigs and was fined accordingly when discovered by local snoopers. The court claimed that the farm was unhygienic.

A national newspaper columnist took up the case and argued that the farmer should be free to raise his pigs. He cited the massacre as evidence of growing religious radicalism in Turkey – which, in all fairness, it was. Mr Tavukcu was reluctantly forced to abandon his farm. He later burned the carcasses of the remaining animals.

Burning is what we have become used to now from the Turks. While I write this, the Turkish army is embarked on the biggest offensive in its recent history against Kurdish insurgents in the south-east of the country. Thirty thousand troops, supported from the air and with heavy artillery on the ground, have advanced along the Iraqi border with the stated intention of massacring all the Kurdish guerrillas they can find. Generals have talked about wiping out the Kurdish fighters. In all likelihood the campaign will fail to meet that objective. In the meantime they are burning villages that are accused of supporting the insurgents.

Pigs and Kurds. Modern Turkey is struggling to hold itself together. On almost every front the nightmare of disintegration appears more like imminent reality. The religious revivalists grow more influential – they have recently taken control of many city councils – and threaten to undermine the secularity of Ataturk's seventy-year-old Republic. The Kurdish threat grows more dangerous as ordinary villagers, who had formerly associated their fortunes with the Turkish state, are alienated by its increasingly indiscriminate violence against them.

This is not the Turkey one encounters in the resort towns along the Mediterranean or Aegean coasts – in Bodrum or Marmaris or any other of the holiday destinations familiar to the millions of Europeans who visit Turkey each year. I have not written about the resort towns partly because there is little that I can add to the vast literature that already exists. There is another reason: they are summer colonies to which Turks, as much as Europeans, escape from the rigours of ordinary working life. In this sense they are on the fringes of the great debate that rages inside Anatolia.

This book is a debate about the relationship between the past and the present. It is about destiny. Is Turkey to be a western European democracy or an eastward-facing Islamically inclined state? It is an argument which, in different ways, absorbs every person who lives within its borders, all caught up in the increasingly tense conflict between custom and change.

In their past, the Ottomans drew strength from the diversity of the many different peoples that made this land their home; for the modern Turkish state, diversity inspires insecurity, and as far as it can, it has repressed difference in the interests of national unity. But time has not taken its side: the Kurds awaken to their ethnicity, and others may follow suit; the religious begin to pursue historic prejudices against each other and the non-believers.

The world has good reason to be concerned about Turkey. It is in one of the most turbulent corners of the globe. On one side it borders the new republics of the former Soviet Union; on the other, Syria, Iraq and Iran; and on the third, Greece and the Balkans. Generally it is said that the gravest threat to peace in the Middle East is the conflict between the Palestinians and the Israelis, but there is a good argument that the more serious problem is with the stateless Kurds.

Turkey is a vital conduit for oil from Central Asia and the Middle East; it controls the headwaters of the Tigris and the Euphrates on which several desert nations are reliant for their water. Turkey has traditionally played the part of honest broker in the Middle East and Central Asia: it is neutral territory on which rival states can peacefully arbitrate their disputes. It played an important role in maintaining dialogue between the Israelis and the Palestinians when most had given up hope of settlement. Turkey is the bulwark of NATO, its easternmost member. Instability in Turkey has consequences that travel far beyond its own borders.

Pessimists – and the Turks are notoriously fatalistic – believe that the country stands on the edge of an abyss about which it can do nothing. But optimists – and I am one of those – believe that it is never too late. For success, Turkey needs to remember its history and take a leaf out of the Ottomans' book. Toleration can be a real asset. Turkey is still home to many different people, and all should feel a part of its great national adventure.

To the outsider, it is precisely the survival of variety – ethnic and religious – that makes Turkey so attractive. I wrote this book a decade after I first visited the country as an art history student, encouraged to study the work of the great Ottoman architect Sinan. It is his mosques that still dominate the picture-postcard skyline of Istanbul. There is still that hint of mighty self-confidence.

This journey starts with another symbol, Noah's Ark, and ends with it. The Ark, so legend tells, landed in eastern Anatolia. It is in any case the great metaphor for this country: an ark of cultures. The story of the Ark can be a story of triumph or catastrophe, of salvation or destruction. It is a matter of perception.

We start, however, with burning. The burning of Noah's Ark.

April 1995

I

The Living Ark

Okay Temiz was the first to tell us about the Ark. Okay is a famous musician. He is the only Turk to feature in Leonard Feather's *Encyclopedia of Jazz*. Not many Turks realize this. He has big audiences in Sweden and Germany. In Istanbul, however, few take any interest in his sophisticated music. Not long after we saw him he took the sad decision to emigrate to Finland. 'Istanbul has rejected me,' he said over the telephone, with angry humiliation. 'There is no room for me here.'

That night, we had arrived just as he finished a concert on the waterfront in Ortakoy, which is on the European side of Istanbul. There was still a sizeable crowd milling around, students mainly – the concert was open-air and free. They were sipping beer, smoking Camel cigarettes, in T-shirts and jeans. Behind them, around the small square, fish restaurants spilled over on to the pavements. This was posh Istanbul – designer clothes, foreign bookshops. It was a fine evening, and cool. There was just a vague breeze but it was blowing away from the shore, sucking up and cauterizing the heavy smells of the daytime city.

This is one of the two things that are immediately obvious about Istanbul. First, the great broth of smell – meat, petrol, salty water, charcoal, leather, cumin, filth – that bubbles and belches wherever you go. Second, the vast tumult of noise that engulfs the city from first light: an anarchy of sound – the booming sirens of the passenger ferries across the Bosphorus, the whine of the smaller caiques, honking taxis, the shoeless boys selling water, and the inchoate articulations of the thousands upon thousands who press their way along the waterfront at Eminonu or through the Covered Bazaar. A long way from here.

Okay is tiny for a drummer: not much over five feet four inches. And he looks unusual for a Turk, his face entirely enclosed by a circumference of hair that starts around his chin, in clumps of off-white beard, and, without any break, banks upwards into a more even-textured matting across his scalp. When he is animated he can appear quite deranged – arms in the air, and the head with its surrounding helmet moving from side to side, and all of it – the energy of it – at odds with the smallness of his body. This is particularly true when he plays. But when he does, and perhaps just because it looks so unlikely, this little man bringing the congas to life or presiding over a kit of drums, it is hugely impressive. He is a very gifted percussionist and has played with some of the best Western jazz musicians. Recently he recorded an album with the trumpeter Don Cherry.

Istanbul is supposed to be a bridge between East and West. But it sits there, a cantankerous old man, pushing Okay Temiz away. Okay is a (small) living bridge between East and West, and full of passion. He is driven out. Istanbul, meanwhile, sits Buddha-like astride a reputation that is in the past, that does not really live. The modern city has filled itself with noise and turbulence as if this is cultural life. It pretends this is vibrancy, when it is emptiness. The city has been the most important in the world but now it is not important on the world stage. Modern Turkey has never really found itself at home in Istanbul, confronted by so many remnants of greatness. It exists like a squatter in the geriatric city, powerless to change very much or to counter the supremacy of the antique and musty past from which the place continues to derive its sustenance.

Okay was boxing up his drums, looking a little sour. It had been a good concert, he said. He meant: I have been forced to play for free again, on the margins of the city. The crowds were slowly ebbing away. He was talking, like a kindly teacher, to a couple of desperate-looking students. Great, they said. Really great. Can we have an autograph? He softened a little.

A couple of hours later we were still in the square, now deserted. Okay had brought two friends and we all sat on a bench looking out on to the water. It was astoundingly quiet. This is one strange feature of the city: it sleeps at night. You could just make out the familiar skyline across the water: the mosques, the palace minarets. They have the character of fortifications in the dark, looming like a defensive line. This is not a welcoming city – grand, yes, fascinating without doubt, but it offers no warm welcome. It has no compassion. Was that what the others were thinking? The Turks are very sad about their city and the way it crumbles.

'Hey, look!' Okay said suddenly. 'Are you interested in Noah's Ark?' He looked very pleased: such an abrupt question. 'Well, you know, Noah's Ark . . . I've been asked to sail on it. Tomorrow. You should come . . .'

Still there was bewilderment.

'Look, I'm not joking. They're going to burn it . . .' Then he explained and we all agreed. We would all go.

Behind us a couple of working men approached. 'Okay, brother,' they said deferentially. 'Will you play for us?' They gave Okay two empty Coke cans.

Okay stood up and laughed. He took two drum-sticks from his pocket, put the cans between his legs, and started to play. He beat them with real feeling. It was a violent intrusion into the night.

The next morning Ersoy, an old friend, and I took a taxi to Sariyer, which is at the extremity of the city, a suburb lapped by the Bosphorus. It was hot. On a hot day Istanbul is unbearable. Every sense is assaulted all at once: the heat and the smell disable the brain and the palate; the noise ricochets between your ears and makes your head feel as if it is made of thin metal; the dust turns your throat to sandpaper. There is the confusion of people and of traffic. The jabbering language, the shouting, the sudden awareness that a car is honking its horn at *you*. You long for space. Up above you a bird wheels and crows, all on its own, without any encumbrance.

We arrived and put all that behind us. This was a smart house, with people drinking wine, wearing fine hats as if they were all going for a day at the races. Istanbul has a very well-defined sense of class, Victorian in its stringency, and just as uncompromising. The women of the upper class look very much alike: peroxide blondes, jellied necks, unnatural tans. On the small quay at the back of the house there were television crews treading carefully in between those women and the other women, who wore red sashes around their trunks, and served the wine.

Okay said, 'Hey, man! This is the craziest performance art.' He was much happier than he had been the night before. Partly he was pleased that he had come in a baseball cap, T-shirt and tracksuit trousers: he knew this offended the sensibilities of the richer guests.

It was simply too hot to drink wine, so we drank water from the bottle because we were so thirsty, splashing it into wine glasses when one of the women handed us some for the sake of decorum. The idea of wine in this heat made me feel sick with thirstiness.

Behind us, moored to the quay, was a great blue tent rising out of the sea. It was made of hemp and it was very tall: a simple triangular shape on a flat barge. On the surface of the barge there was sand. The tent was blue with gold and red motifs – around it there were odd pagan standards on posts, with flailing pieces of wool, and flat geometric faces. The Ark was an extraordinary sight amongst the other small fishing tenders and caiques which were tightly packed along the waterfront, violently bobbing on the wake of each passing boat. The Ark was much the biggest: a solid barge, normally used for transporting lumber and drums of diesel. Berthed immediately alongside it was a two-storey Bosphorus tour boat, decorated with bunting and dozens of Turkish flag pendants. This was for VIPs. Apart from a few hay bales there was nowhere to sit on the Ark itself.

One of the TV crews was interviewing a local politician (he wore a dark grey suit which fitted him like a box). 'We have sponsored this event because it is meant to remind us to take good care of the environment,' he said pompously. 'We do not want to destroy it.' Istanbul, historically one of the civilized world's cleanest cities, is now one of its most polluted, the signs on every stone and on the surface of every crude mud alley. Even the fish stink of pollution. 'We want a clean, fresh sea,' the politician went on. 'Clean like the waters of the flood from which Noah rescued animalkind and saved the environment.' The traffic poured down the straits behind him: great oil tankers from Central Asia, and container ships. One day a tanker will sink and life in the Bosphorus will finally become extinct.

Riding on the surface of the water by the Ark there were cans and plastic bags and a light effluent froth. The environment has become a fashionable cause among the educated rich. This is partly because it is a fashionable western European cause. It has been imported. There is a new consciousness and a new pompousness. Much of the pollution is caused by domestic fires in the slum areas of the city, and by the traffic. Neither problem, however, is in sight of remedy. The city continues to crumble.

The Ark was the brainchild of Ender Guzey, a Turkish performance artist, who lives mostly in Germany but occasionally comes home. He had also designed the promotional poster. There was a copy taped to one of the walls in the house: 'Noah's Ark,' it read. 'Be There Before It Burns To Ashes!'

Okay said the Ark was meant to be an event for all the people of Istanbul. The local radio was to broadcast live reports on its progress down the Bosphorus. It was to sail from Sariyer into the heart of the city and dock outside a fashionable waterside night-club where, after a week, there would be a special concert with ballet and jazz and avant-garde classical music. Then it would burn to ashes.

Ender was wandering around in white jodhpurs and a black straw hat. A little grey pony-tail protruded from the back of the hat. All along the quayside people were watching the spectacle from their balconies, or pressed up against the iron railings along the waterfront. They were dressed more soberly: crumpled brown shirts, and grey trousers. A poor audience.

While they stared impassively at the Ark and Ender's assistants buzzing around it, shouting into walkie-talkies, putting the finishing touches to the sailing arrangements, a gust of tender, ethereal music rose into the sky above the tent. It was the sound of the *ney*, a reed-flute invented by the Islamic mystics, and supporting percussion. Searching for the source of this sweet, heavenly harmony led the onlookers, with much finger-pointing and shouting, to two musicians sitting on stools on the Ark. Okay had brought a large brown and white conch sea-shell, and every so often while the two played, he would raise it to his mouth and blow hard. That brought a smile to the faces of the bystanders. The children shouted every time he made it boom.

Above the mosque on the seafront a column of smoke was rising. At first we thought it might be fire, but then realized it was probably from an open-air grill: corn on the cob or kebabs; the old, empty world of the city; rusty barrows manned by unshaven men peeling stiff green foliage off dirty, banana-coloured cobs, or spooning fat over small fingers of meat on the grill. The Ark projected a different image of the city: self-conscious, sophisticated, politically correct, trendy, enlightened, responsible. This fitted snugly the image Turkey likes to project of itself. It is what it likes to believe about itself.

It was early afternoon when the Ark set off. We travelled aboard the tug that pulled it. A little distance out into the Bosphorus, Okay leaned over the side of the tug and said, 'You know, this has no meaning for me at all. There should be animals on board . . .' Instead there were TV journalists trying to stand up straight and deliver a commentary to camera. Okay became sullen and angry: 'Shit, this really is crap!'

A flotilla of small boats had gathered around the barge. The wind was whipping the water a little, and you could see waves crack over the side, and the expensively dressed television presenters pointing angrily to sodden trousers. Some of the flax panels were being torn away from the blue tent but they held, more or less. I wondered if anyone had ever sailed an Ark up the Bosphorus before. Never like this.

The tug drew alongside the Ark after a while and we were allowed on board. Okay took his seashell and went up to the musicians and started to play it like a trumpet. He was playing a Miles Davis tune. Ender walked up to him with a long wooden tube, decorated, like his ship, in blue and gold. It was filled with beads and he turned it one way and then the other. The rolling beads made the sound of rain. The instrument was called a rain-stick.

The trip was not going well. The Ark drew into various harbours on its way; more often than not nobody was waiting to greet it. There were Sunday fishermen sitting on the quayside trailing lines into the water, their trousers rolled up to their knees. They would wave.

Ender didn't care. He was admired and loved by his friends aboard the barge who were full of enthusiasm and complicated insights. When the musicians stopped, they played cassettes over the PA. 'This one comes from a loft in New York,' said one man. Ender sat cross-legged on the sand, making castles with his wine glass, giving an interview. 'You know, we can't bathe in this water,' he pointed across the straits, 'we have lost the most beautiful part of nature . . . so I chose the Ark as a symbol of regeneration . . . a world myth . . . a global symbol . . .' He thanked his sponsors: the Minister of Culture, the Munich Chamber of Commerce, the Turkish Maritime Agency which had provided the barge. 'It's normally forbidden for a ship like this to be allowed into the straits. Of course, you don't expect this freedom – but it is our country and some rules get broken . . .'

Ender smiled: he had let his hair down and it was trailing over his back. 'You know, this is not so intellectual, but very basic. By the end of the day you will see many people with candles lining the quay . . .' The radio had said that people should buy a candle and light it when the Ark passed, as a gesture. He scooped some sand up in his hand and then opened his palm and let the wind scatter the grains.

'Is the Ark anything to do with Turkey?' the interviewer asked.

'No, it's universal,' Ender replied.

He stood up and ran his hands around the edge of the strange standard in front of the tent. It was a pole stuck on to the deck, about six feet tall, with a wooden plank as a cross-piece. Tacked on to the wood were pieces of a lamb's fleece, unwashed and wiry to the touch. Ender stroked them.

'Noah,' he said. 'I suppose I am like Noah.' He was very aware of himself. He moved slowly, as if he was acting. A woman sitting on one of the hay bales threw him a kiss. He smiled.

The light was starting to fade, the wind was blowing stronger. The Ark pulled alongside at Arnavutkoy, and we ran into town to find food. There was a big crowd in the square where we had been drinking the night before, but only one or two held up candles when we docked.

The Ark passed into the Golden Horn and under Fatih Bridge, coming closer now to the main city. Fatih, which means Conqueror, is the nickname of the greatest of the Ottoman sultans, Mehmet II, the man who retook Istanbul in 1453. It is the only bridge that is named after him and was built in the late 1980s by the Japanese. By then Turkish engineering, which had once been famous for its brilliance and startling achievements – the biggest cannon in the world, the strongest city walls, the finest mosques – was incapable of such a task.

Huge oil tankers were gliding alongside us. To the right stood Rumeli Hisar, the old castle at the entrance to the estuary. Its towers and thick brick walls seemed much bigger from the sea. A bit of history; a hint of imperial arrogance.

Ender was stapling more strands of wool to the standard at the front of the Ark. He had put small lanterns in the sand all around it and these were burning nicely.

Sevim was one of Okay's friends: she was at university in Germany and she wanted to buy a cello so that she could learn to play it. She had classic Turkish good looks: long hazelnut hair and porcelain skin. Ersoy had been talking to her all afternoon and they were both drunk. There was still some wine left in the crates inside the tent. By now people were drinking it from the bottle. Sevim was young and political. She told me that I should read some of the revolutionary Russian writers 'because they really believed in something'. She kept on speaking odd phrases of Russian.

There is tremendous energy and passion in the young Turks, a creativity that will help ensure the country has a much less stagnant future than its present. In the recent past it was a criminal offence to say you were a communist. Today, if you speak too loudly about it, society will freeze you out. There are still prosecutions. Marxism has become a shorthand for the young, however. It means resistance; it means you hate the injustice of Turkish society. It means you are not like your parents who accepted it. It means that you are willing to challenge it.

Sevim's sister, Saziment, was older. The two barely seemed like sisters, Sevim so extrovert and Saziment brooding and quiet. Saziment worked for one of the new private airlines which had grown up since the early 1980s. She was chief stewardess, and she hated it. She hated the corruption. She hated the tedium. She had met Okay on a plane to Spain a few months before and she had kept up with him since. She was sitting, in a pair of shorts, on the side of the Ark, looking miserable. Her luminous turquoise eyes seemed lost and sad.

'How much would it cost to marry an American or a British husband?' she asked casually. There was a precariousness about her. She seemed ready to break down and weep.

'I don't think you can do it any more. Immigration is much tighter these days. The British investigate to see if the marriage is really made for love. I don't know about the Americans . . .'

'I heard it cost five hundred dollars to marry for a green card.'

'I don't know.'

'I really want to leave.' This is something you hear a lot from educated middle-class Turks. Many want to leave: they perceive the emptiness and they fear the vacuum. Old things are nourished by this uncertainty: religion, tribalism, prejudice, corruption. Ataturk's purist secular vision for this country is rapidly decaying.

It was nearly dark. The musicians were playing again. We were sailing past the palace of Topkapi to the cooing of a *ney*.

Suddenly there was some shouting on the other side of the Ark. A motor launch had come alongside, and a large Turk, wearing a spivvy white suit, shouted, 'Is this a sex party?' He had brought some friends; they must have seen the lights on the Ark from the shore. He was shooed away by angry, insulted artists. Ender was furious. How could this be so misunderstood? 'We import these values from the West, you see,' said one man standing beside me.

An hour later we arrived at the seafront night-club. We would have stayed but nobody could afford the drinks. It was close to £10 for a gin. This was where the super-rich young Turks went for an evening. We went instead to a nearby fish restaurant. The girls were talking about what they would eat when Okay, who had been quiet for some time, shouted, 'The Ark is shit!' Saziment looked embarrassed. This was a family restaurant.

A week later. I never saw the Ark burn. By then I had left for Ankara. 'AND THE ARK OF NOAH BURNED,' reported one of the newspapers.

> The Ark of Noah was burning last night as a protest at environmental vandalism in Istanbul and the world. Ender Guzey, the artist and inventor of the boat, said he was very pleased with the response to the Ark, and hoped that people would remember it in the future. Last night he set light to the Ark, but the winds were poor and the materials would not catch fire.

Saziment and Okay were there. 'It rained that day and I think the tent was damp or something,' she told me later. After an hour Ender gave up with his firelighters and decided, after some discussion with his friends, to symbolize the burning by putting a few candles around the boat.

2

The Tyranny of Hindsight

Four hundred and eleven years before Ender's Ark sailed the Bosphorus, another Ark burned in Constantinople. The two could not have been more different. I had discovered it while idling away some time in the British Library, described in an old book published in 1590.

I asked Ender if he had heard of this Ark. It was a firework. The most extravagant firework in the history of Anatolia. When I told him, he said, 'Wow!' He had not heard of it. I am not sure that this book has been looked at by anyone for centuries. It tells the extraordinary story of an English adventurer named Edward Webbe who was taken hostage by the Turks in the 1570s on his way home from Italy. He spent more than a decade in confinement but he had skill as a gunner, and when the Turks realized this they employed him to help construct fireworks for the Sultan. His finest achievement came in 1582 when he built a representation of Noah's Ark, to symbolize the great diversity of the Ottoman Empire, for the celebration of the circumcision of the son of Sultan Murat III.

The festival was considered by contemporary chroniclers the finest and most extravagant spectacle since those of Ancient Rome. It was attended by the envoys of many countries (including England) who were shocked, amazed and quite often frightened by the displays of jousting and riding and, particularly, by the fireworks. The Ottomans had staged festivals like this in the past, but this one, for which the city was given a holiday that lasted fifty-five days, was the longest and most remarkable.

Can we imagine what it was like? A moment of real democracy, according to one historian, in which all people in the

Empire – Jews, Christians, Muslims – gathered to celebrate as equals. The festivals were safety valves. They were to celebrate victory, and to disguise defeat; for births, marriages and circumcisions. They were an opportunity to reflect on the glory of the Empire and its creativity.

This festival, like none before it, underlined the technological advancement of the Ottomans over the Western Europeans – perhaps for the last time. The visitors watched artisans wheel an entire public bath before the Sultan in the Hippodrome. They marvelled at the skill of the glass-blowers who carried before him a huge working furnace. There were robots; there was a big kite in the shape of a mythological bird which could be guided from controls on the ground. There were miniature gardens with trees and shrubs made entirely from sugar carried on boards by a hundred men. There were the grand processions of the guilds and artisans from across the Empire, from the Balkans, Arabia, the Indies and Anatolia, presenting gifts to the Sultan. The Ottomans considered everything as art. This was total theatre.

Noah's Ark was one of the highlights. Webbe wrote of the festival with genuine awe. He had this to say about the firework:

> Whilst I was remaining prisoner in Turkey, and kept in such slavish manner as is Rehearsed the great Turk had his son circumcised, at which time there were great triumphs and free liberty proclaimed for a hundred days space, that any nobleman, gentleman, traveller, Christian or other, might freely, (without being molested) come and see the triumphs there used, which were wonderful: I myself was there constrained to make a cunning piece of fire work framed in form like to ye Arke of Noah, being 24 yards high, and eight yards broad, wherein was placed 40 men drawn on 6 wheels, yet no man seen, but seemed to go alone, as though it were only drawn by two Fiery Dragons, in which show or Arke there was thirteen thousand several pieces of fire work.

In a way, Webbe's story is an introduction to Turkey. East

meets West. Europe meets Asia. Borrowing initiative. Technology transfer in a twentieth-century sense. Webbe was one of the first Englishmen to spend any length of time in Constantinople. He, the slave, discovered cruelty as well as generosity; beauty and hopelessness. Perhaps little, in this sense, has changed in the Western perception of the Turks.

But much has changed in the way the Turks view themselves. When I first read of Webbe's Ark I had no idea of Ender's project. I boarded his raft with an amazed sense of coincidence. But the differences between the two were more pronounced than the similarities. They are very different symbols for very different countries. Webbe's Ark was an entertainment, a self-confident statement of the Ottomans' achievement and of their self-sufficiency. Ender's, on the other hand, was the Ark of failure, when the burning speaks for disaster rather than triumph.

Ender knew nothing of Webbe. Few Turks know anything of the festival or even of Murat III. Why? They have been ignored in official history. Their oversight is not a trivial thing, it is a symptom of something very important to an understanding of modern Turkey: the way in which it has been systematically deprived of its past. Ender had not heard of Webbe's Ark. Perhaps he would never have heard of it, even if there were genuine academic freedom in Turkey. But he was delighted when he found out. This was immediately obvious. The Ark was not merely a symbol of environmental catastrophe, it was also, unexpectedly, a symbol of modern Turkey's political insecurity and intolerance. Istanbul was once an Ark of peoples; now Istanbul is a grey place of intolerance and prejudice.

In 1923, when Ataturk declared the Republic of Turkey, he declared war on much of Anatolia's history. He wanted a propaganda that would justify the construction of an explicitly Turkish nation: strong and independent, a European nation. The Ottomans did not fit comfortably in this official history. They were neither Turkish – the Sultans were the sons of Christian slaves – nor European. Quite the reverse; they presided as Caliphs over the Muslim world. Most important, they had no sense of Turkish identity. They were Greeks, Serbians, Arabs first and Ottoman second. The Empire, in this sense, resembled the modern United States – a vast racial melting-pot.

Ataturk quite literally closed the door on most of the Ottoman past. He wanted to demonize many of the Sultans, to pronounce their failure because this made his success more natural and more spectacular. He did not want historical truth to obscure his purpose. He shut the Ottoman archives, one of the world's greatest historical resources, to all but the most loyal historians who could be trusted to forage for facts that would be of use in the legitimizing of the new Republic. Inside the archives, among the hundreds of millions of unclassified documents, Murat III and Webbe lay buried.

And so did many other things that could embarrass the purpose or damage the self-confidence of the new nation state in other ways. There were papers in the archives that would clarify old arrangements for the self-government of the Kurds; and telegrams that would reveal whether or not the Ottomans had ordered the genocide of Armenians in their territories during the First World War. The memory of the old ethnic diversity in the Empire was banished.

Murat III remains, as a result, a tantalizingly obscure figure. I had tried to learn a little about him, but it proved difficult. There is virtually nothing in Turkish except a few anecdotes, most of them derived from contemporary European travellers who were far from impartial in their approach.

He gets a passing mention in the *Ottoman Chronicle*. It reports that of all Ottoman Sultans he was the one most addicted to women – so much so that he eventually contracted epilepsy as a result of his exertions and died of it. Nineteen of his wives were pregnant at the time of his death, and he was survived by at least 112 children, although not all their names are recorded. 'Sounds a remarkable fellow and quite different from his near contemporary Edward VI of England,' remarked one friendly scholar of Turkish history.

We know a few other things about Murat. He was a poet of some distinction, and smoked opium. He was a patron of the arts, though not as ambitious as Suleyman the Magnificent, who ruled a few years before him. He enjoyed watching dwarfs and dumb people fight each other. He had a red beard. He was obsessed with clocks and would spend a good deal of his time taking them apart. Traditionally he is condemned as a bad ruler with a mad lust for women. But there are many contradictions. Fragments hint at a rather more astute governor. This vicious hedonist was, for instance, also the man who opened up the Ottoman Empire to English merchants. It was during Murat's reign that Queen Elizabeth I secured, for the first time, a diplomatic mission to Constantinople.

'You see, we have no idea really about him,' I was told by another historian – a Turk. 'Not just him, but most of the Ottomans. They don't fit the way Turkey likes to think about itself. They were deliberately downgraded. For so long we were not allowed access and still the history remains intensely political. But we need the Ottomans now – we need them. Turkey is exploding now because it is so intolerant – we desperately need to rediscover the Ottoman blueprint of a diverse society, a no-nonsense, pragmatic and not ideologically rigid society.'

It seems on the surface surprising that modern Turkey does not make more of Sultans like this. At the least, there might be tourist dollars in this kind of history. Imagine a man like Murat as an English king: dead in the bath; having sex; the father of a hundred sons; a poet; an evil man. Museums. Festivals. Train rides, *son et lumière* spectacles, unemployed actors in period costumes. This is show business. But there is nothing.

Ataturk did allow some of the Sultans to escape from the archives. These were men who in one way or another buoyed up his image of the new regime. The two on whom Turkey looks most favourably are Sultan Mehmet, conqueror of Constantinople in 1453, and Suleyman, who took the Ottoman war machine to the walls of Vienna in the middle of the sixteenth century.

Both were indeed great men. They were warriors, poets, just legislators. Suleyman had his flaw: he married his Russian slave-concubine, Roxelana, an unprecedented expression of love in an otherwise rigidly structured life. Europeans respected him for this: the few travellers who ever saw the harem found it an obnoxious slur on decency. It was a living hell for most of the women. All were slaves. Most spent their lives living six or seven to a room and never slept with the Sultan. When he died, the entire harem would be retired and confined to another palace until they too died.

Suleyman's armies were respected for their discipline and their courage. The Janissaries – the professional soldiers – and most of the civil service were Christian by birth. They were forcibly removed as children from families in the conquered territories of the Balkans. This was how the Sultan ensured the absolute loyalty of those who served him. Slaves ruled this Empire.

Suleyman was not only a great general. He was highly cultured, an expert on Aristotle, and a poet. It is to him that we owe some of the greatest architecture in Islam: the great mosques and hospitals of the architect Sinan. The city that Suleyman ruled was far more civilized than London or Paris. Constantinople was both the cleanest and best proportioned of cities. Its markets sold prunes from Egypt and butter from Moldavia. It was the envy of Europe. Many Christians chose to convert to Islam and live there. They were called renegades.

For sixty-five years the doors to the archives – and the whole truth of the Ottoman past – remained shut. Then the Turkish government unexpectedly relented in 1989. A law was passed allowing free access for the first time. It was a monumental decision. Modern Turkey, said the government, had no reason to play with its history any longer. It was no longer scared of it. Would Murat III finally get a fair hearing?

Perhaps the Turkish government was acknowledging a new desire among its people to know the truth. But its commitment to openness is widely doubted. Every historian I spoke to was sceptical. They all said it was a lie, that there was no glasnost, just window-dressing. They said they were still being refused access to sensitive documents.

★

Modern Turkey is exhausted and floundering, like a weak bird that cannot find its nest in a storm. It is also fragile. To the visitor it can appear vacuous, shallow and lifeless. There is a tremendous sense of drift: a listless fatalism engulfs broad swathes of the population. In Istanbul, where the tension is greatest, the people daily confront the solid stone roots of a past from which they no longer receive any cultural nourishment. The mosques and churches in the old city are now submerged beneath a congealing layer of modern squalor; the new city vacantly promotes its five-star hotels and glossy bars.

It was my last day in Istanbul. And for no reason other than idle curiosity, I decided to find out if the Turks still made the fireworks which had so terrified their foreign envoys. Was there any continuity, even in this tiny sense?

I went first to a fire station to ask if they knew of any manufacturer. To her own surprise, the clerk found a local licence. Yes, she said, about two hours from Istanbul. Ersoy and I had the afternoon to kill, so we took the bus.

Adapazari is wholly unmemorable, like many of the towns in the hinterland of Istanbul. It is a precise statement of the colourless urban culture of western Turkey. It has neither charm nor character. It is modern in a paint-peeling eastern bloc style: clumsy cement apartment blocks and patchy green communal spaces. The factory was on the outskirts, hidden behind low-slung yellow-washed walls. There was nothing here that said factory as such; but this was where the taxi dropped us. The gatekeepers in front of the blue sliding doors were surprised. We said we wondered if we could speak to the manager. No, he was not expecting us, we were tourists and we had not had a chance to call to warn of our arrival. We thought that he would probably want to see us.

All over the yard inside were signs warning of the danger of explosion; but women and children were wandering among the barrels. We walked into the largest building. On one side were some photographs of huge fireworks bursting into colour; and on the other was a small cabinet displaying the stock – from small novelty rockets to dazzlers, to great missiles the size of small trees. You could see that all the fireworks were wrapped by hand – the paper was twisted around the wicks – and the printing was fuzzy and poor. You smelt the lack of technology in this plant.

We were taken into the office of the proprietor, an elderly gentleman with a skull-cap, who had long since retired from running the business, which he had left to his sons. But he still had his office and he liked to come in every day. It was a brilliant morning and sun streamed through the windows. There was suspicion in the air, but he offered us a Coke and invited us to sit with him.

His two sons quickly joined us. They watched us closely. We asked how long the factory had been at the site. Initially, it transpired, the old man had made caps for toy guns. That was in 1966. The company had only started making proper fireworks three years ago. There had been, we were told, an increase in demand. 'It is a growing market with the big displays. At Christmas, even ordinary people buy them and sometimes they buy them for weddings, but,' the old man told us confidentially, 'not in Adapazari. The Muslims here are not rich.'

There was a brief silence. Why had we come, one of the sons asked quite tartly. Now this was familiar: the gruff, irritable suspicion of strangers, a paranoia that extends throughout the country. The stranger comes and upsets routine. Strangers are unpredictable; thus they upset things. This is where Ataturk really failed: he never conquered the abiding Anatolian distrust of change. He never properly inculcated a sense of individualism, a sense that a single person can, or even has the right to, change the course of his own life. The Anatolian does not like surprises.

I explained that we were merely curious. I told him about Webbe and Murat, and about Ender's Ark. He obviously doubted our sincerity, suspecting some other motive. But he did not say anything.

'Do you make any special fireworks? Turkish ones?'

The man said, 'No, there are no special ones.'

'Could we see the factory?'

'No,' said the other brother unblinkingly.

'Are fireworks profitable?'

'No!' the old man shouted, as if he was in some pain. 'There is too much competition.' They muttered amongst themselves.

Ersoy leaned across. 'They think you are a spy who has come to steal their secrets.'

'You will not run my company,' said the old man. 'Perhaps we could be partners –'

'We expect rivals,' his son interrupted, 'and we are ready for them. The Americans and other countries send out spies to investigate developing countries. But we are Muslims here.'

In the end they agreed to show us some of the rockets, mainly to illustrate how advanced the factory was, and therefore how pointless any competitive venture would be. They had fourteen kinds of rocket. They were particularly proud of the Satan Rocket which made a trail, one of the brothers said, 'like the devil through the sky'.

We prepared to leave. Just as we stood up to shake his hand, the old man said quite severely, 'The Christian world wants to find out if the Muslim world is as sheeplike as it used to be, unable to do anything for itself. But we make fireworks, and they are better than yours, and that is how it will remain.'

The following day I boarded a plane for Ankara to seek a meeting with the government's chief historical censor: the curator of the Ottoman archives.

3

The Great Dictator

I sat outside the arrivals terminal at Ankara airport, watching a flock of tiny birds chirp their way across the car park and swing in tight formation over the top of the building and away. Bird song. I had never heard it so close to the airport before and for some reason it filled me with relief.

I was nervous about meeting the archivist. Several historians I had met doubted if he would grant me an interview, given the sensitivity of his position.

A few minutes passed, and then, outside the terminal building, a car screeched to a halt. The driver flew out of the door and ran to the front of the vehicle. There was a cat lying in the road, lifting one paw and then another, lazily, as if it was waking from a sleep. But there was blood oozing from its side. The driver, cursing, picked up the animal and flung it high into the air. It landed with a damp thud on the other side of the road. A porter cast a glance across, then lit a cigarette and went back inside the building. Ankara was a long way from the magnificence of the old Ottoman court. It is the capital city of the new Turkey.

Ersoy had said he would pick me up from the airport in his old Volkswagen Beetle; he was late. It would be at least an hour before he came. That was just his way. But I knew this airport. I had waited before at the gates outside the terminal, smoking.

This time, however, I had a companion. He had stepped off the same flight and he was English – shirt-sleeves and Argyle socks. Sometimes you just know them. Foreign and Commonwealth Office. He actually said he was here for a business conference.

'So what is this place like?' he asked after a while. He was a fat man with a round face. His eyes were like currants embedded in a bowl of stiff custard.

'I like it. I lived here for two years, and I think it's a good place. Are you waiting for a car?'

'Yes . . .'

We fell silent. His car never arrived, so he took a taxi. He said to the driver, 'British Embassy . . . yes, that's right. Embassy. Embassy!'

He turned round to me and added, 'Bloody Turks. Good for nothing!' None of the taxi drivers in Turkey speak English, even passingly.

Finally I had had enough of waiting. It was dark and cold. The taxi drivers were beginning to knock off for the night. I hailed one to take me to Ersoy's house in the city. Ankara at night is awful: grey, looming pavements, high off the road, with dunes of filth accumulating on top of them; dopey dry trees which pry between the blue drums of garbage that stand on the pavements; and the sheer stench of it all.

Ankara is Ataturk's city. To the Ottoman élite of Constantinople, Ankara was merely a small town full of peasants and long-haired goats. They called the peasants Turk, which was a pejorative, meaning uncouth and philistine. The climate is hostile: there are heavy snows in winter and parching sun in summer. Ataturk made it his capital city, the centre of his government, to put a symbolic distance between the new regime and the old. Ankara has wide, tree-lined boulevards like a continental European city and special amusements for its secular population: small parks, like the Swan Park with a special lake and a stone bridge, and one or two theatres. The shops are floodlit and full of fashion, and there are cinemas. But there is nothing here that is improvised or accidental. It is just like its history, oddly deformed and monochrome.

Ankara cannot compete with Istanbul, which is the first city of Turkey. Istanbul is where the writers and the artists live; it is where the musicians play. It is entirely appropriate that the Republic's chief historical censor should be based here, and not there, where the archives are actually kept. Ankara is a more loyal subject. It has a veneer of importance: a coagulation of bureaucrats and the military. It makes a comfortable home for them. It is compact, unpretentious and undemanding, an idiot sister to Istanbul. Ankara is, however, truly Turkish. Anatolian. Heavy-handed, bruising, reliable. It has a hard, business-like personality with little sophistication but considerable humour. It has no architecture. It is built in straight lines without any artistry. The roads run like canyons through the town: unthinking stretches of concrete beside which the inner-city dwellers – students and office workers, all victims of the 100 per cent inflation – eke out their difficult lives in dirty apartment blocks, with irregular water in winter and seething pollution in summer.

From the airport, you pass through the *gecekondu*, sprawling shack settlements built from breeze-blocks and corrugated iron. *Gecekondu* means 'made in a night'. This is where the migrants from the villages of the East live, a dispossessed people. These suburbs are not like Latin American slums. They have become a permanent feature of the city and are clean and tidy. They are built on mud, and in the winter they are waterlogged. But in the summer they are as clean as the residents can make them. There is real poverty here, but there are none of the usual symptoms: crime, drugs, prostitution. The people of the East have not given up their self-respect.

The middle classes live on the edge of the town in sedate, homely suburbs. It is the middle classes who have the hardest job to make sense of modern Turkey. They divert themselves with shopping: any kind of electrical item – television, video, CD. Imported items are the most valued. They save hard, only to watch their money collapse in value with the enormous inflation. They buy the newspapers and, like them, their conversation revolves around either family or deterioration. They are depressed. They hunger for opportunities to improve their purchasing power but are relentlessly beaten back by the reality of an economy that seems to serve only the super-rich. Or the corrupt.

Ersoy lives with his parents in one of the smarter districts in what passes for the Ankara green belt, although the grass beside the roads is mangy and unkempt, and it is only a matter of half a mile away that children under the age of ten are working in petrol stations and car workshops. Ersoy has stayed at home because it is cheaper that way. It was not, of course, entirely an economic decision. He is a young man of marriageable age, and convention dictates that men and women do not live together unless they are married. Ankara exerts a fierce moral pressure. Even the most radical young Turk – and Ersoy is one of those – does not challenge it.

His father is an accountant and his mother was a senior manager in Turkish Television. They are good, sound people. As I walked up the stairs of the apartment block, I glanced at my watch – 11.00 p.m.! They would not be happy to see me, and they would be the last to know what had happened to Ersoy.

Ersoy's father was still up. He was in his pyjamas, and he simply said, 'Hello, Tim. How are you?' He disappeared back into the sitting-room before I could answer. There was football on the television: one of the Turkish teams playing the Italian champions Lazio. Half the country would be up with him, praying for victory. We did not talk again: he passed me the phone, and I kept trying different numbers for Ersoy. He said nothing at all. He had not been well, Ersoy told me later. He had lost his taste for surprises.

This was a standard Turkish room: spotless, with low box-like sofas that have hard, low backs, and hard, low arm-rests – one evolutionary step from sitting cross-legged on the floor. There was a glass coffee table and some onyx ashtrays. The carpet was as new, because nobody walked across it with their shoes on. They had spent a lot redecorating the old place. The rough concrete hole in the ground had been replaced by a WC. They had acquired a cordless phone.

After an hour Ersoy arrived in his clanking white Beetle, and we drove off. Ersoy is not a good representative of the average western Turk. He is an exceptional person. He speaks fluent English, much of which he learned from rock records; he writes short stories in English and has read very widely. He has read everything published by Wittgenstein. He spent a lot of his youth, when I first met him, just thinking. His passion was philosophy. To live, he worked night-shifts overseeing computers for a British mining company. Then, about five or six years ago, he wanted a real part of the material world, and he started to work for Turkish Television. He has made a lot of money since but it does not much matter to him. He has never cut his wiry black hair, which he usually wears in a pony-tail. His skin is a deep bronze. He looks like a Red Indian and he likes that comparison because he feels that he is an indigenous person. I met him because he was a friend of a Turkish girl called Hulya with whom I was in love ten years ago. He used to help her translate my love letters. We have been close ever since.

We drove to a relative's flat not far away. He had fixed me a bed there. Despite the heat this place was cold, trapped in freezing shadow by neighbouring apartment blocks. It had been empty for a few weeks. The WC had flooded; the telephone was broken. We sat down and uncorked a duty-free litre of Scotch. Ersoy's girlfriend had left some *borek* and small raisin cakes in the kitchen. His job at Turkish Television was to translate English-language programmes, mainly American and Australian soap operas. 'God!' he said. 'How can you lot watch this stuff? It is hideous.' He said he had started to learn Japanese.

'You know,' he said later that night, 'we are a lost people now. I love my country. I really love it. Ataturk told us we are all Turks, but we all lived for centuries as different people. And now – look – how can I look in a mirror and tell you what a Turk looks like . . .?'

We drank heavily, and smoked. Ataturk was an historic drinker. He sat in his huge pink presidential palace at the top of the Cankaya district of Ankara – the other end of town – and drank most nights until dawn, playing poker. It killed him in the end (he died of cirrhosis in 1938). He made no attempt to disguise any of his addictions: he loved women as well, and foreign diplomats were repeatedly scandalized by rumours of orgies at the palace.

Ataturk's legacy has, for many, become a tiresome inheritance – for the Muslim as much as for the free-thinking liberal. Different communities begin to awake: the Kurds remember that they are not Turks at all and cannot be a part of Ataturk's historical fiction. Other minorities start to question their loyalty to a state which denies their existence. The radical Muslims begin to question his version of their past: they cannot accept that Islam is the enemy of human progress.

Ataturk's state is intensely intolerant. This is what Ersoy meant when he said, 'How can I . . . tell you what a Turk looks like . . .?' Ataturk enforced an identity without mercy. Perhaps even he, however, could not have guessed that the experience of violence at the hands of the state he created would have become such a widespread phenomenon. It has become a common factor, shared between people, like memories of the Second World War, or of going to the same school.

The persistent brutality of the state is an expression of the sheer difficulty Ataturk's successors have had in imposing the logic of nationhood on the people of Anatolia. The victims are on the margins: they are on both the left and the right – intellectuals and farmers; atheists and the religious. Ataturk was incapable of accepting criticism. He would react with ill-tempered ferocity when confronted. His child, this Republic, has the same trait. I cannot say – because I do not know – that the violence of the modern Turkish state towards its critics is not systematic, as many claim, but it feels hot-blooded and irrational. The state loses its temper. The generals lose their temper. The uneducated thug policeman loses his temper.

Ersoy has friends who have spent time in one or other of the country's prisons. Everybody knows somebody who has been jailed, tortured, injured or murdered. One friend, accused of being a communist, was taken to the notorious Mamak prison where they squeezed his testicles so hard that his balls ended up inside his stomach. He would stand in the shower, using soap to help him masturbate, just to check that he was still potent, that – in the Turkish saying – the cock still crowed. He had no success until many days later when, standing trial in Ankara, he raised his fist in the air. Everybody understood his sense of achievement.

But Turkey still has nothing else in which all its many diverse elements can share, even if they wished to. There is still no alternative to Ataturk. His cult lives on: in every concert hall and every classroom, in every office and every tea house there is a portrait of the man: the tawny eyebrows, the general on the battlefront, the statesman in top hat and tails. In every square there is a statue. Even forests are named after him.

Ataturk was a contemporary of Hitler and Mussolini but he was not of their kind. If there is a comparison, perhaps it is with Bismarck, another legendary drinker. Neither acknowledged the sovereignty of history; both rode roughshod all over it. Unlike the German chancellor, however, Ataturk was no intellectual, nor a figure of literary genius. Ataturk did not invent the new Turkey. He imposed it, by the sheer power of his will.

Mustafa was born in Salonika, which is now part of Greece, in 1881. He was awarded the title Ataturk, which means Father of the Turks, more than forty years after he had secured the country's independence. His origins were humble but by no means desperate. His mother was deeply religious and his father, more liberal, was a minor civil servant who left his post in the Customs to set up in private business. He was no entrepreneur. He invested his savings first in a timber business and then in salt. He lost everything and died of drink.

The young Ataturk showed proficiency in maths but was taken to task by his teachers for his arrogant, haughty manner. However, he showed enough brilliance to be given the sobriquet Kemal, meaning mature, while he was still at school. He wanted to be a soldier and at fourteen was sent to the military school at Monastir. Here, for the first time, he learned of the myriad rebellions against Turkish rule that were erupting throughout the Balkans. These were dangerous, violent years.

The reigning Sultan, Abdul Hamit II, was perhaps the cruellest and most paranoid tyrant ever to have ruled the Empire. His mother was an Armenian who had been a show dancer before entering the harem. When he took the throne in 1876, he supported the growing number of intellectuals who called for democratic reform and constitutional government. But he soon betrayed them and constructed a police state. He had an obsessional fear of assassination, particularly by poison. He was suspicious of everybody, even the imprisoned concubines of his harem. After a visit to a museum of waxworks in Paris, he commissioned a wax statue of himself, which he planted in the corner of the harem so that the women would feel that he was constantly watching them.

During the 1880s dissenters began to organize, and slowly an opposition movement grew up: teachers, students, administrators and soldiers. In 1908 the terrified Sultan was forced to accept their demands for a constitution. The following year he was deposed, and government passed into the hands of the reformers, the Young Turks.

Ataturk was among those demanding reform; he was imprisoned on one occasion. But his commitment to change did not secure him political advancement. He was distrusted by those officers who led the constitutional movement. In turn, he publicly criticized them, particularly for their repeated military failures against the rebels. The reformist government, which was becoming increasingly despotic in its conduct, distanced itself from Ataturk. In 1913 he was sent into virtual exile as military attaché in Sofia, where he whiled away his time learning how to dance waltzes and foxtrots with some of the most eligible virgins in the Austro-Hungarian Empire.

But they remained virgins. Ataturk was forced to seek sexual gratification from whores because no respectable European would sleep with a Turk, which must have compounded his already strong sense of rejection, and he contracted venereal disease. Nevertheless he enjoyed the company of Europeans, for their modernism, their rejection of old ways and tiresome tradition, their novelty.

At the same time he was grindingly frustrated; he sensed his destiny and felt as if history was ignoring him. The cold man with the riveting blue eyes made few firm friends, and his ambition never encouraged others to trust him deeply.

He was saved by the First World War. In a series of desperate telegrams wired from the Embassy in Sofia, Ataturk pleaded with the government in Constantinople not to enter the war on the German side. He hated the pervasive presence in Turkey of the Germans, who ran the army as well as much of the Empire's heavy industry. But he was ignored.

Ataturk was a tactical genius in warfare, and it was during the Great War that he conclusively demonstrated his remarkable talents as a soldier. It was the war that made him famous – not just in Turkey, but in Europe – as the result of a chance posting, one of those accidents that are the real substance of history. He was posted to the Gallipoli peninsula in 1915, and his unexpected victory there reflected in full his gift for improvisation on the battlefield. But in human terms at least, it was the most marginal triumph. Tens of thousands died, Turks as well as invading Allied soldiers.

Although news of his responsibility for the victory was deliberately censored, he became something of a folk hero. Nevertheless, he enjoyed no political advancement, and he was sent to the eastern border, where he was forced to watch the resurgent Arabs take Damascus and rout his army.

Finally, in 1919, after Turkey had lost the war, he was given his opportunity when he was ordered to suppress riots in northern Anatolia. The British, who were administering Constantinople on behalf of the Allies, gave permission for his departure. This was their mistake. In the provinces, Ataturk nurtured a popular movement which quickly became an army. Finally this army, which immediately proved its courage and hardiness, reclaimed Anatolia for the Turks. The new Republic was founded four years later.

The important thing about this campaign was that it involved everybody. It was not like the First World War, when starving women fought with starving dogs for black bread on the streets of Constantinople, not knowing why they were suffering or why their sons had died. In this war, people gave up their houses so that they could be demolished for firewood to feed the engines of trains. The struggle for independence is still fresh in the memory of the present young Republic. Every family has a story of its sacrifices and its casualties to tell.

After Ataturk had forced the Western Allies out, he was left with the rump of the Ottoman Empire: Anatolia and a tip of the European continent. He had decided long before that the destiny of this new country lay in Europe. The Turks had to reorient themselves. So he inaugurated the cultural revolution. He trod carefully at first, not wishing to outrage the most conservative elements in a profoundly conservative society. He claimed that he had waged the war of independence in the name of the Sultan; that he posed no challenge to the Sultan's position as Caliph, leader of the worldwide Muslim community; and that he was no enemy to Islam.

But when he judged the time right – and he had a brilliant sense of timing – he tore apart the fabric of Ottoman society. In 1922 the Sultanate was abolished by decree of Ataturk's parliament, which was no more than his rubber stamp. In November of that year the last Sultan left Constantinople with his retinue (which included his barber), under the protection of a British warship, the HMS *Malaya*. An American impresario telegraphed an urgent message to the British Ambassador:

> Hippodrome New York could use the wives of ex-Sultan. Kindly put me in touch with party who could procure them

In his biography of Ataturk, Lord Kinross reported that King George V was wildly amused by this request.

The following year the Western powers recognized the territorial integrity of Turkey in the Treaty of Lausanne. This marked the end of the Ottoman Empire. It overruled a treaty signed at Sèvres in 1920 which held out the promise of self-determination for some of the non-Turkish minorities living in Anatolia: the Kurds, the Armenians and the Syriani among others. After Lausanne it was accepted that only Turks lived in Turkey. The

Armenians did win official status as a minority, but neither the Kurds nor the Syriani were so fortunate. The Greek Christian population of Turkey was later evicted from Anatolia, and the Turkish Muslim population of Greece was in turn ejected by Athens.

Politically Ataturk pretended to be a democrat, but in his belly he had disdain for democracy. It was unruly and he could not control it. He never trusted the people he loved (and he did love them) to make decisions that he considered sensible or rational. On 29 October 1923, when the Republic was declared, he was elected President and acquired complete, formal control over the government and the army. The period of his dictatorship began.

Ataturk's preoccupation was to exorcize the influence of Islam from Turkish society and build in its place a community focused on its ethnic credentials. He once told a friend: 'Religion is like a heavy blanket that keeps the people of Turkey asleep, that stops them from waking up, from moving forward.' During the 1920s, by which time he was turning increasingly to drink, he issued in quick succession a number of laws designed to banish Islam to the periphery of Turkish life. These were not, as some have claimed, designed to eradicate religion altogether. Ataturk wanted to banish it from politics, to break the ancient habit that challenged the authority of the state. He forbade the wearing of the fez, which had become a joke in Europe but not among the ordinary Muslims of Turkey for whom the upturned felt flowerpot symbolized the constant readiness of the faithful to prostrate themselves before God. It was designed to allow the wearer to touch his forehead to the ground during prayer without having to take it off. The notion of the hat with a brim, as worn in Western society – in fact the very word hat – was a source of moral opprobrium in the East. Characteristically, Ataturk was the first to wear such a hat in public, but he recognized its potency as a symbol and the so-called Hat Law did indeed provoke widespread, if temporary, dissent in the East.

He took a hard line against the clerics of the old Empire. He banned the dervish, the mystical orders of Islam. At their least significant they were corrupt charlatans, travelling around the Empire selling cures to the sick; but at their best they were among the most spiritual of intellectuals. They hovered on the edge of Islamic orthodoxy teaching an intuitive existential faith that appealed to the poor, and as such were popular and highly influential with ordinary Anatolians, whom they often educated. But by the end of the Empire they had become a reactionary force. Ataturk thought of them, probably correctly, as vehicles of superstition – fortune-tellers and witch-doctors – and believed that in their decadence they symbolized to many secularists the historic corruption of Islam. Not only did he close the orders, he also banned worship at the tombs of the Hoca, the legendary dervish, who, like Mevlana, was among the greatest thinkers and poets in any religion. This reform too met with violent opposition, which was suppressed with characteristic efficiency. Ataturk was impatient for speedy changes and he believed that the people were ready for them.

The same was true of his language reforms. Ataturk wanted to create a brand-new Turk, freed from the past. But instead he succeeded in creating confusion. In 1928, virtually overnight, heavily influenced by the nationalist thinkers of the late nineteenth century, he banned the Arabic script in which Turkish had previously been written and replaced it with the uglier but more user-friendly Latin version. The religious roared their protest: the Arabic script was adopted at the time the Turks were converted to Islam; it was the script of the Koran; it was an ancient symbol of Muslim loyalties.

Ataturk was not distracted, however. He set up a language foundation which was tasked to make new words. Wherever possible, these words were to be modelled on Western equivalents – Turkey's destiny, according to Ataturk, lay in the West, not the East.

The word-inventors continue to turn out new words at the rate of several thousand a year. And the result is still confusion. Turks speak Turkish, but often they fail to understand each other. The villager in the east of the country, even now uneasy with the new language, uses out-of-date words unintelligible to the educated city-dweller. Ataturk wanted the language to unite his nation; in fact, it has helped to ensure that it remains culturally divided, underlining social differences rather than common ground. In modern Turkey language has become a symbol: the left-wing intellectual, still loyal to the revolution, avoids the old Islamic words; the conservative peppers his speech with them.

The abolition of the Ottoman script had an even more profound implication: it disenfranchised the nation from its past. No longer could the people read the old historical sources, even if they were granted access to them. In an attempt to reconcile past and present, Ataturk founded the Turkish Historical Society in 1925, ordering his historians to describe how the Republic fulfilled the historic destiny of the Turkish people. He insisted that the modern Turks were descendants of the greatest warriors he claimed the world had ever known – the pure Turkic tribes of pre-Islamic times which had settled in Anatolia from the Caucasus. He required his historians to show that it was Turks who had contributed the most to the greatest achievements of the Ottoman Empire. He wanted what did not fit to be rejected. Much of the Ottoman past, with all its racial confusion, was to be ignored. According to Ataturk, the Ottomans had perverted the Turks from their true course. They had imposed an elitist Islamic culture on the original Turks. The Empire had failed because it was racially impure: a salutary lesson, he said, for the young Republic.

This was nonsense, of course, but Ataturk had no scruples about ensuring the accuracy of the nationalist history. It was irrelevant to his purpose. He closed the archives so that there could be no dispute. He had great ambitions for these ancient Turks. He wanted his historians to show that they had played a leading role in the development of Western civilization and, further, that the Turks were the first civilization on earth; the origin of all human achievement. He ordered the invention of a new master race.

On one occasion Ataturk accosted a British diplomat during a conversation about names. He insisted that the county name of

Kent was derived from Turkish (*kent* in Turkish means town). He said this was proof that Turks had once conquered Britain. And he was serious. His historians produced wild new theories to order. There was the Sun Language theory, which maintained that Turkish was the first language and that all others derived from it. There was the theory that the Sumerians, and even the Hittites, were in fact Turks.

Ataturk wanted to teach the nation self-confidence but he taught it isolation. His Turkey was a very self-absorbed place which insisted on self-sufficiency, even in history. In the decades that have passed since he died in 1938, much has happened that Ataturk would find intolerable. In 1965 the government reintroduced vocational education for the clergy, and by the mid-1980s around 10 per cent of students in secondary education were at religious schools. In 1982, after the country's last coup, the constitution made it a requirement that all children had religious instruction. Christian Turkish students are obliged to study the Koran. The religious reaction started as early as the 1950s, when the law that banned Arabic calls to prayer in mosques was revoked. Successive governments discovered that Ataturk had only superficially persuaded the rural voters of his secular reforms, which they distrusted. His nationalism could not fill the spiritual gap once plugged by Islam.

Ataturk wanted Turkey to be a democracy. But when he tried it for himself he found it intolerable (he had no qualms about executing political opponents), and it was only after his death that the country began its first faltering experiments in parliamentary democracy. In the half-century since then, Turkish politics have remained infantile, dangerous and endemically corrupt, and few, if any, Turks have any real respect for the parliament. There have been three military coups provoked in part, if not entirely, by the incompetence of the country's politicians.

After the last coup in 1980, the military ruled the country for three years and then stepped aside for a civilian government headed by a right-wing economist called Turgut Ozal – the only Turkish politician of any international standing since

Ataturk himself. He steered the country very firmly towards Europe, but in other ways he speeded up the corruption of Ataturk's legacy. Ozal was a religious man who had made the pilgrimage to Mecca, and his government was openly sympathetic to the religious conservatives.

He was also a free-market ideologue, much impressed by Margaret Thatcher. He relaxed state controls on commerce and so accelerated the polarization of Turkish society. But he did nothing to end the corruption of the government or its civil service. Nor, despite the outward appearance of liberalism, did he encourage greater social tolerance. Ozal, like Ataturk, was terrorized by the Ottoman model of society, the model of diversity. Ethnic dissent was rigorously suppressed. Ozal dispossessed the people further of their Ottoman inheritance.

4

The Archivist

How can I have come this far without *Yok*? *Yok*, the most commonly spoken word in Turkey, means: nothing, non-existent, negative, you are wrong, there is no milk, I don't know when the shops are open, or when the telephone will be reconnected. It is an all-encompassing statement of powerlessness. It is a gesture: arching eyebrows, a hunching of the shoulders, a look of disdain. It can be said carelessly – lingeringly – which is to insult a person: why do you ask me such a stupid thing? Or fast and angrily. Or softly and caringly.

That morning I stood at the front desk of the Ministry of Press and Information. A man sat inside a glass booth on the ground floor of a miserable block which smelt of urine. It was directly behind Ataturk Caddesi, Ankara's main street, which cuts like a knife through the centre of the city. I had come to see Merih, who was in charge of liaising with foreign writers. She was arranging my interview with the administrator of the archives.

'I have come to see Merih.'

Nothing from the man in the booth.

'I have come to see Merih' – banging, by now, on the windows of the booth to attract his attention – 'in the Foreign Press Department.'

He turned his head.

I raised my voice. 'The Foreign Press Department.'

Nothing from the man.

'Do you know her?'

He turned his back.

'Merih. Do you know her?'

His back still towards me, he said, '*Yok!*' Then he turned around and smiled.

'But you must know who she is.'

'*Yok.*'

I had no option but to leave. I found a telephone box and called her office. A woman told me her surname.

I returned and reapproached the man in the glass booth. This time he was full of recognition, and he let me in.

Merih's office was surprisingly dingy: stained carpets, dusty tables, dog-eared copies of the Turkey year book on the coffee table. She was kind and helpful. She promised to do her best to help fix an appointment with the administrator.

Ersoy was working in a music shop nearby, selling hi-fis to the wealthiest residents of the city. This part of Ankara, at the top end of Ataturk Caddesi, is widely touted as the most up-market. The city is not clearly defined into districts of desirability, but it is at this end of town that all the rich Turks and foreign residents live. It is also the greenest part of the inner city, and the site of most of its foreign restaurants. There are two Chinese restaurants, both of which advertise pork on their menus, but neither of which serves it. There are other strange anomalies. Peas, for instance. It is impossible to buy fresh peas in Ankara. And exceedingly difficult to buy mushrooms.

At this end of Ataturk Caddesi are the imposing former Soviet bloc embassies – large, square, behind tall, thick metal fencing – and the anonymous grey presence of the American government. Ankara has a vast number of embassies, most of them small and unprepossessing. The numbers alone indicate the importance of this capital to international diplomacy. Many countries monitor the Middle East from Ankara – the Turks have unique insight into the region. Turkey is neutral territory: Palestinians and Israelis used to talk secretly in Ankara because both sides trusted the Turks.

Even here, however, the city has no character. It is charmless and grey and ugly. There are building sites simply left abandoned, and gaping potholes in the road. The diplomats are discrete with their social life – private cocktail parties, afternoons by the Embassy pool. Their variety does not spill over and they remain aloof from the Turkish city in which they live. That is the predominant atmosphere at this end of the city: detachment. It is like an island that floats above the flood of noise, filth and sweat which engulfs the rest of Ankara.

Ersoy had a fine collection of American hard rock music, and an expert knowledge of hi-fis. The shop was a smart boutique called Atlantis. Some of the loudspeakers retailed at $3,000 apiece. Ersoy was telling a visiting American diplomat about the benefits of the 'low excursion woofer' when I arrived.

Outside a police car rolled up and down the street with an officer calling out through a megaphone the registration numbers of illegally parked cars. He was shouting so hard that none of the numbers and letters were decipherable. They do not clamp in Ankara. 'I wish they did,' Ersoy said. I recalled a Turkish businessman telling me how he had bid, in partnership with a Western company, to install 1,100 parking meters in the city as part of an experimental traffic control project. The contract was relatively small – just around $1 million – but the prospects were substantial. The civil servant running the tender had told him over lunch (for which he was paying) that it was usual to include in the budget a small commission payable, er, to him: 10 per cent – $100,000. The Western partners pulled out. He lost the tender. And Ankara still had no parking meters.

On the way back to the flat I bought a copy of the *Turkish Daily News*, an English-language newspaper for which I had once worked. It was terribly dull then; the work consisted of compiling foreign news agency reports and editing columns by tedious local academics. In the intervening years it had improved. Some of Ankara's better journalists had joined the staff, refugees from the mainstream Turkish press. Diplomats and tourists read it regardless, because it is in English.

The paper was edited by Ilnur Cevik, a tiny man, always dwarfed by his wives. I had first met him in a beach resort on the south coast, when he was walking his dogs. Ilnur was a remarkable man, an Ataturkist through and through. For many years he thought himself important – politically significant – because he edited this paper, which had easily the smallest circulation in the country. He would write grand editorials reminding the government, in very personal terms, of his policies. It was good entertainment for the expatriates. But it went on and on. And then, almost overnight, he *was* important.

After Mr Ozal's appointment as President, Suleyman Demirel, his arch-rival and the oldest political hand in the country, took over as prime minister. Demirel appointed Ilnur his foreign policy adviser. And what did Ilnur do? Quite remarkably, he built a factory to make underpants. Some, in the Turkish press, reflected – I am sure unfairly – that Ilnur had used his new influence to secure planning permission. Turkish politics are a marvel: no more demanding than a game of British bulldog; infinitely more rewarding.

When I arrived back at the hotel, there was a message from Merih confirming my appointment with the Curator the following morning. There would be an interpreter, it said, to ensure that there were no misunderstandings.

I sat dopily in the back of a taxi making its way to the Curator's office on the outskirts of the city.

His biggest problem is with the young historians. They are humiliated by the difficulties with their own archives when they can travel the world and have no problems with anyone else's. They are a new generation, in their thirties and forties, educated in foreign (usually American) universities, and they insist on openness. They are the iconoclasts who will debunk the old history.

Their peers are slowly taking control of the country: economists and doctors and entrepreneurs. One of them – a woman, Tansu Ciller, an American-trained economist – is now prime minister. Almost without exception, their loyalties are to the urbanized west of Turkey. They do not have a vision for the whole of Anatolia. They are the evangelists of secular self-interest and personal freedom. This new élite acts just like the old Ottoman élite: the intelligentsia and the barons of power in the cities.

The young historians are uncompromising about their right to academic freedom. They want unrestricted access to the Ottoman archives. 'It is not just that we do not know that much about the Ottomans but what we do know has often been tampered with,' one of them told me. I met him one Sunday morning in a downtown tea house. I was late, and he was furious. He refused tea. His whole face, which was thin and drawn, became a fidgeting grimace of disdain when I shook his hand. I was taken entirely by surprise. Punctuality was not generally something that even the bureaucrats of Ankara cared very much about. People assumed delay and inefficiency. Most seemed to wrap themselves up in a blanket of doziness and work through the day in a half-stupor. But not this historian. He was burning with anger.

'Researchers are still thought to be injurious to the state, and that is not going to go away.' His English was erudite and fluent. His tone was breathtakingly arrogant. 'They have opened the archives and whereas it used to take six months, it now takes days to get permission; but the old attitude prevails: the bureaucrats are not archivists but *guardians* of the documents, the *guardians* of the state's secrets. That is how they see themselves. There is a vetting committee which makes sure nothing funny is going on. They say of a document "It's outside of your topic", or lie – very often – that it has been lost. They never say, "Sorry, this is simply too sensitive."' He was disgusted.

When the archives opened, the big question was: the Armenians. The Turks are accused of the modern world's first genocide: the extermination of a million Armenians in the eastern provinces during the First World War. The Armenians say that it was Turkish policy; the Turks, who dispute the figures, say that it was an accident of war. The proof, either way, is somewhere in the unclassified archives. When they were opened, the Turkish authorities said this was proof they had nothing to hide. Their ancestors had not been genocidal murderers.

'They released two sets of documents,' said the historian. 'One was a hand-picked set chosen by old ambassadors to show that we never touched an Armenian. They reproduced these, and they released all the World War One cipher telegrams, but the enclosures were often missing. If there was an Armenian holocaust the world should know about it, and reflect on it.

'We have lived for too long under the tyranny of hindsight,' he went on. 'The past has been simple: everything that explained Ataturk was good – a Sultan was judged to be good because he did things of which Ataturk would have approved.' His face had no distinction: a small beige moustache and similar-coloured hair, cut short, suggested that his origins lay partly among the fair-headed peoples of the Black Sea. But they are famous for their sense of humour, and he had none.

'Do you like Turkey?'

'A stupid question.'

'Why?'

'Turkey is not to be liked or disliked. It exists. Once there was something great and creative about this country. Now it is merely an imitation of Europe . . .'

Ismet Binark is the most senior archivist in Turkey. He enjoys his job, which gives him considerable status and responsibility. He sat in a large, pine-panelled room in front of a picture of Ataturk, smoothing the large mop of white hair on his head down with his hand. Mr Binark wanted this chat to be official; and he wanted there to be no misunderstandings. He had provided the interpreter, a pretty girl in her early twenties, who spoke English with mechanical efficiency: she had learned it at school in Holland. She was taking notes on a large pad while we talked, and she told me that this was the first time Mr Binark had granted an interview to a foreigner.

The first thing Mr Binark said was that he had written many books on Ottoman history. He said these books were very helpful, and encouraged me to read them. 'Once the Turks were very superior,' he said. 'Now it is just the reverse.' The books would help explain how this had come about. 'There are *some* other very valuable books on Ottoman history,' he added.

He was wearing a pink, short-sleeved shirt, and I had an idea from the calligraphic plaques on his desk that he was religious.

So far I had said nothing. He was a big man with an open, smiling face. He was genuinely pleased to be having this conversation. He was giving me a lecture. 'The history of the Turks does not begin with the Ottomans but with the Uygurs who were a pre-Islamic tribe from Central Asia . . . research made on the Uygurs has shown that these people had notaries and kept records in libraries. An article written by a German-Turk says that the first printing machine was used by these people . . .'

The interpreter interrupted: 'It shows how civilized they were.' She was a rather tight little girl: small and mean-faced. She was very neatly dressed, and her face was only lightly dusted with make-up – the work of a perfectionist. She seemed concerned by Mr Binark's enthusiasm. I had the distinct impression that she had decided I was her enemy and not to be trusted.

I could see on the neat desk in front of him a copy of the fax I had given to the information office. I had been told I would have to ask my questions according to the list. The first was: 'How old is Mr Binark? I will ask him his qualifications and about his hobbies.' The last was: 'Why are the Ottoman archives not fully open yet?'

'Really,' I had said to Merih, 'do we have to do this?'

'Oh yes,' she had replied. 'You see, they think you might be an Armenian or something, perhaps out to embarrass the director. That is why they want the list.'

Mr Binark picked up the thin copy paper and rolled it up in his hands. He squinted and looked me over, as a butcher might cast his eye over a joint of meat. He was full of interesting information, reeling it off as a proud sailor would a history of his voyages. The archives were the largest of their kind in the world . . . started in 1845 . . . 150 million records . . . the history of a dozen countries . . . new countries needed them to create their own national histories . . . Bosnia, Serbia, Croatia. 'It is why this country has such importance.' He relaxed back into his chair. There was a short silence. 'It would be unfortunate if you were looking for anti-Muslim propaganda,' he said, as if the thought that I might not be trustworthy had only just occurred to him.

He pushed aside the list and looked at me. I could ask a question.

'What was the significance of opening the archives?'

'It showed that we had no secrets. You see, some had been saying – the Armenians, I mean – we were afraid to open them. But we had no secrets so we invited the whole world to look for themselves . . .'

He suddenly became very serious and leaned forward, placing both his hands palms down on his desk. 'This reform is of the greatest importance. We have recruited 600 new staff. Many books have been published and we are classifying the documents. The archives have been automated and the number of researchers has increased – but,' he held up his hand and paused, 'but there was not *one single* Armenian who came.'

Another pause, for dramatic effect. 'That is comical, isn't it?' Then he laughed. 'Ah, no! I am wrong. One did come but he could find no records to the disadvantage of the Turks. In the past it was sometimes difficult to gain access to the archives but now you know in two days if you have permission or have been refused. There is no limit to taking photocopies.'

He pressed his palms together and pressed them against his nostrils. 'I regret to say that when I was in London in 1972, I had to acquire a letter from the Turkish embassy before I could take photocopies from *your* library!' He put his arm out towards me, like a policeman stopping traffic. 'During my visit to England I was very interested in the history of the kings and queens, and nobody knew about it when I asked them – for instance, on the underground train. Nobody knew the background. You see, the national culture is weakening. Not just in Turkey, but in Britain. For example, the number who go to church on Sundays has fallen. I observed that the churches invite people to come and then give them lunch or dinner to attract them.'

He wagged a finger. 'I do not think I have ever heard anybody talk about Ataturk in Britain.'

I was slightly confused. I wasn't sure exactly what point he was making.

The interpreter looked at me with undisguised hostility. 'I believe the British do not like Turkish history because of the glories of our past,' she said.

Mr Binark looked at her, apparently concerned by her vehemence, and said calmly, 'The Western world doesn't, of course, know the Ottoman script well. Nor the culture. What they knew was people wearing the fez who married more than one woman. The Ottomans reigned for more than 650 years. Of course, if they were not just and equal how could they govern for so long? It is not possible.' He ran his fingers through his hair. 'There is a very striking example. Under Louis XIV when he went to the streets, they blew trumpets. Why? Because there were no bathrooms in French houses they threw pots from the windows and this was a warning. During the same period there were baths in most Turkish houses . . .

'Even – imagine this – the Christian knights did not trust their wives and had special equipment to prevent them having relationships with another' (the interpreter became po-faced and shrewish). 'The Turks meanwhile had widow houses, so that if a man died she could find comfort there . . .'

The interpreter added: 'This is to show how civilized the Ottomans were.'

I looked at her and said, 'Well, it seems to me that the West knows Turkish history better than the Turks do themselves . . .' She did not reply.

Mr Binark spoke. 'Yes, when I was in London I had a friend called Peter, who was studying the history of architecture at Oxford and especially Turkish architecture . . .'

He picked up the telephone and ordered his secretary to bring in some copies of his books. There was one on Azerbaijan, and another on Bosnia, and another on Bulgaria. His secretary wrapped up the books as presents.

The interpreter showed me out. I said, 'Thank you' as we approached the door. She said nothing.

I met Ersoy back at the shop. He wanted me to meet a friend of his. It was late afternoon. We walked past the Sheraton, a tall, cylindrical building, probably the tallest in the city. 'Bloody tasteless aerosol,' said Ersoy as we walked along. The sun was starting to set. It cast a sickly grey pall over the place. I noticed for the first time that there were mushrooms growing in the gaps between the concrete panels on some of the pavements.

The bar was packed with a lot of young men and women. We sat out in the beer garden. Ersoy told me that his friend was a historian. 'He has been banned altogether from the archives.' I was surprised. 'Yes. I mean banned. They don't trust him. He has left-wing views.'

Selim arrived. His face was masked by a massive orange beard. When I caught sight of his eyes, they were dazed, as if he had just been asleep. His lips curled towards his chin in a permanent grimace. He had a woman with him. She wore a dirty old sheepskin jacket.

Selim's expertise is in the history of Trebizond (now Trabzon) on the Black Sea coast. He is one of the very few in Turkey who can read the old Ottoman script. He works for odd sponsors: a university paper here, a conference there. He cannot obtain regular work because he is denied access to the archives.

'It must be difficult?'

'Yes.' His girlfriend smiled.

'To be an Ottoman . . .' The conversation was very awkward.

'Yes, I am an Ottoman,' Selim snapped. He was really angry.

At the next table some young girls were squealing with laughter.

'I am a *freelance* historian,' Selim said with emphasis. 'Not attached to any *particular* university. I make a living writing papers and books. But it is difficult because I am deprived of *data*. I am not allowed into the Ottoman archives. I have to read books. That is my *only* resource.'

'Well, what can you do?'

'Actually, I understand them,' he replied, suddenly smiling. 'You cannot have everyone looking through the old manuscripts.'

There was a silence. Selim was fingering his beer glass. I thought he might throw it against the wall. Such frustration.

Another friend of Ersoy's had joined us at the table. 'What do you read then?'

Quite serious: 'I have already answered this. I read printed books . . . You realize that dissent was difficult under the Ottomans too? That there were few then who could even read and write, and without this you cannot do . . . anything?'

Ersoy, thinking aloud, said, 'Maybe history is not much good in any case. I mean, it does not answer all the questions you really want to ask. You know, Christ didn't tell us the most interesting thing: what did he see flash through his mind when he died . . .?'

Selim looked strangely at him. He said he had to leave, and stood up. His girlfriend followed him and the two walked out of the bar. They had not finished their beers.

I had not asked Selim why he had not been given permission for the archives. The next day I tried to find him. I went to the address Ersoy had, but it was incorrect. There was a dental surgery where he should have been. None of the local shopkeepers knew of a historian living nearby. He did not have a telephone. I never saw him again.

I was, however, given access to the archives. I thought it would be an interesting (little) test of the new openness. It took a few weeks. I had applied to seek out material on Edward Webbe and the firework of Noah's Ark. An official letter arrived at my hotel in Istanbul. I could not achieve much in an afternoon, of course. It would be years before they dug Webbe out of the archives. The vast majority of the material stored here has not even been catalogued. And I do not read Ottoman. But there might be something.

I imagined vaulted roofs and gilded upholstery. The reality was disappointing: plain, low and concrete on the first floor of a block in a side street near the mosque of Sultan Ahmet. There were one or two people I recognized in there, but they did not acknowledge me. Perhaps they did not see me. Perhaps it would not have been politic to have done so.

I browsed along the bookshelves at the back: *The Immortal*

Ataturk: a Psychobiography by some Chicago academics, 1984. Then I found an article: 'Gunpowder in Ottoman Documents of the Last Half of the Sixteenth Century'. The time of Webbe and Murat. The young Republic, lamented the writer, destroyed many documents. There is little left on the subject of gunpowder, he concluded.

I spent a moment looking at all the academics furling and unfurling large rolls of old parchment on the tables in the reading room. Nearest me was a young Turk with long lists of numbers etched on his scrolls, annotating each number carefully into his notebook. These men and women, I thought, were not so much historians as geographers, mapping a land that has been described in no real detail before them. I wonder if this nation will thank them for it.

5

The King of Despair

It started like a food scare. The Turkish government told the people that they were afflicted, paralysed because they were consuming something that did them harm. It warned them that they might not be aware of their affliction. Unwittingly, citizens could become depressed. Negative, hopeless. Ready to give up. In extreme cases the reaction was so violent that it was blamed for provoking suicide attempts.

Special research was commissioned. 'It was revealed,' reported the upmarket newspaper *Milliyet*, 'that 28 out of 681 suicides had chosen to take their own lives in order to save themselves from bottled-up despair provoked by *arabesk* in the cinema, the press and the television.'

Turkey was gripped by a real panic. *Arabesk* is merely a kind of music. Quite suddenly, however, it was being blamed for undermining the fabric of society. The matter was raised in the National Assembly. The government decided to take action. It became the central point of discussion on TV chatshows and in the newspapers. *Arabesk* was held up by its enemies as the reason for the degeneration of Turkish culture. They said it provoked profound despair in those who listened to it; that it corrupted them with the terrible sadness of its lyrics; that it left them hopeless and aimless. It was said by the Establishment to be the enemy of everything decent in the Republic. It is everything that Ataturk despised.

The government decided to ban it. In 1989, the Minister of Culture forbade its performance on Turkish Radio and Television. That had no effect on its popularity. Still the people loved it. The minister adopted a different strategy. He ordered the invention of a less pernicious strain of the music, which could be accepted by the people, an official *arabesk* that sounded the same but was free of the suicidal elements: the excessive heartache and melancholy of the most popular lyrics were to be replaced with brighter, happier thoughts. The tunes were given solid Western pop-style rhythms. 'So that people can dance to music instead of crying,' said one official.

There was a special television programme to unveil it. The minister called it *Acisiz Arabesk* – *arabesk* without the bitterness. Nonsense, said the people, who continued to buy the original cassettes by the million. Impossible. But one of the minister's aides predicted that within months the ordinary Turk would have put the *arabesk* behind him and turned to marching band music 'with its heart-uplifting tunes and national sentiments'.

There were some who counselled caution. One conductor said, 'The point is that bitterness satisfies the people. To eliminate *arabesk* you have to eliminate the social conditions that created it. To cut out the bitterness artificially would be like taking alcohol out of *raki*.'

He was right: the music was popular because it articulated popular despondency. The *arabesk* said that something had gone very wrong indeed with Ataturk's Republic. That is why the government took it so seriously. This was not merely a fight to counter a musical style, it was part of a broader struggle to preserve the purity of the original Republic. That fight continues. In 1989, however, the government lost its campaign against the *arabesk*. The minister responsible has left politics, and his hybrid music is forgotten. The old *arabesk* lives on and prospers. It continues to divide the nation.

Ersoy was late again. I had arrived in Istanbul and booked myself into the Eresin, behind Taksim Square, which is the hub of the city on the European side. The Eresin advertised a free mini-bar, but I had not believed it at the time and it turned out to be just a couple of free soft drinks. I was disappointed that Ersoy was late. His mother said he had left Ankara; and then she added that he had gone walking in the mountains. Perhaps he had simply forgotten to meet me; but that was not like him. One day here or there was of no consequence to him.

I always remember the first time I arrived in this city. It was aboard the express train from Athens. Three days of unrelenting discomfort on unforgiving vinyl seats in the company of two elderly Turkish ladies who insistently and frequently passed a bottle of eau de cologne around their fellow passengers. I had been recommended a hotel in the tourist quarter of the city behind the mighty Sultan Ahmet mosque – the Blue Mosque – which is probably the most famous mosque in the world. In front of it there are lawns and neat flower-beds, behind, there is a maze of tiny streets which lead you – so soon after the mosque – face to face with the dirt, poverty and squalor that are the true hallmarks of Sultan Ahmet today.

Here also was the Hotel Best. It was run by women. We were the only guests. Others used to arrive at night, and we could hear the bed-springs in neighbouring rooms play out little rhythmic concertos over and over. There was one lady I remember. She was not more than thirty, with skin so pale and lifeless it hung off her face, like paper. You could literally see the bones. Her eyes were dazzling: they stood out like emeralds against her bleached complexion, and they sparkled when she smiled. But they were swimming in water. She was always dabbing at them with a tissue. Her hair, now I look back, was the give-away: a few sad red strands. Otherwise she was bald.

I have been back there once or twice. The last time, I could not find the hotel at all, and I have never found any of the women. But these were the first Turks I ever met, and it was my first taste of the *arabesk*.

It is the sound of Istanbul. It is the music of the *dolmus*, Turkey's communal taxi, and the yellow cabs, and the restaurants and the brothels. It was the only thing that would take the edge off the cranking bed-springs: loud, brash and, though I did not know it at the time, dismal and fatalistic. I can understand the drivers now, mostly poor villagers trying to make good in the city, driving around in never-ending circles of need and disappointment. The music does that too, round and round, mourning lost opportunities. This is a typical lyric:

> I have been addicted to every sort of sorrow
> I have been elected to life-long suffering
> I am terribly alone
> Not a single day do I spend without suffering
> But always much suffering.

The Eresin provided an *arabesk* channel on the bedside console. There are private radios in Istanbul now. They pump out despondency because, as is perfectly obvious, it sells exceptionally well. I put on the radio and sipped a free Coke.

I had come to the city for a quite specific purpose: to find Ibrahim Tatlises. Ibo is the biggest star in Turkey; for a decade, he has been a popular hero. He is the closest thing the Turks have to monarchy. The newspapers report on Ibo's presence at a football match, or that he has been taking tea in a city café. Sometimes he beats up his girlfriend; and sometimes they catch him with a long lens, tears streaming down his face. Ibo holds the key to this country, and most especially to Istanbul, which is very largely his parish. Ibo is the Crown Prince of Arabesk. He survived the Ministry of Culture's offensive.

I had bought a couple of newspapers, to test them. They both carried something about him. In one of them there was something about him and *her*. She is something special too: the Queen of Istanbul. She is a sometime actress and singer, an *arabeskci* for sure, but not as artistically sound as Ibo. Instead she is beautiful. Hulya Avsar – the words themselves are voluptuous. She is the innocent villager with wide, sky-blue eyes and an obedient smile. She is the Turkish male fantasy. One of Istanbul's glossy magazines had an article about her feet. There were close-up photographs. They were not perfect. I noticed that on one toe the nail lacquer was cracked. They were stubby things, in any case. The point of the article was that Hulya's feet were a match for those of any of the historic beauties of this century: Marilyn Monroe, Sophia Loren. And so was she.

Hulya is mainly important because she had been – and perhaps still was – Ibo's lover. Their relationship has been long and complex. It is the great romance of modern Turkey. The story has a uniquely *arabesk* flavour to it: doomed, peaks of ecstasy, long troughs of frustration and despair. During one of their separations Hulya fell at the feet of Tanju, Turkey's star footballer, the highest goal scorer in Europe in 1989. The press splashed pictures of the two together during a secret holiday. Editors relaxed normally firm rules about nudity (they black out nipples) to let readers examine, with proper outrage, the full majesty of her breasts while she pranced topless along the beach.

Hulya was born a peasant in Izmir (it's the part she is always playing in her films, with a head-scarf to show her modesty, embroidering lace table-cloths for her dowry). Her mother still is a peasant, and when the story about Tanju surfaced, she weighed in demanding the two get married. They did eventually, but it did not last long. By the time I turned up in Istanbul, Hulya had long since done with Tanju. The word was that she was seeing Ibo, who has never married, again.

Ibo is a vast legend. He is the country's best singer, with a claim to be considered amongst the very best in the world: in terms of the quality of his voice, comparisons with any of the operatic tenors should be taken seriously. Yet Ibo is ordinary, so ordinary: the regulation Turkish moustache, a curly-bobbed crust of black hair on his head, a stupid grin. Mr Turk, full-blooded, straight-talking. No Ataturk here; no blue eyes and blond hair. He is Turk all over, and people feel good about that. He seems just like his audience. He beats his women and so do they. Turkey was scandalized for a few days when Ibo admitted that he had beaten Hulya up once or twice during arguments, and other women too. He was not ashamed. Quite the opposite. He was smiling in all the pictures.

One newspaper asked 2,300 men, picked at random, what they thought about wife-beating. Forty-five per cent supported it; half went on to claim intellectual superiority over their women; and two-thirds saw women as subject to their whim. The newspaper, trying to account for these results, claimed that men were becoming more violent and despotic because they were sexually frustrated. They were frustrated, it explained, because they were not eating enough nutritious food.

In reality, of course, Ibo is nothing like his audience. He is fabulously wealthy – his cassettes sell anything up to two million copies. He has investments in land and in tourism. But there is the illusion of similarity. Ibo started out like them: a poor, uneducated villager from the east.

There are those who say that the *arabesk* is going out of fashion, and, of course, it will. But for now neither the popular new singers of the left, who write music about social change, nor the Western pop imitators have deposed it. The city still wears its *arabesk* badges. In every dolmus and not a few taxis, there are the regulation postcards of a small boy and a small girl weeping. Sometimes they just have a symbolic tear rolling off their cheek; other times it is real crying, as if somebody has just beaten them. It's a small thing, but it says *arabesk* loyalist. So do the extraordinary child-like decorations on trucks and cars. Little stickers here and there, inside and out: an imitation wool fleece on the passenger seat. These are people trying to personalize things, to make themselves feel at home when they do not. Some will be more direct and will have stickers on the dashboard which carry a lyric from a song by their preferred *arabeskci*. The enthusiasm can sometimes cause violence. There have been reports of crowds at football matches dissolving into fighting because of arguments not about their teams but about *arabesk* singers. There is a vicious rivalry between fans of Ferdi Tayfur and those of Orhan Gencebay. Ibo has somehow stayed above all that. Everybody seems to like Ibo; they do not fight over him.

Music is a key in Istanbul: it unlocks the place. It is how people sort each other out. Music divides and unites. It is not just that music symbolizes things about people; it *is* people. Different styles of music in Istanbul are, mainly, different ways of talking about life in Istanbul.

The *arabesk* is not so much a style of music as a frame of mind. It is a phenomenon which frightens the followers of Ataturk because they say it is contrary to everything he set out to achieve. Ataturk promoted two kinds of music: Western classical and Turkish folk. He banned the music of the Ottoman court, which we can call Turkish classical music, because it made systematic use of musical forms developed in Arabia and Persia. Ataturk wanted Turkey to turn away from the East. Western classical music was deemed to be the product of 'universal' civilization. Folk was said to be the essence of pure Turkish culture. The highest achievement in Turkish art would therefore be the union of Turkish folk with classical music.

Gradually, over the years, Ataturk's purist musical culture became perverted from its original course. The old Turkish classical music – the highbrow art music of the Ottoman court – reappeared. Turkish Radio and Television (TRT) eventually relented, and it started to appear on television. The Ataturkist musicians were, and remained, unhappy. They see the art music with all its Ottoman associations and its heavy use of Middle Eastern scales as a symbol of reaction.

But the arguments about the revival of art music were nothing compared to those that followed the emergence of the *arabesk*. It has its roots in the 1920s and 1930s, when Egyptian films and radio became very popular in Turkey. They were the vehicles of a new music which combined Arab songs with some popular Western styles. Turkish film-makers were much influenced by them and started to imitate the films, and their music. The scripts followed strict formulae: most often, they told the story of a tragic love affair, never consummated, which would cost the participants either their lives or their happiness. There were some classical variations: the girl who was blinded when young, becomes a singer to support herself, falls in love, sees her lover die, and, in her grief, recovers her sight. The films generally articulated a dilemma: the hero would possess a basic honesty and decency, and he would find this tested by the corrupting values of urban society, influenced by the West. Usually he was a rural migrant to one of the larger cities, alienated and ill-at-ease with metropolitan life.

The hero-stars of the films (they were called *yesilcam* after the street in Istanbul on which the producers had their offices) of the 1950s and 1960s defined the way in which the later stars of the *arabesk*, like Ibo, would conduct themselves. They rarely married, and seemed incapable of sustaining a relationship for any length of time.

By the 1970s the *arabesk* had arrived in its full maturity. During this decade and the next the music of fatalism and despair became a huge commercial business. During those years there was massive migration from the rural east of Anatolia to the urban centres of western Turkey. This encouraged the *arabesk*, a mix of traditional Turkish folk music, heavily influenced by Arabic popular music, and some features of Western popular music. As in folk, at the centre of the music is an instrument called a *baglama*, a long-necked lute. But in *arabesk* (usually), this versatile guitar is electrified, supported by an army of drummers, violins, and an electric organ. The lyrics may be depressing and fatalistic, but the music is marching-style, and very punchy.

Arabesk started its life as the music of the ghetto, but its appeal now extends much further than the taxi driver or the migrant *gecekondu* dweller. It does not belong to any particular social class. It is only the rich who can afford, night after night, to pack out the wildly expensive night-clubs at which the *arabesk* stars perform.

The late President Turgut Ozal (he died of a heart attack in 1993) was always said to be a fan. It was rumoured that he used to drive along the highways of Anatolia, at the wheel of his Mercedes, windows down, listening to Ibrahim Tatlises tapes. (At one point Ibo thought about standing as an MP.) Ozal certainly recognized the political benefits of patronizing the music. In 1988 he made an *arabesk* song called 'May He Who Doesn't Love You Die' the theme tune to his general election campaign (which he won).

The liberals are horrified. For them the *arabesk* is an exact expression of resurgent tradition: full of old Islamic fatalism. It seems to speak for a country that is tired of Ataturk's secular

Republic. It is music which speaks of confusion and failure. They say that *arabesk* is an anti-culture, but it is not. It is a culture; it is a uniquely Turkish culture.

Ibo is the most difficult man in Turkey to meet. Much harder than Turgut Ozal. I did not have a strategy. Friends in London had told me I would find him by asking his recording company; others said it was hopeless. I did not know where he was performing. The usual places – the night-clubs, the *gazino* – in Taksim were either closed or presenting second-division performers. The big stars were in the summer venues: Bodrum, Antalya. But nobody seemed to know where Ibo was. I had scoured the papers for information. There was a picture of him – the familiar slight podginess – on a beach somewhere. But the caption said that this was him on a beach where he *had* been on holiday.

I left the hotel and went walking into Taksim, trying to figure out what to do while I waited for Ersoy. Taksim Square has the Ataturk Cultural Centre on one side, which is where officially sanctioned music is performed: opera, ballet, Turkish folk choruses. It is a big rectangular building, formal and functional. It was here that the government sponsored a concert of the *Acisiz Arabesk* during its campaign to try to outlaw melancholy in the music. It was this concert which was televised.

Further round, past the lights of the Marmara Otel and the men selling American hard-core pornography from street stalls, is Maksim's. At night the square is thronged with people. A lot of them just stand around, smoking, eating ice cream. They join the wild dogs, who slope in and out of the square, and the feral cats. I observed one dog asleep inside a glass-sided cash dispenser booth. Istanbul has an enormous population of both animals. Their origins remain a mystery. I have yet to meet a Turk who keeps a pet. To live in this jam-packed city with an animal would be sado-masochistic. This is not a pretty or refined square. It has few trees breaking up the rigid contours of concrete. It is difficult to see why people gather, except to survey the simple hum of urban activity and plug into it. Whole families were walking up and down, just yards from the kerb and the frenzied traffic. Every word they said must have been drowned by the noise.

They would have paused outside Maksim's, the home of live *arabesk*. But it was closed. A huge square grid on the front wall of the grey theatre building – a strange parody of its French namesake, with imitation Parisian features – used to scream across the square in a blaze of neon with the names of the night's performers. The great stars of the *arabesk* used to play here. But it was deserted when I arrived: the place had been gutted. A sad, stray letter hung from the grid. One of the street vendors said there had been a fire. I wondered if it had been started deliberately.

It was early for Taksim – perhaps ten o'clock. I continued across the square towards Istiklal Street. The air quivered with the beat of hard-line *arabesk* from all the *pavyon* – the brothels, bars and night-clubs. All around, when I looked up towards the sky, were flags making Istanbul's bid to host the Olympics in 2000. Istanbul wanted to claim its place as an international city of great standing. It wanted to stop all those elderly Europeans who say, 'Ah yes, Constantinople! Of course, it used to be a great city, and so civilized.'

Once this area, Beyoglu, had been a place of legendary hedonism in Europe, the heart of a sensational party that came to an abrupt end with the First World War and, later, Ataturk. It was a party for the foreigners in the city: the white Russians, like Basil Zacharoff, the famous arms dealer, and the French, and the Jews, and the Armenians, and the Levantines. They call this era – the twilight years of the Ottoman Empire – the Belle Epoque, when they danced the polka des Anglais in the ballroom of the Pera Palas hotel. Little remains on Istiklal to mark the marvellous extravagance of those years. The town-houses suggest some of the elegance: the ornate Parisian stone decoration, the fine metal work on the balcony rails, the wooden window shutters. Now there is extravagance of a different kind, brash and without refinement. Istiklal is full of expensive shops and little arcades that have been refitted with bars and restaurants. I stopped in one of these arcades, the Flower Passage, with a cold beer, watching an accordionist entertain some Japanese tourists. It had been carefully restored, and yet, after all the work, it finished up with no character at all.

I drifted up one of the tributaries off Istiklal into the Jazz Stop. There was a big neon sign. Jazz seemed interesting. It made a change.

The club was down some steps and it was empty. I guessed that it must originally have been a brothel. It had a belly-dancing floor space, lined with mirrors. The seats and tables were shrouded in almost indecent darkness.

In here they were playing a kind of rock music: old covers mutated, transformed with just a hint of the Orient. I wasn't disappointed: familiar features on a foreign face. The band was good. Some were Turks, the guitarist was a refugee from Bosnia.

After a few drinks, I thought about Ibo. I could see by now that there were a few people hiding in the shadows. There was a man standing behind the bar wearing a torn T-shirt and a bandana, and on the small stage another man was miming some riffs on a guitar to the music. On the stool beside me was Ahmet, who was an electrical engineer and before that had been a merchant sailor. He had some clipped whiskers on the tip of his chin, an unusual arrangement for a modern Turk, but elegantly Levantine. He hated the government; he hated the army; he hated Ibrahim Tatlises. I asked him how he would go about finding him.

'Why are you interested in him?' He paused. 'The guy is a danger to our country.'

'So how do I find him?'

'Easy. Ask Cahit.'

It was, in fact, that easy. Cahit was guitarist with the Moguls, one of Turkey's best-known rock bands, and also a famous film score composer. He wrote much of the music for Tatlises. The two men had become friends. Ahmet told me about the Moguls. They were not the band performing that night. 'God, if they were this place would be full,' he said.

In the 1970s they had been huge. The American company, CBS, signed them up for an album. Their blend of Turkish melody and Western rock was very attractive for a time. Once they were awarded a prestigious French prize for their music. The year before the Moguls won it, it was given to Pink Floyd, and the following year to Jimi Hendrix. But their success did not last, and the band split up. Cahit went on to work as a barman in Amsterdam. The drummer Engin, who owned the Jazz Stop, had run a kebab restaurant in Paris.

Eventually they had all returned to Turkey. A few months before I arrived, the band had re-formed. So far it had been a success, but the biggest challenge lay ahead. The Moguls had been invited to perform at the Izmir International Fair, which during the 1960s and 1970s had been the greatest cultural event in Turkey. It was – and comparisons to the great arts festival of 1582 are not misplaced – the most prestigious arts event in the Near East. There was intense competition to perform at Izmir. In the golden days of the late 1960s, the Moguls were one of the headline acts; this year it was Ibrahim Tatlises.

What a contrast that was: old-fashioned concept rock and the garish unsubtlety of the *arabesk*. The two men should not, according to normal social conventions, have been friends at all. But they were. Turkey has a quiet cultural density which, when you find it, is always unexpected.

You could make out the posters. There were photographs of four young Turks with long shoulder-length hair and bell-bottoms. This was the 1970s, unmistakably. There were the collars too – great floral affairs with thick flanges; and in one poster, these men were wearing traditional Turkish folkloric costumes of a kind that today only tourist guides or show dancers wear. It was a telling costume, designed for a foreign audience.

Ahmet was looking at the posters. 'We need them back,' he said. 'Turkey needs them back.' He sounded quite despairing when he said this. The sentimentality was surprising. The 1970s were years that many Turks prefer to forget: they may have been the years of the Moguls, but they were also the years of chaos. *Midnight Express* has fixed them in the European conscience. Most Turks have not seen this film. For them, those years are filled with memories of street anarchy between extremist political groups which claimed hundreds of innocent lives.

When I met Cahit the next day, I sensed that he knew the age of the Moguls had passed. They were a band for the idealism of a youthful Turkey that could still remember the freedoms of the 1960s. The blend of Turkish and European music and what that symbolized – cultural union with the West, equality with the West – does not make sense to most Turks any more. People are more comfortable looking East to Islam. The *arabesk* thrives on this. The new Turkey is more hard-headed and less naive.

The band was having a rehearsal before the performance in Izmir. In the morning, Istiklal was different. Cold. All the shadows were gone. The milling crowds were aspiring, smiling consumers. Mothers and daughters. The *Istanbullu* are among the best shoppers in the world, with such a tradition of it: careful and demanding. In the big international shops they give you a shirt in a plastic bag; but in the small stationery shops they wrap up your pencils in gift paper, and finish it, like a florist, with a ribbon bow.

In the Jazz Stop the lights were on, and the fully used sense of the club was exposed: the curled-up edges of the posters, the black panels around the room that are dented and look as if someone in a rage had spent some time punching them out of shape. There was a black labrador asleep on a seat near the stage.

Engin (forty-five) was standing by his drums, laughing at some joke. Cahit (forty-eight) was beside him, a giant with a shaggy clump of grey hair tied up in a pony-tail. Behind them there was a poster in intense bright colours of a young Elvis Presley with a fluorescent pink face.

They played a song called 'Isizlik Ortasinda', which means 'In the Middle of Nowhere'. 'You are in the middle of a crowd,' said Cahit, 'but you still feel lonely, in the dark.' It was written, he explained, to mark a shocking incident of religious violence in the central Anatolian city of Sivas just weeks before. Thirty people had been murdered by Islamic extremists. It left liberal Turkey dazed. The song had no words, the vocal line was hummed by the band without their instruments. It was like a plainsong chant, a heartfelt plea for moderation. They sung with the full force of their years: tired old men suddenly exhausted by the intolerance they had struggled for so long to challenge.

Cahit was worried about the Moguls in Izmir. 'I do not want to break the magic,' he said. He did not want to be reminded that Turkey had no room for his idealism. Ibo, on the other hand, could not fail. 'You need to think about that,' he said. 'I do a great deal. Here I am writing that music and this. How do I make sense of that myself . . .?' He smiled. He had stopped worrying about it. Life is too short. He agreed to introduce us to Ibo.

Ersoy finally arrived. I had moved to a new (cheaper) hotel in Aksaray, which is across the Golden Horn from Taksim. The hotel itself was in the middle of the Eastern European quarter. It was full of Romanian whores with hair the colour of vanilla ice cream, and hard eyes. The men, in shell suits, were filling canvas sacks with cheap jeans and shirts which they would take back on the cramped coaches that ferry them out of Eastern Europe. Many of the shops around here had signs in Hungarian or Polish. In the evening, some grotesque Ibo parodies – huge, fat men in white linen suits with incompletely shaved faces and clumps of thick hair protruding from their nostrils – came to the reception and sat with the women. Nobody took much notice. Their husbands were too busy running up and down the stairs with gigantic sacks of cheap shoes and leather jackets.

Ersoy had not been to Istanbul for a while and he had noticed all the Olympic advertising. 'All this and we will lose; a dreadful waste of money . . .' I listened to the radio in the hotel room. A man from Izmir was proposing to swim to Northern Cyprus in protest at some government policy. I have always liked the Turkish sense of humour. I told Ersoy we were going to Izmir, and then he went to sleep.

While we sat in the plane flying down to Izmir the next day, we both read the Turkish Airlines magazine. There was an extraordinary article about the city.

> The bay of Izmir where we used to fish in the late 1950s today harbours barely a living creature. The once clear waters now emit the smell which has come to characterize the city. The two- and three-storey neoclassical houses along the esplanade, with their porticoes and gardens adorned with statuary, have been swept away to make room for eight-storey modern apartment blocks.

The airways magazine is supposed to promote Turkey.

Izmir is Turkey's third city, and one of Anatolia's most famous. In Greek, it is Smyrna. Aristotle was born here. Some say it was founded by the Amazons and others by the Lydian King Tantalus. Alexander the Great rebuilt it, and it became a cosmopolitan entrepôt of Levantine traders. There was a wide diversity of religion: Christian, Jewish, Muslim. 'The colourful cultural mosaic which characterized pre-war Izmir has virtually disappeared today,' reported the Turkish Airlines article in a long lament about its deterioration. This was the city in which Onassis had lived until 1922, and it was the birth-place of the French singer Dario Mareno.

After the First World War, Greece invaded Izmir, with the connivance of the British prime minister Lloyd George. The Turks reclaimed it, and a dreadful fire, probably arson, consumed much of the city centre. The site of the fire is where the Culture Park now stands. This is the home of the annual trade fair where Ibo and the Moguls were to play.

Most people remember Izmir for its clock-tower. This ornate clock, on its spindly tower, stands with its face to the sea, surrounded on the other sides by shops and office blocks. A gift from the German Kaiser, it was erected by the despot Abdul Hamit to mark his twenty-fifth jubilee. Abdul Hamit was obsessed by time. Murat III had the same fascination. This clock symbolizes most of the things Ataturk hated: the folly of the Sultans.

When you arrive by plane, the whole place looks a shambles. Izmir is one of the messiest, most confused cities in Turkey. From the airport the view is of scrubland and high-rise blocks, cows grazing between apartments, tractors on the motorways, bags of flour in huge canvas bags on the roadside. As you drive past them, the *gecekondu*s of Izmir feel as if they are merely impersonating urban life, not aspiring to it. Izmir is warmer than Istanbul (there are palm trees) and life is lived at a slower, more leisurely pace. It is, however, a town which has attracted many eastern migrants, and they have brought Islam with them. Many women in Izmir have taken the veil; and there are new mosques sprouting in the suburbs, foil on the domes, not yet covered by cement. These are no-nonsense places of worship. Nothing fancy. The skin is of cement, just washed with white. This is also a place of no colour; there is no clean colour anywhere, just shades and haze.

When we arrived at the bus terminal in the centre of the city, our first priority was to buy tickets for Ibo's show. It was bound to sell out fast. We passed some posters – IBRAHIM TATLISES: MEGASHOW. Not just Ibrahim, but Hulya Avsar as well. The two of them were pictured as caricatures sitting side by side on thrones. The King and Queen of Turkey. There were no posters for the Moguls. We found a ticket-seller in one of the bookshops near the clock-tower and reserved some seats. The clock was covered in scaffolding. There were no men on the frame; it looked old and quite rusty.

On the way to our hotel, we passed a bath-house which had this slogan (in Turkish) painted across its windows: THE MODERN SHOWER. PEOPLE CAN TAKE ONE.

This was the first day of the International Fair. There were huge signs at the entrance to the large park, and inside, in between the gardens, were dozens of pavilion buildings. The Indian one had little Taj Mahal-like arches around the sides; the Romanian one was just a box, straight up and down. In between the pavilions were fountains and long, shallow pools of water. The park was set out, topographically, as a circle: the concrete footpaths that crossed it went on and on for ever, round and round, encircling a paradise of consumption. Outside, there was a grubby city with a stinking harbour. The water was dead, slurping over a filthy polluted sludge that heaped up along the waterfront. It smelt like a latrine. In the distance, some Nato warships were moored.

To the people inside it must have seemed like a marvel, like window-shopping in a dream: German cars and the latest in Italian cookware. Renault had constructed a large model of Zeus in their pavilion with flashing blue lights for eyes and Mozart booming through the speakers. The Turkish stands were less well attended. They displayed hand-made hunting rifles from Konya and gas heaters, irons and toasters. ASELSAN, the Turkish arms company, had its own pavilion, showing some hi-tech muscle with complicated pieces of military hardware. There was no one at all inside that building.

In the middle of the park young men and boys were jumping off a tall green tower attached to a practice parachute. They screamed with laughter. This was where the army sends its trainee paratroopers. But today it was open to the general public. There were fun fairs and fast food joints and music for every kind of Turk: popular, *arabesk*, classical. There was a huge screen outside the entrance decorated in golden streamers with the names of all the *arabesk* artists appearing at the fair. This was an opportunity for poor Turks to see the big stars. There were booths in which a woman would read your future from your palm; there were others in which a computer would do the same job for less cash. There was a queue of conscripts waiting in line for their turn. There were stalls where you could have your picture taken besides cutouts of the big stars – all the men were choosing Hulya Avsar. A mini-Turkey: all the bits and pieces were there in the park.

I had picked up a local newspaper. Tomorrow was the anniversary of the liberation of Izmir from the Greeks in 1922. Yet more celebrations. But this was not what was preoccupying the locals. The main front page story stated: 'EVERYBODY SAYS THEY HAVE NO MONEY . . . BUT THAT IS NOT HOW IT IS . . . 200 PEOPLE IN TURKEY HAVE BOUGHT THE NEW MERCEDES C SERIES.' Another story on the front: a 'beautiful blonde' English tourist who had lost a leg in some holiday accident said her real aim in life was to be like Princess Diana.

There was a picture of Ibo (playing football) and Hulya (swinging from a roof beam). Ersoy and I thought we would try to find the *gazino* in which Ibo was performing. The theatre (it was a huge *gazino*) was next to an Italian stand, full of electric water-pumps, and opposite a row of tarot kiosks.

The doorman laughed in our faces: Ibo was not even allowing *photographers* near him, he said. A second heavy said that he spent his time in the afternoons swimming in the pool of the Buyuk Efes Hotel, if he was not in his room at the Hilton. But he counselled us, 'He does not like to answer questions.'

Not far away large crowds were beginning to gather. The official opening ceremony of the fair was to start shortly. Large tented pavilions had been erected for the VIPs, and they included foreign diplomats as well as businessmen. The ordinary people were forced to strain for a glimpse of the stage behind these tents and through the lines of hard-looking armed Turkish police. There were sharpshooters on surrounding roofs. The Opposition leader, Erdal Inonu, was the guest of honour. He was the son of the Republic's second president, Ismet. But Mr Inonu had not had much success as a politician and he had recently announced his retirement. He had been a professor of physics before he became a politician, a man of sweeping intellect, who had no gift for rabble-rousing. He said a few nervous words and then disappeared in a screeching of car rubber.

That night the Moguls took the stage in an open-air disco in the middle of the park. During the day they were very confident, upbeat. But in the end only a handful of people turned up for the show. Their equipment played up as well. There was wild feedback and by the end the small audience was demanding its money back.

This was what Cahit had feared: complete lack of interest. Nevertheless it was a shock. Engin and Cahit were shouting at the stage-hands – the tickets were too expensive, the time was wrong, there was not enough publicity. Everything – except the obvious. The manager arrived, smooth in a pink open-necked shirt. He spoke good English and the first thing he said to me was, 'I studied, of course, at the London School of Economics – you know it? – and I lived in England for fourteen years . . .' He was trying to calm Cahit down, patting him on the back like a dog. Then I noticed his friend. The liquid eyes and the promise of innocent sensuality. You *felt* her presence before you could see her: a force-field of cheerful sexiness. It was Hulya Avsar, skipping around like a girl, forcing a smile out of Engin and laughing all the time. It was so inappropriate, all her laughter, but everybody laughed with her. She was wearing jeans and a little leather jacket. The manager was patting Cahit, saying, 'It really doesn't matter. The Moguls are a great band. They are a great band.'

Hulya's eyes fluttered with disappointment when Cahit told her what had happened. 'But I *so* wanted to hear the Moguls,' she said with proper emphasis. Engin looked at Cahit, and I thought they were going to get back on stage. 'But there is another night, maybe?' she continued.

And Cahit said, 'Yes, of course.' He knew her and he kissed her like a brother. Then she flew away, with the manager saying, 'Tomorrow, then, Cahit. Tomorrow.'

I have often thought that Ibrahim Tatlises was like Frank Sinatra – thick with the mobsters, a lot of singing brilliance, and never past it. Ersoy argued that he is more like Benny Hill. 'Not at all like Sinatra,' he scoffed as we walked through the *gazino* to his dressing-room. The guards were there: sharp suits and pistol bulges. They were all smiling at Cahit and looked quizzically at Ersoy's pony-tail. These men had stiff brushes of trim black hair on their heads, and strip moustaches. They were not liberals or open-minded. Nobody said anything. One man did approach Cahit: Ibo was not here, he would arrive shortly. We were to wait.

The *gazino* was built beside a small lake in the park. It was called the Swan because the man who ran the boating business on the lake had a number of paddle-boats in the shape of swans.

Across the grubby lino floor was one dressing-room marked

'Hulya Avsar' and opposite, another marked 'Ibrahim Tatlises'. A good throaty noise was coming from Hulya's room: she was shouting at her assistant. Her voice, deeper than I had remembered, had a nasty I-told-you-so edge to it. Ibo's room was in darkness, which was a surprise. The backstage was grimy and seedy. On the walls next to the dressing-rooms there were some Constable prints in dirty plastic frames. These were familiar English scenes, in rose-red and gold. They gave the place a completely inappropriate air of genteel respectability. I kept on thinking: what if these people really do love each other? Hulya's assistant whimpered from behind the door after a graceless torrent of abuse, and then opened it an inch to shout at a boy sitting on a chair outside, '*Sis!*' Hulya, the peasant girl, wanted a kebab.

We were still waiting for Ibo, and all the bodyguards – they had been growing in number – were pacing around anxiously. He was late. The show should already have started. Cahit said in English, 'He has four or five bodyguards – one carries the drugs and another his gun . . .' He laughed.

Ibo could not read music but he wrote the lyrics and took a big hand in arranging the orchestration. Cahit said, 'He knows, he really knows about music . . . he makes the impossible possible – a crazy man but very intelligent. Once he came to my house in Istanbul and I said, come alone without your bodyguards. He arrived and he said hello to the wife and then he ran into the kitchen and to my amazement he rifled the cupboard for food . . . he said he was hungry. What a person!'

And then he arrived. The men had anticipated his arrival by a few seconds. They stamped out their cigarettes, straightened their hair. He was wearing a grey suit with lapels so well pressed that they looked sharp.

He seemed to be very nervous. His eyes were swivelling around his head, panning across the room, taking everything in. He saw Cahit and went towards him. Cahit said casually, 'I have some friends here who want to talk to you.' He smiled, but his hands were electrified. He had no pocket to put them in, and they were constantly on the move, clasped together or stroking his throat. He did seem nervous. Ibo had a soft, effeminate face, when you looked at it closely, and his voice was hoarse. It sounded as if he was ill.

He made a joke. 'Look!' he said. 'I have just been to Istanbul to open a restaurant and I've just eaten twenty *lahmacum* and I feel sick . . .' Everybody laughed. This was the caricature: Ibo, the King of the *arabesk*, eating *lahmacum*, a village pizza, very popular with the urban migrants. The food of the *arabesk*.

But he did look sick and I could believe that he had just eaten that many. Perhaps it was his restaurant – he knows how much money there is to be made out of the *arabesk*. 'I really don't want to talk about it, I'm sorry.' Ibo had already said 'sorry' three or four times. He was constantly concerned that he might be causing offence. 'I'm sorry for looking so ill,' he said and, 'I'm sorry for not having more time.' This was not the wife-beating machismo I had read so much about.

Finally, after all his apologies, he shook our hands, stretching out a fat, warm hand. Cahit said to everyone within earshot, 'This is the biggest man in Turkish music, if not in Turkey, for fifteen years.' He was nothing like I had expected.

Ibo was like a mascot for the underclasses: somebody who had broken free. The story of his life is swapped and embellished by every poor boy who wants to be a rich man. But what exactly had happened? How did he get his break? Since this is one of the central popular legends of the Turkish Republic (much to Ataturk's chagrin) I asked him if the traditional story was true. He looked odd, mystified, when I asked, as if I had broken a promise. Cahit said, 'Ibo, it is only one or two questions. No harm done.' He shook his head briskly, as if to clear it.

He was shuffling his limbs, like a boxer limbering. Finally, he said to Cahit after pulling a series of agonized faces, 'Look! My private life is trawled over all the time – but if you are serious then it's fine . . .' He was standing next to Ersoy, looking him up and down. Quite without warning, he suddenly thrust his hand inside the breast-pocket of Ersoy's shirt. He seemed quite distracted, the hand foraging inside the pocket autonomously. It found a pen and began first to stroke it up and down and then to pluck at it. It seemed, at the time, quite natural. Everybody in the room was staring at him, as if they could look nowhere else. If Ibo had asked to keep the pen, Ersoy would have handed it over without a word. Ibo had started to fiddle with the cloth of Ersoy's shirt, and now he was staring directly into his eyes, peering very closely. Ersoy, meanwhile, was mesmerized by the activity in his pocket. Perhaps he had a simple motive. Perhaps he was searching for a tape-recorder.

Ibo started to talk in strong, accented Turkish. 'I was a worker who bends iron structures on buildings so that cement can be held in place – do you know the word for that? No? You see, when I talk about iron you might think I am talking of fence work, but no, it is much more important than that. I can understand everything about a building and if you leave it to me I can do it all. Everything . . .' He thrust his hand into the pocket of one of his retainers to produce a packet of cigarettes. The man lit one for him.

'One day some people appeared in Urfa [which is in the far south-east]. They had an old Volkswagen van which had a big boot loaded with tapes and 45 rpm records and they were selling them. They asked the locals if there was a singer. "Is there any young guy who can sing?" they said. And they recommended me. I was singing, you see, while I was doing my day job. Then in Elazig I produced a tape with them but it didn't sell too well – a few copies maybe in Urfa. And then I sang a song called "The Shoes on her Feet", and that made me famous. Of course it was not my song. It was an old folklore song, a genuine piece of folk. But the song made a killing and so my story started. That's the truth.'

There was a pause. He heard a shout from Hulya's room and smiled.

Cahit looked at me. I was to ask another question.

'People say that *arabesk* is bad for the soul . . .'

Now Ibo was quite serious. 'I am a folk singer but the *arabesk* is at full swing, and it sells, and so I sing *arabesk*. That's simple.' He looked at Cahit, who nodded his head. 'In any case, if the music

. . . if both the playing and the singing is good, and it doesn't disturb your ears . . . if it is this . . . then every music is all right. There is nothing called bad music. When I listen to Western classical music . . .'

He started to mimic it, as if he was putting on headphones, closing his eyes.

Hundreds of people were waiting for Ibo in the auditorium of the Swan a few minutes later. We had seats at the back. In front, there were the rich people, sitting at tables and eating and drinking *raki*. We sat with the poorer ticket-holders. The women, rich or poor, wore head-scarves, almost without exception.

The show started. Everybody was cheering and applauding. Everybody was excited. The violins and cellos ripped and roared in unison phrases and the *darbuka* (a small goblet-shaped drum) whipped the rhythm along. The place tingled. The backing vocalists swayed and clapped their hands while a zither pinged up and down scales. The orchestra was in dinner jackets, which seemed awkward attire as so many of them, like the zither player, were involved in hard manual labour. Picture the scene for a moment: the sound – the swaggering microtonal scales, which rest strangely in Western ears – and the vision of these men in formal evening wear. It has become a matter of ritual in modern Turkey for senior politicians to wear a top hat and tails on important public occasions, as if they were dancers or conductors. Ataturk set the style, embracing the dinner jacket as an emblem of the smart secular society he wanted Turkey to emulate. Today it seems oddly anachronistic. That Europe has passed, but in Turkey it lives on as a central statement of loyalty to Ataturk. To the foreign eye, it seems more a commentary on the country's motionless. There are times, as when the President, in his tails, lays a wreath at the mausoleum of Ataturk each year, when it actually feels as if you are stepping backwards in time.

Hulya came on first: not the retiring little schoolgirl who had come backstage at the Mogambo but a *femme fatale*, as everybody best knew her, in a low-cut red dress with slicked-back hair.

And then, sort of stumbling on to the stage, came Ibo, playing the clumsy idiot, in a duck-egg green suit and blue shirt with a blue handkerchief curling over his breast-pocket. I was beginning to understand the way in which these two had managed to manipulate the national imagination so brilliantly.

The show, which was really a pantomime, was clever. Tonight Ibo and Hulya sent up their public personalities. The two lovers: he, a blundering fool from the east, and she, a sophisticated seductress. That is what Turkey thinks they are.

Right at the start they were arguing, much to the audience's amusement. Hulya was complaining about the posters for the show. She said that she should have come first on the billing and he said, 'But I am sure that you are! Go check the poster.'

'Can you read?' she shouted back.

'If there was a university in Urfa then I would have gone,' Ibo replied, and everybody laughed. The idea that he could have gone to university was so ridiculous, especially in Urfa, in the far south-east, among the Kurdish peasant farmers, so far away from here.

Then Ibo sang.

> Would you look for me and find me
> If I won a disowned grave?
> Would you still love me
> If I was pitch-black smoke?
> Who am I to deserve your love?
> Where is the end of it?

His voice was utterly unexpected: sweet, strong and very pure. Ersoy was impressed. 'He really is a bloody good singer,' he said.

It must be irritating, sometimes, to have to keep playing the part of Ibrahim Tatlises, when there is so much talent and sensitivity. Ibo was very close to his audience; he understood what made them laugh or fall into a melancholy silence; he treated them as if they were his family. He wandered around, stroking heads, kissing the hands of the wives. He was keeping Turkish culture alive, not killing it. I wondered how many of his critics write him off without ever having properly listened to his music.

Ibo directed the show; he was the centre of everybody's attention. People could not take their eyes off him. I had the impression that a woman next to me was trying not to blink while he was on stage. Her eyes were stretched unnaturally wide. He was kissing little girls who were lifted up on to the stage by their proud parents. One small girl, wearing a cardboard tiara with silver glitter stuck on to it, had come on to the stage and was belly-dancing by his side.

Next he sang a sad song, which had the audience very quiet. I have seen grown men cry to *arabesk* music before. It becomes a very personal matter; a way of talking about yourself. Taxi drivers on long overnight treks start to talk about a film as if it were their own life. Turkish men do not like to talk intimately about themselves, but they can do so through these films.

Ibo appeared in pain when he sang this song.

I'm walking on thorns
I'm wounded
As I proceed slowly
Where are the people
Who started with me?
If I return they would throw stones on me
Until I die.

And then he sang a lighter number.

I put some leblebi nuts
In a dish
I press them down.
I like every part of your body
Except that you are a little short.

The audience which had withdrawn into mournful silence after the tragedy of the first song, burst into hilarious laughter at the second.

After this a transvestite walked on to the stage, a big man, nursing gigantic breasts, in traditional Anatolian peasant dress. He shouted at Ibo, 'Don't you remember me?'

'No,' said Ibo.

'But you remember the forest?'

'No.'

'Ah, then, you will remember when we used to put our Levi 501 jeans on and climb up the minaret on the Urfa mosque? And when we hung our feet down, over the edge, like people at the seaside?'

'No.'

'Then you remember the day the Turkish troops landed on Cyprus, you landed on me?'

Everybody, including Ersoy, was laughing. This was a very Turkish joke: the 501s and the mosque. Such a stark contrast.

Then Hulya came back on: she had changed into a very regal black outfit with big puffed sleeves. Two boys came up and tried to give her roses. She ignored them and started to sing. She was not good at singing. She was much better at acting. This was a whining *arabesk*. The men clapped in any case. When she had finished, boys brought trayfuls of confetti to the front of the stage. She took the trays and showered herself with confetti. She let her wrap slip from her shoulder to reveal the full crest of her breasts.

This was the climax of the show. Ibo came back on, pretending to be an opera diva. He was prancing around, talking in a grand, pretentious accent. The band struck up with 'O Sole Mio'. The audience understood at once. The Turks have heard of Pavarotti and the rest; no European has ever heard of Ibo. Tonight he would prove that he was their equal. This was 'Iborotti'. Ibo puffed out his chest and sang the aria with great skill.

Out from the wings walked somebody wearing a dinner jacket and a beard, like Pavarotti. He said, 'Mama mia' a few times and then he started to sing 'Allah, Allah! Allah!' which is one of the most popular *arabesk* tunes. It was very funny.

The crowd rose to its feet.

★

Far away, an assassin plans Ibo's end. He has a new weapon: a boy pop star. This young man is a new phenomenon, a pop star in the Western mould – not like Ibo, a friend of the family, but a minor deity. It is the first time in Turkey that teenage girls have fainted in concerts. Tatlises is part of people's lives; Tarkan, on the other hand, is like a hamburger: a packaged commodity, easy to eat and to throw away. Turkish parents and the Turkish press have gone into a spasm of anxiety. Is Tarkan the future?

Orhan, however, was delighted. He is the assassin: the promoter, the boyfriend of Tarkan's manager. The controversy does him good. There was to be a concert the following day, a huge open-air event in Istanbul which would more than demonstrate the growing popularity of his product. Orhan was a loud-mouthed Turk who had lived for several years in America, a bulky character with a belly that was almost perfectly circular, wearing shorts and a Hawaiian T-shirt. He imagined himself to be an American and spoke with a cultivated New York rasp, somewhere between Brooklyn and the Bronx. His flat was in a peeling apartment block just off Taksim Square. There was a huge amplifier in the middle of the sitting-room, which was otherwise empty except for a sofa, some large cushions and bottles of liqueur. A half-drunk whisky tumbler stood on the television. All around the room were empty glasses with dried kisses around their rims. On the front of the amplifier was the word MOTHAFUCKA. Orhan played the guitar when he was not living off Tarkan. He was good, but he had never made any waves in Turkey.

He spoke nicely of Tarkan: 'This guy, *man*, I mean, he's nice. He's singing right, real good. And suddenly he became a lover of young girls – and now all the fathers are very angry. When he comes here, all the girls are on the street – and this is very new, like the Beatles, Elvis.' He offered bottles of beer. 'He likes the animals – you know, the bears and the birds – and he is *very* nice. You see what the women like about him?' He walked into the office and produced a promotional photograph: this exceptionally beautiful boy was hugging a shaggy dog. 'This is what the girls like. I've had thousands in my life. They are very stupid.'

Tarkan had only recently become big. He had in fact only recently returned from Germany, where his parents had emigrated shortly after his birth. They were farmers from the Black Sea coast and returned because they found life abroad difficult. When Tarkan came back he learned how to sing Turkish classical music, but he wanted to be a pop star and as soon as he could he was trying to meet record producers. Now, at the age of twenty-one, his posters were all over the city. He had just performed in front of 90,000 in Ankara – the largest concert in the capital's history. He sold 400,000 copies of his first cassette.

Orhan admitted that he too would have liked to become a star. 'It's easy to be a Turkish star,' he said. 'Anyway, I'm going to leave this country. I am going to settle in the Caribbean.'

The concert was in Atakoy, an upmarket suburb near the airport. Orhan had said that there would be a cocktail party before the concert for all the local dignitaries who would be attending. The concert, he said, was being staged to mark the opening of a local recycling plant. 'Tarkan is into the environment,' he added.

I arrived a little early. The stage had been constructed in the middle of an estate of high-rise tower blocks. On the balconies, the older generation set out chairs and barbecues. Old women wearing head-scarves passed round salad bowls; their husbands bent over the charcoal with matches.

Below, in front of the stage, the teenagers were congregating. The police had put up barriers, but these fans were very small and slipped easily between the rails. Most of them were no older than thirteen. Above the stage, there was a banner advertising an Opposition party slogan. The establishment had already recognized Tarkan's value, a sure sign of his popularity. There were some men in jackets and ties, nailing the banner firmly on to wooden supports. Still, it looked dangerously insecure.

Behind the stage was a municipal building in which the VIPs were congregating ahead of the party. Several dozen girls were crowding around the entrance, shouting at the security men to let them see Tarkan. Orhan was inside, asking why the cocktail party had not already started. Some politician had not yet arrived, he was told. The VIPs were a mixed bag: poorly paid civil servants and the political élite. All the perfumes co-mingled in this confined space. Together they smelt like petrol with a hint of lemon, like some kind of industrial pollutant.

The minister had still not arrived, but the pressure on the security staff was intense and they decided to open the cocktail party without the guest of honour. There was a stampede to the drinks and then people relaxed. Outside, there were a few thousand by now. It was beginning to feel unsafe. Children (and some parents) were squeezed tightly together just a few feet from the stage. The barriers had been removed and in their place stood a line of policemen trying to keep the crowd back. Already some of the cannier girls were working on the officers. 'Oh, please, why do you hurt me so much?' one said. 'It hurts me.' The policemen looked very uncomfortable.

Orhan came up in the darkness, watching the crowd like the captain of a ship scanning a heavy sea. He was dragging somebody behind him, quite literally, by the scruff of the neck. 'What in the *fuck* do we do about this?' he said, laughing and clapping the man on the back.

The man said, 'My girlfriend said that I look like Tarkan, so I called Orhan.'

'Well, doesn't he? I mean, a fucking *double*!'

He did sort of look like Tarkan: black wavy hair and clear green eyes. 'We might use him as a double.' The man was also from the Black Sea coast. He was a chemistry student.

Then Tarkan emerged on to the stage. There were crowds on either side, trying to touch him. He had slicked black hair, a T-shirt under a black silk shirt and skin-tight striped trousers. He started to sing. There was a lot of sex in his performance; more than I had anticipated. The music was hugely predictable: Euro-pop – Italy, France, all the same, with the merest ghost of the Orient in some of the harmonies.

He stopped after the first number. A large politician clambered on to the podium and took the microphone. He spoke about the importance of the environment.

'You are young,' he said. 'You must not repeat the mistakes of your parents . . .' Orhan was beside me: 'Fucking politicians!' he said.

The music started again. For a few seconds the police held the crowd back, then they gave up, throwing their arms into the air. The children surged forward until they could touch Tarkan's feet. 'Jesus,' shouted Orhan, suddenly alarmed. Some of the children were lifted off their feet in the rush and left lying on the ground, crying. I looked around. Orhan had walked away. He was sitting on a wall, on his own, drinking.

6

Sisi

A few years ago, transvestites walked in fear on the back streets of Istanbul. The police would sometimes come across them, and pierce their false breasts with knives, or slice them off altogether. Occasionally the police stabbed a transsexual with real breasts. Transvestites were among the most victimized of the city's minorities. They still suffer, and have to keep a low profile if they are hawking for business on the streets. But they have a unique and influential place in Turkey. Ataturk banished the Ottoman Empire, but he could not exterminate the eunuchs. It is said that Turkey has more transvestites per head of population than anywhere else in the world, except Brazil.

Bulent Ersoy is the most famous of them. She was a boy until she had her operation (in England) ten years ago and became a girl. She was then effectively exiled to West Germany, because the Turkish authorities prohibited her from appearing in public. This was under an old law decreeing that women are only allowed to perform in public with permission. For Bulent this was denied on moral grounds.

Yet she became one of the most popular artists in Turkey. Her cassettes sold in hundreds of thousands. She was a friend of President Ozal, who loved the *arabesk*. She persuaded him to let transsexuals marry, and he lifted the prohibition on her performance. On this single issue, Turkey was far in advance of most of the European countries it seeks to emulate. Bulent has since reportedly married a West German boyfriend.

But the Turks are not consistent about sex. Mr Ozal was also responsible for setting up the Committee to Protect Public Morals. This organization has the task of censoring the sex magazines which have suddenly started to appear all over the country. *Penthouse*, one of the mildest, has attracted fines in excess of £1 million for pictures likely to 'pollute the minds of minors'. The demand is there: the new private TV stations have recognized the commercial shows. There is even a transvestite newspaper, *Natasha*, which started recently in Istanbul. The editor asked one newspaper reporter, 'Are there any transvestite newspapers in England?' He claimed that his paper was 'selling like freshly baked baklava. I'm having lots of fun.' Turkey has a special interest in cross-dressing.

Bulent Ersoy is adored and reviled. She is both a role model and a moral obscenity. She is a symbol of confusion. In the past people have tried to murder her. She was injured when bottles were thrown in one Istanbul night-club, although this was a demonstration of affection, or frustration, not of hatred. The most serious attempt was made five years ago, when a young man, a member of an outlawed paramilitary group on the extreme right, demanded she sing a nationalist song. He wanted to hear her celebrate his patriotism. This was in a dusky club in Adana, which is in the far south. Bulent refused as it would have upset the flow of her show. So the young man shot her.

She survived. Doctors were quoted afterwards as saying, 'We were very surprised at the strength of her body, after all the . . . well, you know what I mean.' After the gunman had been taken into custody, he said that he was sorry, that he had not intended to kill her and that he was agitated by a large bar bill. His mother condemned him for his rashness and begged 'Bulent *hanim*' for compassion and forgiveness. The distraught night-club owner declared, 'She can't die. She stands for so much. You see, she is so Turkish.'

Bulent prefers to think of herself as a classical singer now. She tries to disassociate herself from the *arabesk*, the music that made her famous. But transvestite and transsexual culture in Turkey is part of the *arabesk*. It is on the margins of society, turning tradition upside-down. That is what Bulent sings about – a world turned upside-down – and that is what she represents.

I had heard that one of the 'new wave' transsexuals, the

generation after Bulent, was intending to stand for the Turkish parliament. She wanted to be the country's first sex-change prime minister. Her name was Sisi.

The editor of *Tempo*, a popular weekly news magazine, had promised to put me in touch with Sisi. *Tempo* is the chronicle of the Turkish sexual obsession. In one recent issue it had disclosed that the new big thing was the blow-up male doll. There was a big colour spread, with a photograph of a woman in suspenders hugging one of these life-size dolls, which had hair painted on to its chest. The doll was called 'International Lover Boy' and the promotional literature stated that it featured the 'full service suction mouth' and came complete with 'solid 10-inch realistic penis which vibrates and ejaculates'. They were newly imported, the article said, and demand was exceptional. Most popular were those modelled on Hollywood stars. The 'Kevin Costner' was one of the most expensive. You could buy a transvestite model, which had both a penis and breasts.

In another way, *Tempo* was a product of the economic enlightenment that has taken place in Turkey, from the centralized Soviet-style planning of the 1930s to the free market of the 1980s. This is the age of the Turkish entrepreneur – alert, self-obsessed, open to suggestion, and short-sighted. Among the most successful are the promoters of the sex industry, which flourishes. There is little obstruction to its growth. Moral objections from the religious right have not stopped it. Sisi has not only survived but claims she has made a fortune. Her story is a story of the economic revolution.

Kursat Basar, the editor of *Tempo*, worked in a large printing works on the outskirts of Istanbul. He had a wild look: his hair was unbrushed, and stuck up in tufts at angles to his scalp. He was young, in his early thirties. His office was huge, with a big wooden desk. It was rather like meeting a bank manager. The Turks have an obsession with offices. The room was glass-walled so that from it Kursat could survey his dominions: an open-plan floor packed with journalists and designers. He was dwarfed by the room. His desk was quite tidy, with everything in its place.

The first thing he talked about was his novel-writing. He had written one or two books. He appeared to be making it clear that *Tempo* was merely the day job. He seemed embarrassed by it. He picked over the Turks' interest in sex, provoking it with half-naked pictures of working women, and glorifying it in the text. But this was a sort of family affair. To discuss it with outsiders was embarrassing.

I asked him about the dolls. 'They sell too much in Konya,' he said. 'It is the new best-seller . . .'

Why did he, as an expert, think that the Turks had such an unexpected fascination with transvestites? 'You know, I can't understand why it is so big here. I think it is a tradition from the Ottoman. This thing is about impersonation. Perhaps that's it. I mean, Turkey is about impersonation . . . but maybe it's just because the Turkish man will fuck anything . . .'

Outwardly the Turks appear to be sticklers for sexual decency. In many parts of the country, a woman will find it difficult to marry if she is not a virgin. The police in central Anatolia will raid hotel rooms occupied by unmarried couples, and force the woman to go to hospital so that her hymen can be inspected. If it is not intact, she may be branded a prostitute and fined accordingly. Prostitution is legal in Turkey but only when practised within government-licensed brothels. I once had to barricade myself inside my hotel room while travelling through the hinterland of Anatolia for fear that the local police were going to raid the room and humiliate my girlfriend.

While they are locking up wanton unmarried women, the same Turks are buying records from their transsexuals. Ottoman culture was both crude and bisexual. Modern Turkey has the same genes. Kursat said that a Turk living in Germany had become leader of the gay movement in Berlin. 'He wants to make a gay liberation movement in Turkey but the police will not allow it.' Then he found me some telephone numbers for Sisi. 'Oh look,' he said, 'I have some numbers for Bulent Ersoy. Here is her mother-in-law's . . . but wait a minute, how can she have a mother-in-law? Fuck, this country is weird . . .' The numbers were all wrong anyway. They had been changed a few times since he last phoned them.

Back in Laleli, Ersoy was waiting in the hotel. A new busload of Romanian prostitutes had arrived; *Tempo* had already written an article about the changing sexual culture of the district. We tried to telephone Sisi. Her secretary said first that she was at home, but busy; then she claimed that she was out. We made it clear that we wanted to ask her only about her political ambitions.

Ersoy and I went for a walk towards the mosque of Beyazit, near the University of Istanbul, at the entrance to the Covered Bazaar. This is the first mosque of the Ottoman Empire, dedicated to the son of Mehmet the Conqueror of Istanbul. More recently, it has become the focal point of Islamic revival at the University, as female students insist on their right to wear the traditional headdress in overt defiance of the secular terms of the country's constitution. Behind the University, casting an unrivalled view across the Golden Horn, rise the minarets of the Suleymaniye mosque complex. This is the masterpiece of Islam's greatest architect, Sinan: monumental and unpretentious. The complex had baths and hospitals, a library, even an asylum. This was Islam as a social religion, uniting people, providing for them.

From here we walked through the jumble of antiquity to the Hippodrome: the Byzantine chariot race-course. During the reign of Justinian, this place erupted into violence as warring racing factions ransacked the city. Thirty thousand are said to have died. Centuries later, the Hippodrome was where Webbe displayed his fireworks. By then only a few witnesses to that chaos remained: the Egyptian Obelisk of Pharaoh Thutmose; the Serpentine Column brought from the Oracle at Delphi in the fifth century. Where the gigantic race-course once stood there are now gardens, surrounded by tourist shops.

We wandered into the courtyard of the Blue Mosque of Sultan Ahmed, which is built on top of the ruins of the Byzantine great palace, and above part of the Hippodrome race-track. It is the largest mosque in the city, staring impassively across the Golden Horn, its six minarets like spears against the skyline. Inside it is not a building of sensitive artistry: it is decorated with thousands of Iznik ceramic tiles, but it is dark, full of shadows, slightly forbidding. It remains a very popular place for worship.

Just as we arrived, the *muezzin* started to call the faithful to prayer. On the edges of the courtyard traders were offering guidebooks and pointed shoes and camels. Some Romanian holiday-makers were taking pictures with very old metal cameras. One of them was wearing a fez. On one of the walls in the courtyard, by the entrance, was a pay-phone, and Ersoy looked at his watch and then tried to call Sisi again. Every time he got an answer, the *muezzin* howled, and he put the phone down. I was not sure whether this was a recorded chant – perhaps in such a prestigious mosque it would not be. But the public address system crackled like a tape, and the call to prayer was terribly distorted.

Ersoy tried again when the noise had abated. But by this time the secretary had gone. Another person answered and promised that Sisi would call us at our hotel when she was ready to see us. We assumed that this meant she would not see us. Perhaps it was the hotel number. She would know that we were staying in Laleli, and she might think we were in the sex industry.

We walked back up the hill. We stopped briefly at the Erenler, an old café in a kilim market in the courtyard of an old *medrese*, where working men and tourists smoke a *nargile* and drink tea. There were dozens of people, mostly Turks, sitting on the carpeted benches, and a couple of boys running around with wet plugs of tobacco and hot coals. The *nargile* is a long-term project: an hour or two at least. Istanbul Turks have not lost one ancient accomplishment: the ability to relax. The city appears to be in a constant state of turbulence, everything in turmoil. But this is superficial: the reality of an individual life is much less active, much more stationary. Much more idle.

The coffee house is just the other side of the Covered Bazaar, once an organized community of tiny shops and now a sprawling junk market sustained by tourism: cheap old-looking tea sets, a thousand kinds of white Meerschaum pipes, enamelled plates, ceramic tiles. It rolls down the hill towards the spice market and the Golden Horn: a wild entertainment of sharp-eyed carpet salesmen and furious foreigners, lost and fleeced.

We continued down the hill past Beyazit Square. Ersoy talked about the growing number of children in the city who sniff glue. Somebody had just produced a magazine to try to raise money for their welfare. There is destitution in Istanbul but there are few down-and-outs. There are a few homeless children (the Turks call them 'Underbridge Kids') who hang around the Galata bridge. But there are far fewer than most people expect.

When we arrived back at the hotel, we tried the telephone again and this time it seemed more positive. A woman asked us to explain why we wanted to talk to Sisi, and said that she would meet us. That, of course, could not be guaranteed. But if we wished to wait for her at an agreed place, she might or might not join us.

The coffee shop of the Etap Marmara Hotel in Taksim Square is called the Café Opera: it is bright and smart, and expensive, but it has no class. It is where the *nouveaux riches* come to drink coffee and eat pâtisserie. You can look out of the windows at the front and watch the huddled masses of the office workers passing by on their way home at night.

We sat there for a long while. Ersoy said eventually: 'We have been stood up, which is a shame, because I have heard that she is very beautiful . . .' I had already resigned myself. It is dangerous being a transsexual in Turkey. You have to be careful. There will always be some right-winger ready to assassinate you. Sisi had no idea who we were and we had given her no references. I had said that we were friends of Kursat Basar, but he had left Istanbul for the weekend, so she would not be able to check that. Ersoy, however, argued that we should wait. 'She will be late, if she is coming, just so she can keep us waiting . . .'

The waiters asked who we were waiting for. When we said Sisi, their faces grew graver but the service improved.

We asked them what she looked like. 'Will you tell us when she comes in?' I said.

'Oh yes, sir, I will show you,' replied the waiter.

Over the loudspeakers they were piping some music from the Austrian Tyrol. Oompah music with accordions and men in lederhosen clapping.

Some minutes later, the waiter rattled through the bead curtain on the kitchen door and pointed to a beautiful woman sitting on the bar beside us. How long had she been there? Neither of us could remember her coming in. She was very thin, with short black hair tied up in a bandana. Her eyes were black. She had a pair of golden glasses swinging on a chain and a camp, but tasteful, leather and sea-shell necklace. She wore a pair of black jeans and a fiery orange waistcoat. Once she had turned around, she was instantly the centre of interest in the café. Everybody was scrutinizing her. As she came down towards our table, she stopped to survey people and to bask just for a moment in their pleasure. It was remarkably easy to forget that this astonishing woman had been born a man.

I did not know, at first, what to say. She broke the silence. 'Profiteroles! I will have profiteroles with thick cream.' And while Ersoy spoke to the waiter, she took out two packs of Davidoff Lights and put them on the table in front of her, as if she was marking out territory. Her English was almost non-existent, but she wanted to show that she knew some. It was chit-chat – Did I like Istanbul? Was this my first time? – and she laughed politely when I replied. She had long curly lashes and a hint of deep velvet lipstick. Her voice was deep, but soft as well – it *could* have belonged to a woman. Every time she slipped on a word, she giggled and patted my sleeve with long bony fingers.

I said that we would like to ask her about her political ambitions. 'Oh yes, that is what was agreed,' she said. Then she spoke in Turkish. She was writing a new constitution for her party, but she was worried that the electoral system would not win her many votes. She said she had thought about joining forces with one of the other more marginal parties. She talked about the Kurds, and then about the Islamic extremists. 'They would accept me because I would draw all the marginal votes . . .' She was quite right. The far right would probably embrace her. 'There is no social democracy in Turkey, and the Muslims feel it just as much as we do. We are all marginal people. The root of Turkey is rotten. We must change it. We cannot have people told that they are wrong or anti-social just because they want to wear a bra and earrings!'

Something was making me feel uneasy. Sisi looked like a woman – she had a perfect milky complexion – but I knew that she was not a woman. Was she exciting or disgusting?

She was militant. 'People do not know how to fight for their rights. You ask me what I want to do? It's all about showing the way. I own my own personality . . .' She was not angry; she spoke coolly, slowly, dragging on a cigarette. 'Before me, people like me were forced to make money by selling themselves. The police did everything to destroy their lives. But that has all changed. I took the stage in night-clubs and became famous – I showed a way out. Now there are many who do the same and no longer have to make money through prostitution. There are still some. I tell them: "Buy a car so that you cannot be caught so easily."'

Sisi said she was twenty-six years old. She claimed she was rich and had made most of her money from pay-for telephone services on which she breathes heavily for the pleasure of many, many thousands around the country. The government has now banned sex over the telephone but before it did, she was making around £10,000 a month. Who knows if that is true? She claimed that she had more callers than Prime Minister Suleyman Demirel (who is now the President). 'Demirel was getting 100,000 minutes a month. I was getting a million minutes.' Most surprising was that so many people were prepared to pay to hear what Mr Demirel had to say.

Outside a police car wailed. More people were pressing anonymously along the pavement on their way home. Sisi heard the siren. Did the transvestites still have a problem with the police? 'No, there is no problem with the police.' She had changed. She was suddenly circumspect. The police inspire fear in most Turks. 'I am not saying that because I have to. It's the truth. They used to come and pull at our clothes. But today they are not so harsh because I showed the way. The police cannot come up to you and beat you up. That is what used to happen. Now we can beat them up . . .'

She looked around. People were still staring. 'Tonight Michael Jackson is here,' she said. 'I have an invitation, but I am not going to go. If it was Madonna then I would go – even if I had to pay. She is a symbol of a way of life, which is not just about sex, but starts with it.' She winked at Ersoy.

Her idol, however, was the Italian porn actress turned MP, La Cicciolina. 'You know that she became an MP in Italy? It is a reflection of the political possibilities on the sexual margins . . . she was also among the hundred best-known people in the world, according to some survey or other, and that's the best way of making us normal, by having a few of us famous. If it happened in Italy, which is Christian, maybe it can happen in Turkey.' Sisi claimed that there were 10,000 transsexuals and 40,000 transvestites in the country, and a huge, if mainly closet, community of homosexuals. She is confident that there will be little resistance to her standing for parliament. 'If we are talking about homosexuals, at least 10 per cent of MPs are. Of course, I know that because I have screwed them.' She put her bony hand on her breast, and, while smiling at a woman at a nearby table, squeezed it.

'Look I didn't have much of an education, unlike you clever boys. I was expelled five times for wearing panties to school. Five times. That was five years ago. Now it's so much easier to be a TV. Twenty years ago for a man just to experiment wearing women's clothes was a surprise. But now a kid says, "Look, Mum!" and it's not so bad.'

She became Sisi seven years ago after being attacked by the police during a holiday in the resort town of Kusadasi. They victimized her because they believed she was a homosexual. 'They put me in a coach and sent me away. And I swore, through my tears, that I would have vengeance. I swore to God. They cut my hair. Can you imagine? So I was sitting in the coach, always crying.' Last year she visited the town for the first time since then, to perform in front of the governor. She was singing with Ibrahim Tatlises. 'I lived, you see, I preserved my honour.'

Now she is famous, she is not humiliated. Instead, she humiliates traditional Turkish convention. It is a dangerous game: somebody nearly killed Bulent Ersoy. Sisi does seem reckless, yet calculating, quite in control. 'I have exposed my breasts in front of Turgut Ozal,' she said, in evidence of her daring. 'Before, in the 1980s, Bulent accidentally exposed a breast and she was sent to jail. Now there have been thirty-four complaints filed against Sisi but I have never had a sentence.' She talked about Sisi as if she was talking about somebody else, as if she liked to keep the two distinct: the man and the woman. She was both, perhaps she could never be just one or the other.

She was extremely jealous of Bulent. 'In terms of art she is nothing. Everyone has to accept that. When the sex lines started I was making a killing that even I could not believe. I can't say why. It wasn't just sex. I hired a crew to write some of the fantasies so that for the first time in Turkey you wouldn't always have to listen to the same tapes. Bulent could not do the same because she was afraid that Sisi would beat her.' She dragged daintily on a Davidoff. 'I had the operation when I was eighteen and I *am* a woman. According to me, no one can be a woman after she is thirty, and even if Bulent (who was older than thirty when she had the operation) had her vagina over her forehead I wouldn't see her as a woman. There is no way you can be a woman just wearing women's clothes. It is about your soul.' She stubbed out her cigarette. 'I don't know any woman who wears size forty-three shoes like she does.'

Sisi giggled loudly when she talked. 'It was my father who persuaded me to have the operation.' People at the next tables were outraged. 'He was an ambassador. Austria was the last posting and then he came back and died.' She relished the shock on the faces of our immediate neighbours. 'You know that the Turks like buggery? I toured the south-east seven or eight months ago. They sacrificed the sheep in celebration of my arrival wherever I went because they are all faggots. I had many proposals – ten times more there than anywhere else. But they are so limited. "Such a shame you had to cut it off!" they said.'

She asked Ersoy to order her another plate of profiteroles. 'Last year I was about to marry a Swiss man,' she went on. 'He was *so* nice. Fifty-eight years old and very rich. He had been separated from his wife for three years. He told me that he would divorce her,' she popped a profiterole into her mouth, 'so he came here and he stayed at the Hilton and I stayed with him. We flirted, and then he extended his stay and we lived together properly. I said, "We Turks are keen on our lovers" and he said, "I've been married for twenty-five years and I've never found such happiness." He was an MP and I asked – *I asked* – him to marry. I said, "Would it upset your career as an MP?" and he said, "No, because nobody would recognize you as a man." So anyway, we still see each other. That was three years ago. We still call each other from time to time.

'He was a nice man, and he was the one who said the Swiss passport was important, not me! I told him I didn't want to marry him just because of that. But I was frightened because I felt that I belonged to my country, that I was a Turk. I called it off because I didn't want to become a Swiss . . .' She paused then. Was it true? Was she really the one who had called it off?

'He was *so* much more energetic than me. He had a twenty-seven-year-old son, but even if he had been seventy-eight he would still have impressed me. But I was afraid, because what is important is not to sell something but to give it.'

I was confused: was she selling herself to this MP, I asked her, but she did not answer the question.

'What is important is that I find myself a foreign husband.'

There was a little silence then.

'It must be upsetting not to be able to have children . . .'

'It's a very sad thing not to have a wonderful thing like a child. But there are millions of infertile women. I consider myself one of those. If I get married, I can hire a mother for my child . . .'

For a moment, she was a lost person. She stopped talking.

Then she went on, 'Children might be difficult in any case. I intend to become prime minister. I want to be the first in the world. And I want to go into history for it. I want to have sex in the toilets of the Grand National Assembly. I have had sex with MPs and ministers' (she names some names, and I believe her), 'one of them lost his position because of me.' There had been a scandal some months before. 'These minister lovers . . . you get fed up discussing the state of the Turkish economy . . .'

She was the second nude for *Playboy*'s edition in Turkey in 1991, and she has since been the cover girl in eight countries. But when we met, she was planning her most controversial publicity offensive. 'Oh, I must tell you. This is simply so awful. I've gone into partnership with *Hurriyet* [Turkey's biggest-selling paper] and with a toy company. We are going to produce fifty thousand baby dolls called Sisi. The idea is that we challenge readers to break Sisi's virginity. In the womb of the dolls there is red paint. All of them are numbered. So you break the dolly's hymen, and then you look for the number and three of them will win the right to sleep with Sisi for the night.' Sisi unpeeled a fresh packet of Davidoff, slowly pulling off the cellophane, and laughed. 'It's a good prize . . .

'Boys! Boys! Now, of all the people I have slept with it is the Russians who have the biggest cocks – like this!' she said, and spread her arms out wide. 'No, really, as large as that. But I have always been told that the English are the more sensitive: not like the Russians – bang, bang, bang – but slow and passionate.' She whispered, 'I have never had an English man. How long are you here for? Because we could just do it, and nobody would ever find out that you had had Sisi. It could be our secret.' One of the waiters was lingering just behind the table, waiting to take the profiteroles away.

She glowered. 'You must live! Few have enjoyed Sisi. She always says, "Allah! Allah! I welcome huge cocks!"' The waiter was polishing a brass banister with his tea-cloth, shaking his head.

Through the doors of the café came Sisi's friend, the owner of Turkey's first erotic radio station. She was middle-aged, with a fat wedding band on her finger. She had come to take Sisi away, and Sisi stood up to leave. Her legs were very thin. Then she ran out of the door. She had left her number on a piece of paper by an abandoned packet of cigarettes. The note said 'Seyhan Soylu'. It was a man's name. It was her real name.

7

The Miracle

The bottom of Istiklal Street – the fine end, near the tunnel, which feels like part of Paris and where the unwashed buildings have a fine lace of black filth across their surface – used to be a colony of European émigrés: white Russians fleeing the 1917 Revolution, French, Greeks. And there were Jews – there were several synagogues in the quarter – and Armenians. The warmth has gone with them out of this part of the city. It was built for one world – tail coats, champagne, orchestra – and it is lived in by another. It is like an abandoned theatre, dark for decades, in which the sons of the stage-hands continue to live, but quietly, keeping off the stage.

Inside one courtyard were a dozen cages full of song-birds making a raucous din. To the left was a doorway, and a sign saying *Jamanak*, which is Armenian for time. The Armenians, who once thrived in this city, inadvertently inspired the modern transvestite cabaret culture that now flourishes a few hundred yards away. It was the Armenian canto, the music-hall singers of the late Ottoman Empire, who were the first drag queens in Anatolia. They were hugely popular. But there are no *zenes*, as they were called, left in Turkey today. And there are very few Armenians.

Jamanak is the only Armenian newspaper in Istanbul. Ersoy was worried that their office would not be open to him because of the way he looked – his jeans and pony-tail – and because he was a Turk. This was a real fear: he had never knowingly met an Armenian. 'I don't even know what they look like,' he said. There was a plaque on the door: Dentist. It must have been an old one.

Nadiye was sitting behind an Apple Macintosh preparing the pages for the day's edition. It looked as if it was printed by hand – the strange characters on thin newsprint. She had been editor for two years. The paper had remained a family business since it was started in 1908. It has been published every day since, and there have been some very dark days, like those during the Great War when hundreds of thousands, perhaps millions, of Armenians perished during fighting with the Turks along the eastern border: the modern world's first genocide. As in a disaster at sea, the bodies of the dead should be left in peace, but they are still manipulated by both sides for petty political propaganda of the meanest kind. Expatriate Armenians insist, as if it happened yesterday, that responsibility somehow lies with modern Turkey. The Turks, defensive as ever, insist, as if they were responsible, that it was not a planned genocide but a consequence of war.

It is extraordinary how short the memory is. Just a few days before we arrived at *Jamanak*, there were reports that Armenian soldiers had been killing Azeri civilians in their bitter war in Central Asia. It was alleged that the Armenians had skinned them alive. The Armenians who continue to live in Anatolia just try to keep their heads down.

It was an Armenian who printed the first newspaper in Turkey. And in the last century there were many Armenian newspapers. They were published not just in the cities but also in the provinces of the east, until the local Armenian population was exterminated.

The family who run *Jamanak* were friendly and delightful. They try to keep alive the promise of what once was: the old tolerance of the Ottoman Empire, the Great Diversity. The persistent abuse hurled at the insecure Turkish establishment by the Armenian diaspora has undermined the level of official goodwill towards those who continue to live in the country.

But those at *Jamanak* do not want to leave the country, nor should they: it is their home – they are merely practising their right to be different. And the truth is that nobody takes much notice. Nadiye, a beautiful, self-confident and elegant woman wearing smart trousers and a soft jumper, said, 'Those who went away don't know where they went.' There was a moment of silence after this, then Ersoy, who had so far said nothing, looked at her. 'It hurts me to know that all your people have left – it is not good for us.'

Nadiye was not comfortable answering our questions. There was a measured calculation in everything she said. A concern. By reflex, she did not trust us. She wanted us to speak to her husband, the managing director. So we waited in his office. The walls were covered with front pages, some dating right back to the birth of the newspaper. They were covered with a slimy yellow film of age. The telephone books on the table were dated 1980.

Nadiye did tell us, always with a smile on her face, that six journalists worked for the paper. But she did most of the work. Her son was eighteen and he wanted to go to journalism school. 'He hopes to work on a Turkish paper,' she said. *Jamanak*, which is four pages long, does very little reporting of its own. Generally, it translates articles from the Turkish newspapers. It still has to send a copy every day to the Interior Ministry for vetting. It would be easy for the Turks to close it; and frankly, if they did, few would care. But Nadiye is careful and, for now, the censorship is merely a formality.

In fact there is a much more serious problem for the paper than the Turks. The new generation does not speak much Armenian. Today there are just 1,500 who read the newspaper and can understand the script. What was once the language of commerce in Constantinople is on the edge of extinction. 'We are very determined,' said Nadiye. 'It will go on.' But in the schools Armenian children attend, the language they are taught is Turkish. Nadiye's son knew Armenian because she had made a point of teaching him. But her husband preferred to speak Turkish at home. The two of them talked together in Turkish. There was a framed picture of Ataturk above his desk. Opposite, there was a photograph of the French mime artist, Marcel Marceau, stretching his mouth wide open to frame an empty word.

The physical paraphernalia of the Armenian heritage is still visible in Istanbul: there are old schools and there are thirty-two churches. But for the most part the people have blended. They go about their business quietly, as Turks, until it is Sunday and they pray in Armenian, or they have private parties, dancing, perhaps, or a play.

Nadiye went to make some tea, and when she returned she said that there was not really any censorship, and that if she had given that impression then that was a mistake. 'I am sure the Ministry does not even read it any more.'

She showed us the paper. The front page was full of the news of a big political scandal in Istanbul. The governor and the Opposition party were accused of corruption over the awarding of contracts. There was a story about two Russian professors who had come to Turkey and had gone to an Armenian church one night. There was a short item about two Armenian boxers who were competing for the European championship.

The classifieds – Tonight: A Dance Party; Monday: A Play Reading; Come And Eat Sausage At The Shop Of Apikoglu – were a window on a private, busy community. 'It is very important to many of our readers,' Nadiye said. 'If it arrives late, then we will have many phone calls. All Armenians spend their time reading.'

Despite all the outrages of the past, there are still 60,000 or 70,000 Armenians in Turkey. Many of them are village folk from the east who have emigrated to the city slums. This is not *Jamanak*'s constituency. The newspaper's readership is amongst the wealthier educated élite who have lived in Istanbul for centuries. They do not live in the heaving poverty of the *gecekondu*, but in the tranquillity and gentility of the Princes' Islands, which are in the middle of the Bosphorus and can only be reached by ferry from the mainland. They still ride horse and carriage along the paved streets of the Islands' settlements. It is charming and quaint. Muslim Istanbul goes there in the summer to have barbecues and picnics. Nadiye's son is one of several students who are responsible for delivering the paper to the

Islands in their satchels, so that elderly Armenians can sit on their verandas and while away their long afternoons.

The Turkish press continues to hate the Armenians. Every so often, it will write at length about the 'Armenian conspiracy' to overthrow the Republic, and report how Armenians are funding terrorist outrages on the streets of Istanbul. *Jamanak* keeps its cool. Baba, the owner, had recently written an article entitled 'Keep your hands off Turkish Armenians': there had been a backlash, and one of the right-wing Turkish newspapers had accused him of being a terrorist. Nadiye paused. 'Throughout our history we have often been provoked, and each time it seems people have had to leave their homes.'

Her husband had still not arrived. She asked us to return when he was back. She was full of smiles when we left. Ersoy was quiet as we walked through the courtyard. He said, 'I cannot imagine why Turks are so prejudiced against the Armenians. Such terrible ignorance!'

The next day we returned to the office. Nadiye's husband was not there but in his office sat Mr Yervat Gobelyan. He was in his seventies, had a big puff of powdery white hair on his thin head and was wearing a pair of black plastic sunglasses. Nadiye said grandly that he was the chief writer; he said he was a professional interpreter. At first I thought that he was blind, but he could see clearly enough. He was looking about for his books – he had written quite a number – so that we could see them. He found two: *Baptized by Soil* and *The Ninth Wonder of the World*. They were compilations of short stories in Armenian. It was that script again: ancient and indecipherable.

The Armenians were allowed to keep their language under special provisions in the treaty that recognized the existence of the Turkish Republic. It recognized them as a legal minority, unlike the Kurds, and gave them the right to publish in a language that was not Ataturk's Turkish.

The old man was suspicious of us. He said that he wondered why we were so interested in the Armenians. 'I will not complain about Turkey,' he said, 'if that is what you want. I am as much a

Turk as the next man, and no man should forget it. My uncle died for the Turkish army at Gallipoli.' He took his glasses off and rubbed the lens with his tie. 'He died for the Turkish army. He used to hammer at copperwork and he couldn't hear someone warning him of a bomb.' He held his tie, which was thin and black and tied tightly around his neck, in both his hands as if somebody was going to snatch it from him.

Nadiye was standing by the wall. 'Turks and Armenians enjoy good relations,' the old man continued. 'I am sure that all those who have left miss Turkey. Here the Armenians go to the Islands – they want to smell the air, and they can . . .'

Ersoy asked after a moment, 'Do many Armenians marry Turks – you know, Christians and Muslims?'

And he replied, quite sharply, 'No, I have never heard of such a match.'

Ersoy thought he had caused some offence, and was embarrassed. The old man, noticing this, said, 'You know, of course, that the captain of the Turkish IQ team is an Armenian.' He laughed.

Ersoy asked, 'How did *Jamanak* report the massacres? I mean, it must have been difficult.'

'I don't know,' he said. 'But let's be honest: I don't believe that they said Turks kill Armenians. Look, we are not sure if the truth will ever be found out. Whatever it is, in any case, what is it good for? Everyone wants to know – but who is going to teach us? Everyone says different things . . .'

Nadiye's son was parcelling up copies of the paper and putting them in his satchel ready for distribution. Nadiye was sitting at her keyboard, tapping away, humming some tune. There was no other noise. You could just make out the birdsong through the window.

The old man was looking at Ersoy. After a little silence he said: 'You know, I have seen Ataturk and I have spoken to him.' He was reaching out to him, to say we all share the same memories. He looked out of the window. 'I was a child then and I was swimming, and Ataturk was there on board his first yacht. Ataturk called to us kids that he was worried we might drown. We shouted back, "Don't worry!" He gave us lemonade . . .' He was so proud of this memory. When the Republic was celebrating its tenth anniversary, he wrote an article in *Jamanak* entitled 'To see Ataturk; to Love Ataturk; and to Understand Ataturk'.

Nadiye's husband arrived while he was talking. He embraced his wife at the door, then shook the old man's hand. He was a big, shy man, and said nothing for a few minutes. Then, 'Do you want to see how we really live? I mean, how it can be really lived in this city? Do you? You should go to the Balat church tonight. It is the night of the miracle.'

The old man clapped his hands. 'Of course! Of course!'

'The miracle?' I asked.

'The miracle,' said Nadiye's husband. 'It happens once a year. On this day, the legend is that a sick person will be cured in the church. The church is full of Christians and Muslims. Sometimes it is a Muslim that is cured. It is true. People have been healed. One year, there was a man – a Muslim.'

The old man said, 'Mevlana says that if you want to be close to God, instead of entering the mosque, enter the heart of the smallest Christian church. It's about tolerance.'

Ersoy turned to me and said, in English, which the others did not understand: 'You know, he is a real old Istanbul man; a man of real nobility.'

Outside in the courtyard a boy was feeding a small yellow bird through the bars of a wooden cage.

The Armenian church in Balat, on the Golden Horn, is a huge vaulted building, fenced in by high stone walls. It was difficult to find. The taxi driver got lost in the warren of tiny streets until, first, we heard the noise of hundreds of people, and then we saw a great mob walking slowly, jamming the streets, towards the bulky church. This is the Old City, a mystery to Istanbul's politer society. It is poor and the houses are falling on top of one another. There is no space here. Every inch is crammed with people and bricks and washing. It is where the soul of the modern city resides: a real life of squalid hard work on the margins of civilized society. It is real indeed, a vivid, warm-blooded life in the crumbling tenements, between the tiny restaurants and workshops: children with dirty faces slipping out of a sweat shop or a tea house to go home to sleep; dogs barking; faceless women hanging out their washing. Here the metropolis has become a hamlet and recovered its identity. In the darkness, it was like entering a medieval world. Closer to the church – by now we were on foot – there was the rough unwashed smell of sheep; and the crowing of cocks.

At the entrance to the church, beyond the wall, there were hundreds of people milling around, of every age and of every district: dark-skinned, blue-eyed, children, pensioners. Inside, the church was packed. At the back some smart wardens, Armenian women wearing pearls and expensive sweaters, were shepherding poor Turkish women in cheap skirts and worn shoes into the pews. At the front, a man in a suit was standing by the altar with three others, some in cassocks trimmed with fine silver braid, chanting. This was not a formal choir; nobody was taking any notice of it. It was rough and out of tune, a drone. I asked a man in a blazer, who was standing by the entrance, what the music was. 'Is it plainsong?'

'No, it is a psalm.' And then he said, with great politeness, 'Where are you from? Are you from Ankara? I have a friend in Ankara. Do you know Mr Turk? From Ankara?' He looked at Ersoy and waited.

Ersoy did not know what to say. 'Ankara is a big city,' he replied. 'There are maybe many Mr Turks.'

'Really,' said the man, quite surprised.

'There are so many Muslims,' I said, looking into the church.

'Only tonight. Tonight we are all together.'

It is difficult to express how extraordinary this all was. It was very bright: all the lights were on. 'They will be on until the morning,' said the man. 'Until the miracle. We will just wait and God will pick one person, and cure him. I mean, he might. He does not always do so.'

There was movement everywhere: people were circling around the pews, Muslims and Christians, with no segregation.

Families were sitting on the pews, some praying, others eating picnics of sausage, yoghurt and bread out of small canvas bags spilling on to the pews. Boys were being cuffed around the head by impatient parents. Elegant Armenians from the European side of the city were carefully pouring tea from thermos flasks. Some had brought blankets. There were the women in head-scarves, pulling the cloth tighter around their cheeks when their eyes met mine; there were wealthier Armenians in sports jackets and Milanese trouser-suits. There was the persistent whine from the makeshift choir at the front and, behind, a lighter hubbub of conversation. In the middle of the church it was incredibly loud. It sounded like a public swimming pool and had the same air of profanity. At the back, old men behind collapsible wooden tables covered in green baize were selling candles or proffering silver plates for donations to the upkeep of the church. It was like a fête. There were Christians buying candles for Muslims, walking them to the trays of wood ash which stood on pedestals among the gleaming white pillars of the church, and helping them to place the candle firmly upright and then to light it. The Muslims were precise as they planted their candles. This was new for them.

There was such an air of expectation. 'There will be a miracle tonight,' said one Muslim man. There were many disabled in the church, physically disfigured, with hunched backs, or without limbs, dragging themselves along the aisle.

There were the mentally disturbed. There was a man whose head shook with tremendous, rhythmic violence against one of the walls. A small boy watched him and held his father's hand tightly while he tried to tear bread from a loaf.

Ersoy was very moved. 'They all look the same.'

This may be the only place in the world where Christians and Muslims meet to worship seriously. There were Muslim men kneeling on the floor between the pews with their palms raised up to heaven, and others, sitting beside them, holding their palms pressed flat together, reciting psalms. One Muslim man was watching a Christian on his pew, and clumsily put his hands flat together in imitation. These are people who keep their distance in their daily lives. That night they shared the same purpose: they sought mercy from the same God.

Ersoy walked out of the church and said, 'I don't know what to say. Why can't it always be like this?' Out here was one of the strangest sights. In the churchyard there was a mass of people, crowding round and shouting, proffering money. In front of them were three or four butchers, bent over marble slabs streaming with blood. They were cutting the throats of sheep. Every so often they would wipe their hands on their stained aprons and take another wadge of notes, and reach for a lamb, take its head between their knees and, with a firm action of the knife, stab its neck. Some of the poorer families could not afford sheep, so they presented cockerels; the poorest gave up chickens. There were pools of blood all over the yard, and the air smelt of it: warm and sweet.

We walked back inside. The church was full of kitsch: a neon-edged crucifix above the altar and another cross outlined in light-bulbs. The simple Corinthian columns that held up the roof were topped with gold enamel. Lining the walls were the lavish portraits which are so characteristic of Armenian Orthodox churches. The largest was a depiction of St Michael slaying the Dragon which featured a silver belt stuck on to the canvas. The Christians walked confidently up to the painting and lightly kissed the saint's buckle. A Muslim, uncertain of this ritual, watched a man kiss it, and then followed slowly, raising his lips to the icon. Some of the peasant women were working themselves into a frenzy, beating their breasts and scratching at their eyes. It did not seem out of place.

Ersoy went back to the warden who had inquired about Mr Turk and asked him what this was really all about. 'Many years ago,' said the warden, 'at a church outside the city, on this night, a woman passed out during a vigil, shouting the name of another person in the church. That person was disabled, but when his name was called, he could stand up and walk. Tonight a believer is supposed to pass out and name the handicapped person who will be cured.'

'Have you seen people cured?'

'Oh yes,' he replied. 'Two years ago Ali, a Muslim, was healed. Ali had an illness. He had fallen in love with a German girl. He had been refused. He became very ill – he couldn't walk or speak. But here in the church someone passed out and shouted his name, and a girl put her hand on his chest and he was cured. If you wait till the sunrise there's a great chance you will be witness to such a miracle.' He looked at both of us. 'This is the only place in the world.'

'Do you like having Muslims in your church?' asked Ersoy.

'This is the house of God. Unless you wear a hat, or smoke cigarettes and drink, it doesn't matter.' The church was full of light, pouring through the lead crystal candelabra.

Downstairs in the crypt you could buy bottles of water drained from a sacred well. The warden was walking us around. 'This church doesn't actually have a well – in fact, it used to be a Greek church. It is in another church that there is the well. But now, while everybody is concentrating on the miracle, this hardly matters.' There was a long queue of people waiting to buy the holy water.

The warden took us into a side chapel where people were filing past a painting of the Last Supper. Muslim followed Christian, kissing the figures in the painting, cupping their hands and speaking a few words. The painting was dirty, the figures indistinct. There was an altar with a depiction of the Madonna, and Muslim women, sometimes beside themselves with emotion, made the sign of the cross before the Virgin, whose silver hands held the baby Jesus, and looked down at them with pursed, tight lips. Sometimes they did it wrong, drawing circles across their breasts.

And permeating everything was the smell of the sheep. Outside, the sheep and the chickens were being slaughtered with more speed by now as the crowd grew larger. The drains were overflowing with blood. There were drops of blood inside the main door, on the marble floor. 'People want a miracle so they make sacrifice,' the warden said. There were students and factory workers, in pressed blue jeans and filthy smocks, pressing chickens into the hands of the butchers. It was a medieval festival, dark with the crooning of cocks.

Outside the walls there were cages full of birds, and shepherds keeping their flocks off the roads, out of the way of angry car drivers making their way into the city. There were dogs barking; and boys sitting on top of the cages, auctioning the birds. 'Cocks – one hundred and ten thousand lire!' one shouted. 'OK! OK! One hundred thousand lire – you are poor, you do not have to beg.' They were laughing and drinking cans of Coke.

There was a local government office building opposite the church. On the wall there was a sign: 'Rubbish Will Only Be Collected on Friday'. What would be done with all the corpses?

There was something fraudulent about the way we were simply watching this great, desperate ceremony of pleading. So we decided to leave. We thanked the warden and shook his hand. Ersoy stopped by the cages and said, 'I am so proud of this. In the middle I did not want to ask questions. I didn't realize they'd be so willing to talk. You know, I didn't want to disturb the peace at all. I am a Turk, the people that killed the . . . we are talking genocide – and I feel guilty. And they are so friendly to me. I wish this was always the way. It shows the potential . . .'

From inside the church you could hear women screaming.

Several weeks later, Ersoy telephoned the church to find out if there had been a miracle. One of the wardens said, 'There was no miracle this time; but we wait for next year.'

8

The Trojan Wars

In 1599, a decade after Webbe left, Thomas Dallam sailed from Gravesend to Constantinople aboard the *Hector*. He had been asked, at short notice, to make the journey by none other than Queen Elizabeth herself. He later wrote about his travels, and at the start of his book he gives the reader a handy list of all the necessaries he had to buy for his voyage.

These included one hat (at 7s 6d), a dozen handkerchiefs, ingredients for the cordial Rosa solis, prunes, sun-dried raisins, spoons, and two pairs of stockings. Thomas had never travelled out of London before. He was an organ-maker, famous throughout England for the meticulous craftsmanship of his instruments. Queen Elizabeth wanted to make a gift of one of his organs to the Sultan. She wanted Thomas to build it once it had arrived in Constantinople.

Thomas had many adventures on his way to the Sultan's court and saw many exotic and legendary places, but none excited him more than Troy. The *Hector* first arrived there on 15 July. 'A greate parte of the gate is yeat standinge, with som hudge peecis of this myghties wales that hathe bene,' he wrote. 'I and some more of our company went a shore and sawe some monimentes in Troy, peecis of wales, sutchins [escutcheons] and marble pillares.'

But his investigations were disturbed by the arrival of two Turkish galleys up the Dardanelles. Thomas and the others were called back on board by their worried captain and they sailed on past Troy. The Turks were notorious for demanding presents of visiting mariners, and the captain hoped to escape them, but he was unlucky. The Turkish admiral sent over a galley to demand a gift. The captain explained that there was an organ which was destined for the Sultan but otherwise there were no presents aboard. Finally, however, he found a couple of finely made Holland chests and some tobacco, which seemed to satisfy the Turks, and they went on their way.

Thomas was then able to return to Troy. 'We saw more at large the rewins of the wales and housis in Troye, and from thence I brought a peece of white marble piller, the which I broke with my owne handes, havinge a good hammer, which my mate Harvie did carrie a shore for the same purpose; and I brought this peece of marble to London.' Europeans have taken their hammers ashore so often since Thomas, and plundered so much of Troy that, above ground, very little remains of it at all.

Thomas Dallam assumed that this ruined town was Homer's Troy. Alexander the Great, on his way to Granicus, made a pilgrimage to Troy, the legendary home of Priam and Paris. Xerxes came to make sacrifice. The Ancient Romans believed this was Troy as well. They used to come on package holidays from Italy to see the town of Priam and the plain on which Hector and Achilles had fought. The Roman Senate granted Ilion, as it was then known, special privileges because Aeneas was a Trojan. But in the age of science there has been much more scepticism about the existence of this fabulous city. Can we really believe that men fought a war for ten years over a faithless woman? But it is like Noah's Ark: some people have a need to prove that Troy exists. This was the brightest city on earth, the strongest, the most civilized. The romance is overwhelming. To find Troy means you have found Odysseus, and Helen, and Patroclus.

After Dallam came ashore with his little hammer, amateur scavengers arrived to rob Troy of its marble. In the last 200 years the scavengers became known as archaeologists, and the great scientific search for Troy began. This little mound of earth, which the Turks call Hisarlik, is a place where great reputations have been made and lost. It is one of the great obsessions of Western European culture.

Professor Manfred Korfmann, a German archaeologist, has for the last six years been robbing the mound of its final mysteries. He may be the last who will earn celebrity status from Hisarlik. When he has finished with it, there will be little left to tell. Some details perhaps, but nothing of general interest.

The Troy which Korfmann has been exposing is far from the glamorous cosmopolitan city of which Homer wrote. Probably the Greek was just exaggerating. But Korfmann's methods, like those of a pathologist cutting up bodies in a post-mortem, are very scientific and painstaking, and do not encourage imagination or beautify their subject.

Just, however, as everybody thought the argument was settled, a young Swiss academic called Eberhard Zangger published a book in which he claimed that what Korfmann has been digging up is Troy *and* Atlantis. The local Turks (or Trojans), who rely on the tourists for their livelihood, are delighted by the prospect of having both on their doorstep. But Korfmann will not have Mr Zangger's name mentioned within his earshot. Korfmann's relations with some of the local Turks, who wish to exploit Troy (or Atlantis) to make money, are also sometimes strained. The relationship between Germans and Turks is not always easy.

It is not only Troy. Anatolia has long obsessed the Western archaeologist: many have desired to possess one part of it or another. The Turks have long refused to believe that the West has given up its imperialist ambitions on their territory. Today, the archaeologist sees in Anatolia a great trove of treasure which it cannot trust the Turks, by themselves, to preserve. There is real prejudice: a vision of the Turk as incorrigibly irresponsible. Nothing irritates Turkey as much. Nothing undermines its self-confidence as much.

I had waited for months to hear if my request to meet the famous Professor Korfmann would be granted. He has a prickly and rather fierce reputation, and is known to dislike wasting any amount of time with the media. His critics said there were two reasons for this. One was that journalists and writers are ignorant of the detailed work he is carrying out at Troy (which is true enough); and the other is that he views them with suspicion. I was granted an audience, however. His assistant had forwarded a fax. I was to go to Troy for three days to meet him.

Hisarlik is about twelve miles north of the town of Canakkale, on a hill overlooking the Dardanelles.

The country along the road to Troy was unexceptional. The fields had been harvested and the stubble was being burnt. There was the odd brick-box house, some painted, others not. There were long flat bungalows with mud extensions beside the electricity pylons. Some of these homes were thatched with branches.

The dominant colour was brown, except for the odd field of sunflowers, which bobbed about in the wind like demented black eyes on springs. The landscape was scorched by the heat. Sometimes there were telegraph poles from which the farmers hung dead birds as decoys. Sometimes you could see the old gun emplacements, ruined reminders that this strip of the Turkish coast along the Sea of Marmara has been much fought over. It has hosted two of history's most tragic conflicts: Troy and Gallipoli.

Soon the holiday villages started. They resembled military camps. At a distance, the rows and rows of identical white and red villas looked like barrack housing. Most were unfinished. The brick shells stared through windowless eyes towards the sea. The sea reminds you of the immensity of this country. You have travelled for hours without seeing any edges: miles and miles of farmed land, stretching on and on; then a glimpse of the sea, and a reminder that it has an end.

The coach passed through Gelibolu, a charming town: blue-rinse wooden traditional Ottoman *yala*, with wrought-iron windows. In kiosks around the small harbour tours of the Gallipoli battlefields were advertised. The guides sat outside shelling nuts in the shade of plane trees. There was not much business.

The ferry to Canakkale leaves a little further along the thin finger of land on the western side of the Dardanelles at Eleabat, where boys were swimming in the water, playing with the inner tubes from old tyres. It was not a long crossing, and that day it was fine and warm. It was nearly the end of the summer but there was still heat on the water.

The first thing you see when you disembark is a café called the Intellectual. But Canakkale, once you have reached it, is not a romantic town, nor is there much evidence that it has been hard fought over, apart from bits of cannon from the First World War mounted on stands in the high street. Canakkale was where Xerxes crossed into Europe with his 100,000 soldiers on his way to Greece and has a long history of violent confrontation.

I took a taxi from here to try to find the archaeologists. Korfmann had said three days, and this was the first. I did not want to waste any time. When I told the driver I was going to Troy, he said, 'It is good for the tourists. But I hate the Germans for taking it all away. What do they do for us, these Germans? Why are there so many Germans here in any case?' It was the usual story: he thinks that the Germans have come to steal Turkish treasure. 'My father used to collect old coins,' he said a few minutes later à propos of nothing.

We arrived at Hisarlik, the site of the excavations at Troy. You pass a few buildings at the entrance – a hotel, trinket shops and a fast-food café – and then you drive down a neat avenue with rose bushes growing in carefully tended flower-beds along a thin central reservation. The first vision of Troy is the Wooden Horse, which has been erected just inside the entrance. Children were waving their hands through its giant mouth. It was built of clinkered wood, like an old ship. Apart from the horse, there was nothing spectacular about Troy.

I paid off the cab driver and asked one of the attendants in a crumpled blue overall where I could find Professor Korfmann and his assistant Matthias. There was no sign here of any archaeologists.

'He has gone,' said the man.

'Where?' I asked. The man shrugged his shoulders and strolled off. I waited a moment and then chased after him.

'But they have not left Troy?' I asked.

'No, no,' said the man. 'They work in the mornings. That is when they work. In the mornings, when it is cooler. And now they have gone.'

He looked at me again and then walked me over to a small gate by the side of the museum. He opened it and said, 'You must wait here. Nobody may enter.' He disappeared behind a wall. I could just discern some tents. But otherwise the place seemed deserted. There was a curious haze, which made it hard to see clearly into the distance.

After a while a young man appeared, waving his hand. He had blond hair and a cheerful, angular face. He was wearing a broad-brimmed sun-hat, just like an archaeologist. This was Matthias.

'Welcome,' he said. We shook hands.

'What is that behind the fence?' I asked.

'Oh no, that is the forbidden area,' he said, smiling. 'Only those who work are allowed into it. Anyway, I hope you have had a good trip. I have made a reservation for you at the hotel up the road. You will want to rest now?' He spoke with a soft accent.

We both stood in the shade by the museum, watching for a moment as the breeze scuffed along the earth.

'I would like to rest,' I said. 'But I wondered also when I can see the Professor . . .'

Matthias looked fragile. 'Herr Korfmann cannot see you straight away.'

'But perhaps I can see him this evening?' I asked.

'He will decide,' said Matthias. 'But we are expecting you.'

'See you later, then,' I said.

And he replied, as if I had startled him, 'Oh yes, no doubt, no doubt . . .'

I made my way back up the avenue towards the hotel. Light cirrus clouds drifted like feathers across the pale blue of the sky, but they did nothing to stifle the heat, which thickened as evening approached. Dusk can be dreadful so close to the coast and a floodplain of fresh-water streams. By now, Troy was alive with midges and mosquitoes.

Next door to the hotel was Heinrich Schliemann's house. Schliemann was the man who discovered Troy, or claimed he did. The simple wooden shack was not the original article, of course. It was a replica made by a German television crew when they came here to film a documentary. Schliemann lived in it for years while he dug away at Troy and made himself famous. This shack is still standing, according to a notice beside it, 'for the pleasure of visitors'.

So much has been written about Schliemann: he was a good man, a bad man, a strange man, a visionary. He was one of the great driven men of history.

He was born in 1822 in the village of Neu-Buckow in north-east Germany. His family lived in humble circumstances. When he was fourteen he worked for a local grocer as an apprentice. But Schliemann wanted more from life, and worked with incredible diligence to educate himself. He had a great skill in languages and he exploited that ability to the full. By the end of his life he was able to speak eleven fluently and to read nearly double that number.

At the age of twenty-four he became the St Petersburg agent of a German firm that dealt in Indian indigo, and he made himself rich through commerce. This arrogant merchant had a taste for adventure that was unusual among his contemporaries. He travelled widely, keeping scrupulous notes of everything he saw. One of his most recent biographers commented: 'If the diaries reveal a lonely figure, letters to his family suggest bossiness and a terrible need to succeed.' He survived a shipwreck and participated in the Californian Gold Rush.

Schliemann was brutally decisive. Once he had made his fortune, he abandoned his Russian wife and three children for a new life in the United States. Once he had divorced her, he sought a new bride. He wanted a young Greek girl and asked friends in Athens to find him one. They selected the sixteen-year-old daughter of a local businessman. She was called Sophia.

Schliemann was obsessed with Homer, and now, in his forties, he decided to discover Homer's Troy. It was a quite conscious plan. He had American citizenship which made it much easier for him to win a permit from the Turkish authorities to excavate in Anatolia. He chose to treat Homer's poems as careful histories of a real past.

Schliemann made his first visit to Canakkale in 1868. While he was there, he met the local American vice-consul, Frank Calvert, who, like him, believed that Troy was in that area. Calvert argued that the old city was under the ruins of Hisarlik. Schliemann started to excavate in 1871. The conditions were awful: the plains below Hisarlik were malarial and crawling with scorpions and poisonous snakes. He had no interest in later Greek and Roman residents of Hisarlik, and he directed his eighty local labourers to discard anything they found that was superimposed on what he believed was the City of Priam. As a result, much of that later legacy was destroyed.

In 1873, after two years of inconclusive digging which had produced no real proof of Homer's Troy, Schliemann claimed victory. On 31 May at 8 a.m. he found a hoard of treasure. There were cups and vases, all of gold, and two fabulous headdresses. He was convinced that this was Priam's treasure as reported by Homer, and that it was proof that Troy did really exist. He wrote later:

> While following up the circuit wall and bringing more and more of it to light, I struck at a point lightly north-west of the gate a large copper article of the most remarkable form, which attracted my attention, all the more as I thought I saw gold glimmering behind it. In order to secure the treasure from my workmen and save it for archaeology, it was necessary to lose no time; so, although it was not yet the hour for breakfast, I immediately had the *paidos* [the work-break] called, and while the men were eating and resting I cut out the treasure with a large knife. This involved risk as the fortification wall beneath which I had to dig threatened every moment to fall on my head. And indeed I should not have succeeded in getting

> possession of the treasure without the help of my wife, who stood at my side, ready to pack the things I cut out in her shawl, and to carry them away.

Schliemann told at least one untruth in this account. His wife was not with him when he found the treasure.

He had promised the Turkish authorities that if he did find anything, he would share it with them. Instead, he stole it. It was a precedent which has haunted archaeologists working in Turkey ever since. He smuggled the hoard to Athens. He dressed the dour Sophia up in the jewellery and took photographs of her as Helen of Troy. A plain woman, she seems ill at ease in the famous oval print. The diadem, with its long chain tassles was designed for a younger woman.

Schliemann's find was undoubtedly a remarkable one. Its implications thrilled the world. Was it possible that Helen and Achilles and the rest of Homer's cast had really lived? But there were many dissenters. Among those historians and other archaeologists from whom Schliemann sought approval, there was scepticism. There was evidence of fabrication – small lies, but enough to undermine his credibility. Some said that Schliemann had bought the treasure himself and then buried it. The criticism eventually abated. In 1880 he donated the find to the German people and it was then put on display in Berlin.

Schliemann returned to Troy later in his life in a final attempt to prove to those critics who continued to doubt the find that it belonged to Homer's Troy. Very quickly, however, during that excavation the team discovered new things: unexpected and unpredicted structures were unearthed. It became obvious that Schliemann had been wrong all along. The treasure he had discovered could not have belonged to Priam. It belonged to a much earlier Troy than the one Homer could have written about.

Nobody knows if Schliemann ever acknowledged his error. His assistant, Wilhelm Dorpfeld, claimed years later that he did. Schliemann died in Naples in 1890, at the age of sixty-eight, following an ear infection.

When he first embarked on his quest, archaeology as a science was in its infancy. Prehistory – the history of mankind before the existence of written records – was obscure and mysterious. Schliemann's excavation at Troy was the first systematic attempt to delve into that distant past. He has been credited by some as the father of modern archaeology. But he was also a thief – more of a prospector than an archaeologist who had no compunction about inflating his own legend. Schliemann gave the impression that he was the first to have located Troy at Hisarlik. In fact, an Englishman had suggested that this was the site of Troy in a book published in the year of the German's birth. Schliemann knew the book but never publicized his debt to it.

When he left Troy, he had, in some ways, done more harm than good. He had demolished much of the site, literally digging a trench through it in his search for Priam's city. In doing so, he had destroyed much of what could have been this city, but that is a historic irony and not one that would have given him any pleasure.

It is a century since his death, but everybody is still sensitive about Schliemann. To many Turks he was the archetypal European – the thief who poses as a friend; dishonest and arrogant. He had betrayed their trust by plundering Troy and had stolen one of the most unique and beautiful memories of their ancient past. He was a symbol of those European predators who, in the twilight of the Ottoman Empire, stalked about looking for booty. In particular, Schliemann stood for the arrogance of Germans.

Korfmann is the most recent German the Turks have allowed near Troy. There are those who bitterly allege that he is another Schliemann, motivated by self-interest, a hunger for fame and a place in history. One Turkish archaeologist told me, 'It should be Turks who run the excavations at Troy. They will have the lot otherwise. They will steal it all.'

One of the most striking things about the actual excavations at Troy are the signposts around the site, which Korfmann put up, damning Schliemann's memory. One told visitors he was

'AN ARCHAEOLOGICAL TREASURE HUNTER WHO ILLEGALLY TOOK FINDS OUTSIDE OF THE COUNTRY'.

Mustafa saw me looking at the shack and asked me if I was the guest of Korfmann. 'You have a special rate on your room,' he said, smiling. Mustafa was the owner of the Hisarlik Hotel and he was chief tourist guide to the mound. He was small, with a swarthy face and bright, mischievous eyes. He was probably in his forties, but he looked younger. He spoke good, disciplined English.

On the ground floor of the tiny hotel, which had a handful of rooms, mostly occupied by people coming to visit Korfmann, there was a souvenir shop. It was packed with a coach-load of European visitors. There was a sign: 'PRICES ARE FIXED. PLEASE DO NOT BARGAIN'. The shop was crammed with trinkets and novelties, all to do with Troy. On coat-hangers above the cash till were T-shirts bearing the legend 'A Golden Apple from Troy'. There were tea sets and handbags with little wooden horse motifs, and there were overflowing trays of little horses, in plastic and wood (and match-sticks) and metal and stone, for the mantelpiece, or the wall, or a key-ring. If you sent postcards from the hotel, Mustafa said, while I was looking around the shop, 'They will be stamped from TROY – I have an arrangement with the post office!'

The shop attendants were all wearing the same T-shirt which said DOORMEN in German. On the counter was a telephone, which is why I had come in. I wanted to call home just to say that I had arrived. The man behind the cash register said, 'It doesn't work to Italy or Greece.' Mustafa, who was looking in the other direction, turned and said, 'I don't know why . . .'

It was early evening by the time I had finished in the shop, and I took a stroll down to the mound and the museum. The heat had dissipated a little; but I was still sweating. Most of the coach parties had left. There were a few cars. They all belonged to Turkish visitors. Turkish tourists? Sometimes they are overlooked, but the Turks take a big interest in Troy and many come every year to see it.

A breeze touched the leaves on the trees around the planked Horse. There were no children screaming around it now. It was very quiet. The air was strongly perfumed: roses and some other fragrance that I could not readily identify, like peach. I walked past the small museum and on to the mound. From the top you could see across the flood-plain of the Scamander to the Dardanelles and the battlefields of the other Trojan war at Gallipoli. Homer called Troy the windy Troy. But it was only a breeze when I stood on the top. All around you are jumbled-up stones. Everything here had been dug up and confused. You could walk up a step, and pass through a thousand years of history. Was this really where Paris brought Helen?

I had read so much about the disappointment of Troy – how nothing much is left, no great temples, or palaces – that I was pleased to find chunks of wall, and pieces of gate, and a ramp. So long ago. The Tower of Troy IV, built between 1800 and 1300 BC, is commemorated by a few huge blocks, but it is beautiful, self-confident masonry. In the Temple of Athena, from a later city, there were bits of marble left, although most of value was taken by Schliemann to Berlin. Everything here speaks of something departed: old sections of wall lying in pieces, scattered and broken, discarded chunks of ancient temple, weeds, dirt. The ruins have a certain vulnerability and sadness. The place feels abandoned and unloved.

I remembered something Mustafa had said: 'Korfmann keeps it all private, you know. He does not let outsiders into the excavations. He does not let me in . . .' He smiled, but he was deeply hurt. Korfmann had made this his secret garden; Mustafa wanted it for himself, and he believed he had the better claim. He accuses Korfmann of being selfish, which is a serious charge. It is saying that Korfmann is like Schliemann.

They were odd rivals. Korfmann had access to knowledge, and he kept it from Mustafa. Korfmann wrote about Troy, and so did Mustafa. He had written a guide-book. Both men had dedicated their lives to the place. One man will go down in history; the other will not.

Korfmann's new excavations are the first at Troy for fifty years. After an American expedition in the 1930s, the site fell back into the possession of the local people. They lived around it. Fifty years later they were evicted to make way for Korfmann. Mustafa's family was one of those forced to move. The new dig was now fenced off, with heavy rope, from both locals and tourists. During the day guards patrolled the area wearing T-shirts saying GUARD in German.

One notice announced: ABOUT 70 TURKISH WORKMEN ARE BEING EMPLOYED. This meant that seventy families, possibly more, rely on Korfmann. This made him the most powerful man for miles around, probably as far as Canakkale. The notice continued: 'All finds are going to the museum at Canakkale . . . our most important concern is to safeguard the ruins from further destruction.'

Even if this mound is not Homer's Troy, it is still the most famous and important archaeological site in the Western world. It is a unique window on the Bronze Age, during which human civilization reached heights which today we can only partly appreciate.

Troy's history started with the discovery of metal in around 3000 BC. It was then that the first residents came to the mound. Their lives were difficult and short. The area was malarial and many died from the disease. In the coming centuries Troy grew to absorb and reflect the culture of surrounding civilizations: Egypt of the Pharaohs; the Hittites of Central Anatolia; the Achaeans of south-eastern Greece. At Troy archaeologists had found the first potter's wheel, the first bronze in Europe and evidence of the first stratified society. The Trojans were importing pottery from as far away as India. They were buying pomegranate seeds, African blackwood, quartz, amber, hippopotamus' teeth, and ostrich eggshells. It was a prosperous and sophisticated community that had time for leisure and for luxury.

And then, after only a few years of apparent instability, it was as if somebody switched off the light. In around 1200 BC the great civilizations of the Eastern Mediterranean suddenly collapsed. There was an epidemic of vandalism. Many buildings were destroyed, cities were abandoned. People who had once lived in houses on streets with sewers now lived very basic lives in mud shacks in small vagrant communities. Troy was abandoned and burnt. Commerce seems to have dried up. The international economy disappeared. Literacy was forgotten for more than 300 years until Homer rediscovered it around 800 BC, and wrote the *Iliad*.

There was no single reason for this. The end came because after decades of continuous warfare, some of the most fluorescent cultures that have ever existed were exhausted, and weak.

Back in the hotel, Mustafa had said that people come to Troy for many reasons. Perhaps some of them hope that we will never know the precise truth. At first people came because Troy was a good place to make war. Now people come to read Homer and imagine what might have been. Mustafa had said, 'The *Iliad* is a book about peace not war.' Homer wrote about people; he wrote about the jealousy of Achilles – and we can all identify with that.

On a noticeboard in the hotel, Mustafa has a selection of press cuttings. Among them were reports of Eberhard Zangger's 'discovery' that Troy was in fact Atlantis. Korfmann dismissed this, as most archaeologists have done, as fantasy. But Mustafa is more positive. It can only be good for business. 'I have already decided to update my guide to include a new chapter on Atlantis,' he said with a tight smile. It was another way of expressing his hostility to Korfmann.

Zangger's book, *The Flood from Heaven*, is probably the most outlandish and controversial work written by an archaeologist in a decade. The orangey dust-jacket painting is of a swirling typhoon engulfing some small Greek rowing-boats, with bolts of lightning lighting up the sky. It is not very good and could be the cover for a science fiction book. It does not help the credibility of Zangger's argument.

The foreword is encouraging. Written by a leading Cambridge academic, it describes Zangger as an 'expert' and his book as a 'daring venture'. It is 'not yet another charge of the hobby horse brigade . . . [but] a plea for freedom to think along new lines . . .'

Zangger argues that Troy and Atlantis are the same place. The only source for the Atlantis myth is Plato, who wrote about it on two occasions and at some length. There are fundamental prima facie defects in the idea that the two are the same – notably, the fact that Atlantis is supposed to be a lost continent. Equally difficult is the fact that Plato states that Atlantis was destroyed by a flood 9,000 years before he wrote the story – a lot earlier than the Trojan war was fought. But there are compelling grounds for believing that the story Plato was telling was another version of Homer's epic. Zangger says that he was simply the victim of confused oral history.

Among the many points he makes in defence of his thesis is the fact that the name Atlantis means 'daughter of Atlas'. Ancient legends state that the Trojans were descendants of Electra, the daughter of Atlas. Zangger makes all the geography fit too. There are springs mentioned in Plato's account near Atlantis, and Homer mentions hot and cold springs too at Troy; there are, in fact, some old springs near Hisarlik. Atlantis was supposed to stand in front of the pillars of Hercules. In the Zangger model, these are the Straits of the Dardanelles. There is a lot of detailed (and, to the layman, convincing) archaeological argument. In some senses the book should have provoked very little controversy. Does it matter that Troy is Atlantis if it is Troy as well? Zangger does not argue that the mound at Hisarlik was not Troy. Why should anybody be upset by the fact that it might also be Atlantis?

But they are. In the book, Zangger gives two definitions of crankiness, to declare his own awareness of the danger. But the precaution has not helped him much. He has been condemned by most of the authorities as a fool. Without doubt, Atlantis has always been attractive to frauds and dreamers. More than 50,000 books have been written about the lost continent. Writers have argued that the legendary urge of the lemming to hurl itself into the sea is a consequence of their desire to migrate to Atlantis.

People have looked for Atlantis in Andalusia, and South America and Outer Mongolia. One investigator found the island in the Sahara; another in deep space; and Sir Arthur Conan Doyle said it was at the bottom of the sea.

There have been some historic frauds on the Atlantis trail. Paul Schliemann, who said he was the grandson of Heinrich, claimed to have discovered it in 1912. Schliemann said that his grandfather had left a letter before he died which was to be opened only by a member of his family who was ready to commit himself to archaeology. He then broke the seal and discovered in a vase, which accompanied the letter, some coins with the inscription: *Issued in the Temple of Transparent Walls.* The letter described a vase which was labelled: *From King Cronos of Atlantis.* Schliemann announced this and then said he intended to write a book giving all the details. But he never did, and later it was revealed that Heinrich Schliemann did not have a grandson called Paul.

It was still light when some of Korfmann's crew arrived at the hotel. They were instantly recognizable walking up the road: an odd bunch of misshapen men and women; tall and gangly, or short and squat. I was writing up some notes, a little hazy with beer. It was still hot. The group came to the tables and each person scrutinized me before ignoring me.

A few minutes later Matthias arrived outside the hotel in an open jeep. He waved at the others and then came across to me. We sat down at a table near the noisy crew who were laughing and shouting for beer. Matthias said, 'I'm sorry I'm late.' One of the women at the other table, older than the rest, shouted out, 'I don't care about Troy!'

We ate lamb. We did not talk much to start with. I could feel intense hostility directed towards me from the noisy crew. Every so often Matthias would catch the eye of one of his colleagues and smile.

'How did you become an archaeologist?'

'I trained to be a priest,' he said. 'I studied theology.'

Matthias was not an archaeologist in any case. He was in

charge of public relations for the dig. He liaised with the press and he was responsible for making a video of Korfmann's work, a visual record which would be presented to the commercial sponsors of the Troy expedition. There were only a few days left before this year's excavation would be over, so Matthias was busy. He talked for a while about theology and said that his favourite theologian was Soren Kierkegaard, the Danish existentialist. Kierkegaard had a hard, obsessive vision, full of pain and self-sacrifice. Matthias was very skinny, as if he had been systematically deprived of food over a long period, and he was nervous, but he was sincere. He was interested in talking about Eisenstein and how he wanted to write a film script.

'What is Korfmann like?'

'He is a big man . . .'

'He is a general?'

'Yes, you are quite right,' he said.

'When will I see him?'

'When he is ready to see you.'

'Do you have any idea of when that may be?'

'No, I am sorry. He may not see you at all. But I hope he will. Really . . .' He was sorry for the uncertainty. His whole face pleaded the case for his powerlessness.

Just at that moment, as the light was closing in, another jeep came to a noisy halt outside the hotel. There was one passenger. Everyone at the table waved to this figure, who waved back. Matthias tapped me on the shoulder, just to make sure that I knew.

Korfmann was bigger, more bulky than I had imagined. He came across to the tables and made a joke with the crew. He saw me, and realized that I was an outsider. He did not introduce himself and walked across to the fast food restaurant opposite the hotel.

Matthias had said that I could come and spend the next day with the crew if I wished. They woke early, he explained, because the heat forced them to work in the mornings. After lunch it was too hot to dig. I was worried about Korfmann. I would not pass up an opportunity to meet him, even by chance.

I had spent most of the night awake, victimized by mosquitoes. Mustafa had put nets across the windows of the rooms in his hotel, but they were no obstruction. I arrived at the team camp just as the archaeologists were rising, shortly before 6 a.m. It was dark and cold but there were no insects. For a while I stood outside the encampment, by the giant Horse, waiting for Matthias to come out. But nobody appeared. So I unlatched the gate and walked unobserved into the compound. I walked over to a light and as I grew nearer I could see a handful of the crew milling around a caravan which was the canteen. They were nursing cups of tea and coffee.

I could see Korfmann sitting on a bench on his own. I decided to approach him, to remind him of my presence and his original invitation. He saw me, and for a moment sat quite still, holding his cup in the air. Then he shouted, 'Who let you in? Matthias?' He ran towards me, and said in staccato, heavily accented English, 'What are you doing? What are you doing?' He pushed me towards the bench. 'Sit, please, while I sort this out!' He rushed towards one of the huts, waving his hands above his head. He looked quite mad. Then he came back: 'Look. Nobody is allowed in here. Nobody. Do you see that if one pearl goes missing from Troy then they will say that we are disorganized or are stealing their treasure and they will ban us?'

'But I am not going to steal a pearl.' I was thrilled by his paranoia.

'They must not see you in here . . .' He was quite frightened.

He escorted me from the camp and asked me to wait by the Wooden Horse. 'You can watch me give instructions to the workers. I am sure that this will be of interest to you.'

I stood outside for a while, and then through the shadows came dozens of Turkish labourers wearing cloth caps, their jacket collars pulled up around their necks to keep out the cold. They had barrows and picks. Korfmann stood on a low wall and told them to form into a semi-circle. He looked like a preacher, reading the roll-call. And when he had finished, stopping once or twice because some of the men had not turned up, he jumped down from the wall and waved the men to work. There was more light as they walked off towards the mound. Some were in very ragged clothes.

Korfmann approached me and motioned me to follow him towards the mound. He was going to inspect the excavations. His contribution to the Troy debate has been significant. He has established that the town was much larger than previously thought by discovering that there was a large settlement outside the walls of the citadel which Schliemann found. He has also unearthed evidence of burning at the level which could, in terms of its age, be Homer's Troy. Evidence of fire is evidence of catastrophe; this could be evidence of the Trojan war, which ended with the sacking of the city. Korfmann said quite sternly that he was merely digging the mound at Hisarlik. He was not searching for Troy. 'You can play with *your* fantasy, if you like.' He was both sensitive and suspicious.

He hurtled around the dig looking like an officer at war or a boy scout in his khaki jacket and canary-yellow shorts. He had dusty walking shoes and a black floral kerchief which added an absurd hint of effeminacy. His English was fluent but irritable. He did not feel comfortable speaking it. He used it to inspire fear in people. 'Janey!' he shouted to one woman deep in a trench brushing the dirt floor. 'Yes, it's a nicely structured level. Nice.' She did not say anything in reply. It sounded as if he was chiding her.

The night before, one of the crew had said that the notices on the site referring to Schliemann had been recently changed. Originally they were not so harsh. 'I don't work in the shadow of Schliemann,' Korfmann said. 'You should be aware of the mistakes and the successes of our forefathers. We are here. We are standing on people's shoulders and we have a broader view. Schliemann is a person to whom we owe very much – especially in Troy.' The sun was beginning to crawl into the sky and the air starting to thicken.

You could see that he was anxious about something. It was

the workmen. One of them was ill, he said. He was worried that the site was therefore not working at maximum productivity. He suddenly became angry, stomping his feet into the dirt, and then he relaxed completely, and smiled. His face was large and flat, like a plate, without any prominent features, topped with a short clump of dusty hair. He stood in his safari jacket, surveying the dig like a benign plantation owner. 'I understand these people very well, better than they know themselves –'

It was not just one man who had failed to turn up for work, however. Several were absent. He seemed full of understanding now: 'Today is pension day and the workmen have to go to Canakkale to pick up their pensions.' I suspected some of them were retired. He looked me coolly in the eyes: 'You know that they call me Osman Bey, which is a great mark of respect. My cook at an earlier dig could not pronounce Korfmann, so she called me Osman. It is difficult for the Turk to pronounce certain consonants together: RF – *rrrf* – as in Ko – *rrrf* – mann,' he said, rolling his tongue, by way of demonstration. 'It is a great honour to be called by a Turkish name.' The name Osman is the name of the first of the Ottoman rulers.

We passed another hole in which some old Turks were digging. They were hacking at the rock with pickaxes. He stopped and shouted down, 'Mustafa! Mustafa!' He turned to me. 'I bring clothes from Germany for the older villagers. You see – one man has a pair of blue slacks. It's not so necessary now, but some are really poor. They are happy now. This one likes to think he's my father.'

'Do they fit well?' Korfmann asked him.

'Thank you! Thank you, brother!' came the reply.

'Now dig along that line. No. No! Not *that* line. Concentrate. Yes, that line. Good!' And we moved on.

Now Korfmann was bounding back towards the camp. He took me inside. 'You can see certain things in here. But it is important that *they* do not see you.' Inside the camp there were some huts and tents. Under one huge awning were trays and trays of pot shards, all being sorted. Some of those without any intrinsic value were being used for making concrete. 'This is as they did it in Roman times,' Korfmann said.

There were some permanent stone buildings in the camp, and inside these women at computer terminals were listing bones and drawing maps, while others were cleaning skulls and making models. There was a rostrum camera taking pictures of pottery fragments. Hi-tech archaeology. Korfmann confided: 'You see, I cannot let strangers all over the place. Troy is too special to make mistakes. I have ministerial problems.' This is a very fragile business, digging into Turkish history. 'One year we have fundamentalists inspecting the site, the next not . . . sometimes they are fundamentalists; sometimes they are nice people.' The Turkish government appointed two representatives to supervise his excavation and make sure that nothing is purloined. Some were more interventionist than others.

Korfmann had momentarily made me his guest, and he insisted that we linger a while in his office while he attended to some problem in one of his laboratories. Matthias popped his head around the door on his way to film the excavations. He was amazed at the speed with which Korfmann had evicted me from the camp that morning. 'I was really surprised he allowed you back when in his eyes – you could tell – he was going to tell you to go.' He disappeared.

Korfmann returned and his secretary asked him a question. He brushed her sternly aside. 'Now I can't make an appointment, I have no time.' I was the full subject of his attention. After a few moments the great archaeologist, who must be in his mid-fifties, asked me if I would like some breakfast. I nodded my head and he led me across to the canteen which was empty except for the cooks, all of whom were local women. 'There are girls here,' he said. 'Usually there would only be men.' He was right. It was unusual. 'But they have known me for a generation. I have known some of them since they were children.' There were tea and bread and olives, and smelly cheese and boiled eggs. Korfmann did not eat or drink.

'Why is Troy so important?' I asked him.

'The Turks say they came from Troy,' Korfmann replied

after a moment. 'Everybody said they came from Troy. Sultan Fatih said, after conquering Constantinople in 1453, that it was revenge for Troy, and that he had come from Troy. The Europeans in the Middle Ages believed that they came from Troy; the Franks believed, as did the Romans, that they were descended from Aeneas, who was a Trojan, according to the legends. The chroniclers of the eleventh and twelfth centuries say that the Franks came from Troy via the Balkans. Troy was a holy city.

'The Fourth Crusade went into this area, not Jerusalem. The locals asked them why they came here. The European knights said, "Have you not heard of Troy?" During the Middle Ages the Europeans knew that Troy was here – there are books and paintings to illustrate this. It is not all Homer . . .'

Korfmann stopped for a moment and I asked, 'What do you hope to achieve?'

'I want a National Park in this area – a Peace Park. We could call it the Gallipoli National Park. So many Trojan wars have been fought here . . . it is an idea. It should not just show cannons and tombs. It is a cry for peace. Troy should deliver the message: peace is better than fighting.'

Korfmann was born into Nazi Germany, and he carried that burden with him. It was what moved him. I was delighted and embarrassed by his sudden sincerity. He was exposing his burden to a stranger. He had first planned to become a teacher. As a student he travelled extensively through the Middle East and he learned Arabic. 'Life. I saw life. I wanted to improve my knowledge; to understand something about human behaviour, and if you are interested in human beings then you must know of the past. I am not an archaeologist who is interested in the past. It all has a meaning for the present.' He looked blankly at the wall.

'I learned that a nationalist can never be a good archaeologist – somebody who is interested only in their own culture.' He was picking up speed. He was giving a speech. 'You must be a liberal and wish to understand people. We are travelling in Troy at different levels of time. The aim is not to find good things but to understand different people.' He was looking not at me but at one of the small windows. There was light streaming into the canteen now, and by the stoves the girls were giggling with their mothers.

'What I can see now, as a pre-historian, is that whenever cultures are threatened or change, there is the inclination to make one group an enemy because they are different. They have different clothes. The Germans say to the Italians, "Hey, spaghetti eaters!" And then our worst examples, the Jews . . . the Jews . . .' He paused. 'We can see that. Where there is weakness there are scapegoats. Troy tells this story. Now the world is becoming more uniform. The Germans eat French cheese as well as sauerkraut. People sing the same songs at rock concerts. I hope they can understand each other better. I am an archaeologist, but I am interested in peace. Archaeologists are not just people with a brush.'

Korfmann solemnly announced that he would die with Troy. 'It is the last site of my life.' He was experienced in the Bronze Age, and was relatively young when he was appointed in 1988. 'I had a good life expectancy,' he said. 'It is not a personal excavation – *ja*, you know that. It is not a German excavation. The time is over when foreign archaeologists work under the flag of a visiting nation. I was born in Germany but I am not proud of being a German . . . I am not proud of being a German.'

One of the girls was standing on a chair trying to reach up to a fly-paper that was dangling from the ceiling. There were fly-papers everywhere. 'This is not cultural imperialism. There are Americans here and Britons. This is not owned by Manfred Korfmann but by all the world . . .'

Quite suddenly his mood changed. I was to leave now. He had to return to work or he would get behind. The thought inspired panic in his eyes. He stood up while I slurped down the last of my tea, and then walked quite briskly towards the gate. As we strode towards it, a glamorous-looking, middle-aged Turk called Emil appeared – an odd sight among all these dreary archaeologists with her peroxided hair and stylish dark glasses. Korfmann stopped abruptly when he saw her. He appeared to be frightened. 'Who knows who we will have next year!' he whispered. And then he looked at me as if he had forgotten that I was a stranger. Emil came across and they chatted. She was a society type. Perhaps her husband was big in the ministry and this was a nice diversion for her, to oversee the excavations. She was not an archaeologist.

He did not introduce me to her, except to say that I was here to talk to him, and as soon as she had gone, we left hurriedly for the gate. I said, 'Thank you' to Korfmann, and he said nothing. He had already turned his back on me. As I strolled back towards the hotel, I remembered that I had forgotten to ask him about Zangger and Atlantis.

That afternoon Mustafa was hanging around in the café, so I asked him if he would take me on one of his tours and show me Troy. He was keen to know what Korfmann had told me. 'No!' he said after I had described our conversation. 'Did he *tell* you anything?'

Mustafa was angry – visibly so – because he was not granted access to the new excavations by Korfmann. This anger was always there. It humiliated him. 'It makes me sad,' he said as we left the shop and walked towards Troy. Then, after a little while, he added, 'Why are the Germans so sensitive about disappearing objects?'

Mustafa was most bitter because he had propelled himself by his own hard work above the poverty in which his parents had lived their lives. After studying economics in Istanbul and English in London he became a guide fourteen years ago. Troy should have been his, but it had been snatched away. He told me about his parents, how they had run a souvenir shop by the mound until the government – to make way for the foreign archaeologists – had forced them out and demolished it. 'All the olive and the almond trees belong to my family.' Once they had expelled these latter-day Trojans, to let the experts into Troy, the state built the fast-food centre and the hotel which Mustafa now runs. None of the locals inconvenienced by the forced evictions were compensated. Is History so important that it should ever dispossess the living?

'I would like to see what it looked like. I mean to see it rebuilt,' he said as we walked up the mound. 'People walk about and they see piles of rubble. They are very upset. It is bad publicity for Turkey, all this rubble.' He had never been able to understand the fetish for ruins, for *preserving* ruins. Why should the past not be put to work for the living?

We had reached the site of the Temple of Athena, which Schliemann destroyed. All that remains today is a tree. 'When I reach this point on my tour I tell the story of Schliemann. I like to shock the Germans in the group. I want to make them know what they did.' He liked to stand under the tree and point down around the mound. 'Now, Schliemann!' he said to his tour parties. 'Over there you can see what he destroyed.'

Mustafa was banned from the excavations. At the end of each season Korfmann took a party of invited archaeologists on a tour to show the new finds. But he did not take Mustafa. 'I protect Troy more than anybody but I cannot jump over the fence. You know, I really wanted to be an archaeologist. Once I asked Korfmann if I could take part. He said it would be very difficult for me to start work at 6 a.m.' We walked on through the layers of Troy. He was burning with the humiliation.

While we looked at the stone walls of the ramp, Mustafa told me the story of the Japanese television crew. They had come a year or two before, with documents from the Ministry of Information. They went to Korfmann and presented their papers and said that they wanted to film Troy and the excavations. And he refused. 'They were surprised,' said Mustafa, laughing. 'He was very sharp with them.' They approached him the following day with their papers but he refused them again. Naturally enough, this was confusing to them. Korfmann was merely a German archaeologist and their papers had been signed by an official of the Turkish government. Korfmann, apparently, was nervous that they might be intent on stealing pictures of the excavations.

The Japanese then left the area, only to return a few days later in a helicopter. They flew around Troy once or twice with their film camera rolling and flew away again. Korfmann watched them, powerless, from the ground. Mustafa was pleased to remember that story.

Just as we passed the gate, Mustafa stopped and looked around at me. 'You know, once we were in a group and Korfmann turned to one man and said, "Don't tell Mustafa everything!"' You could see it had hurt him. His face drooped as he was telling me. 'Then I said to him, "Why don't you tell me? Why don't you make an exception for me?" And he replied, "*You* are not an *exceptional* man."' He was shouting when he said that. A couple standing in the car park, getting ready to go home, turned with a start, as if a gun had just been fired. 'Korfmann even told the guard not to let me take pictures of the excavations. He was worried I might make a . . . *postcard*!'

Mustafa was not a real Trojan. The modern Trojans are Turks of Bulgarian extract who came as refugees during the pogroms of the nineteenth century. The village of Hisarlik was founded in 1877 after the Russian war. By then Schliemann was already here. There was a short stretch of narrow-gauge railway by the shack at the front of the hotel, used by Schliemann to carry away his excavated waste. The rest of the railway had gone. It had been adapted. Local peasants now used the rails as sturdy beams in their houses.

We arrived back at the hotel and sat, more calmly, at a table, watching the sun dip elegantly over the horizon. A man with a shaggy head of hair and a thin face came to sit at the next table. He was an important academic – a professor – who worked with Korfmann. He was an expert on animal bones: an archaeozoologist.

'Why is Korfmann so sensitive about Troy?' I asked.

'The copyright. It is his.'

'And the jealousy?'

'*Ja*, this is a personal feature.'

Mustafa looked sternly at the professor. 'Will you take me to the excavation?'

'You are not allowed to ask this question, Mustafa. Ask Korfmann.'

An aeroplane buzzed overhead, and Mustafa jerked his head skywards, smiling. It was a clear blue sky, but we could not see the plane. Still the drone went on and we searched for it. Then Mustafa spotted it, far away, banking over Troy. It looked like an old single-propeller plane. It was going backwards and forwards, rolling on each turn. It seemed as if the pilot was having some fun, and it seemed to us, who could imagine the rage of the small white archaeologist on the ground, defending his secrets, quite provocative.

I asked Mustafa, 'Is it the Japanese again?'

'No, they wouldn't dare,' he said, his head still crooked skywards.

The following day was my last in Troy. I had asked Matthias to see if I could have another meeting with Korfmann. I wanted to ask him about Atlantis.

I walked down to the site. A young bearded archaeologist came out of the camp to sit on a bench beside the Wooden Horse and shelter from the sun. He was an American, Brian Rose, a professor at Cincinnati University, and was co-leader of the excavation with Korfmann. He was an expert on the late Greek and Roman periods. He was not interested in Bronze Age Troy.

'What do you say to all those Turks who say you are stealing their past?' I asked.

'Now, *this* we are sensitive about,' he replied, but quite calmly. 'The Schliemann shadow follows us all – we try to be very careful about rules on the site. It's more than just Schliemann. It's the taking of antiquities in general. You know, how Xanthos was taken to the British Museum; the Pergamom altar to Berlin – all taken when the Ottoman Empire was in trouble. The Turks are understandably upset. As archaeologists we become accomplices in the murder of civilizations that we have sworn to protect . . .' He spread himself out on the bench, and smiled.

'Prof Korfmann tells me he would like to make the place into a Peace Park.'

'Manfred is fifty years old and he is *very* conscious of being born in Nazi Germany. I grew up during Vietnam. There is an idealism . . . All we say to the Turkish government is: Think about it.'

The Turks, however, are not persuaded. They want to develop this section of the coast to build roads and hotels. They do not want to turn it into a massive protected National Park.

Korfmann suddenly appeared from out of the camp. He walked quickly, almost running, towards the mound. I chased after him. 'Herr Professor . . . please . . . one or two more questions . . .'

'No, no! You cannot expect me to find a relaxed atmosphere with seventy people.' He was nervous, under visible strain.

But he reappeared shortly afterwards. 'Quickly, please, I do not have time to have social conversation!'

'Atlantis,' I said. 'What about Atlantis?'

He turned towards me: 'Atlantis!' He stood up and paced around. 'This is the case of an outsider who is working on problems that are not in his field. Atlantis! No one is going to look for Lilliput. Or perhaps I will next be told that Troy is Lilliput . . . It is a satire. We are not looking for the Trojan War or for Atlantis. You never will find Hector or Helen. *Never!*'

He calmed down. He invited me to stroll inside the encampment. 'I respect history. Atlantis is a satire . . .' He paused. 'The aim of everything I do is conservation. A lot of Turks applaud us for protecting the ruins of their country, and the landscape. It is one of the few resources they have left.'

Just then, somebody came up to him with a document for his signature. I watched while he selected a pen from his jacket pocket, and then as he signed his name. He did not sign it Korfmann. He signed it Osman.

Now my audience was over. When we reached the compound gate, Korfmann asked, 'Did Mustafa guide you around?'

'Yes,' I said. 'Some parts.' There was a pause and then I asked,

'Why do you not include him more in the excavation? He seems bitter about it.'

'He is very eloquent,' Korfmann replied.

'Eloquent?'

'Yes, he is very clever; he is a businessman.'

Lost since the Second World War, Schliemann's treasure has finally resurfaced in the possession of the Russians. The hoard was taken by Russian soldiers after the occupation of Berlin. It was then stored in great secrecy in the vaults of Moscow's Pushkin Museum. Only one person had access to the collection. The young museum curator who discovered in 1990 where it was hidden was sacked for making that fact public. But now the Russians have formally admitted that they have it. It may not, as Schliemann had hoped, have belonged to Priam. But, by all accounts, it remains among the most spectacular finds in history. The treasure includes two headdresses, about 4,400 years old, which are each twenty feet long and made up of 4,066 leaves, 12,171 golden links and a necklace of 8,700 gold beads.

The Germans claim that it is rightfully theirs; so do the Russians. The Turks have said it should be returned to them. But nobody is listening to them.

9

The Lovers

> The springtide of Lovers has come, that this dust bowl may become a garden; the proclamation of heaven has come, that the bird of the soul may rise in flight. The sea becomes full of pearls, the salt marsh becomes sweet as kauthar, the stone becomes a ruby from the mine, the body becomes wholly soul.
>
> *Mevlana*

In Konya, you can touch the spirit of Anatolia.

At the bus station I was met by a man in an old yellow Murat. The bus station was orderly and clean, with tended squares of green grass. The driver belonged to Ali, who had offered to help me find my way around the town. I had come for the festival of the *asik*, which takes place every year in Konya. The *asik* are wandering minstrels who improvise their words and songs. They are the storytellers who reinvent the great epics of the long-distant Anatolian past. They are fewer than they used to be but in the villages and towns of Anatolia they remain very popular. Konya was once a great centre for the *asik* and this is why the festival is held here each year. *Asik* means lover.

Konya now is a centre of more fanatical religion. There is increasingly alarmist talk about Turkey becoming an Islamic state along the lines of Iran or Afghanistan. It is a tiny possibility, almost unimaginable. But in Konya there are indeed Muslims who wish to return to the life of the Koran.

It is the unofficial Vatican city of Turkey. There are mosques on every street corner and everywhere you can see men building new ones. Secular Turkey fears Konya because it believes that the radical imams who live and teach in the town seek a return to medieval society in which men and women are separated and private morality made subject to public scrutiny. It is terrified that these imams are merely the agents of some foreign power – Saudi Arabia or Iran. Turks are prone to conspiracy theories, and none is more hotly debated than this one. Many actually believe that there is a secret plot to take over the country and impose religious government.

The fear has grown because recently the Muslim traditionalists' Welfare Party, which has its headquarters in Konya, has started to win seats in local elections. It now controls the major cities of Turkey: Istanbul and Ankara. Bars have started to serve alcohol only inside. Many more women have taken the veil.

Konya has often been a source of outrage. Some years ago the mayor, who is a Welfare Party member, tried to segregate public transport for students at the local university. He said that he had done so because the female students had asked him to. But the Turkish press howled about fundamentalism, and the mayor abandoned the plan.

Ali says that people exaggerate Konya. He is proud of Konya. When I arrived, he was sitting behind his desk in a huge carpet gallery that had two floors and was empty of customers (as they always seem to be). The walls were draped with carpets and the shop boys were constantly examining them for hairs and dust. Ali was a young man, quite alert and intelligent, not conventionally handsome. He was clearly wealthy, immaculately dressed in blue blazer and tie. He said he was hungry and asked one of the workers to fetch some food. Later the man returned with a kebab wrapped up in a newspaper, and *ayran.* The kebab consisted of great black hunks of meat, hacked off the bone. There was nothing else: no salad or onions. Ali ate it quickly, with his hands, smearing grease over his face. 'This is a local delicacy,' he said. 'The Konya kebab.' From outside, while we ate, came the constant sound of grinding from the spinning jennies in the carpet factory next door. In the yard next to the shop there were vast heaps of fleecy wool, dyed bright blue and red, which stretched like fields to the back of the building.

Ali had arranged a hotel for me, and after lunch he drove me into the town centre. He was a gentleman; a burgher of Konya.

In the shop a man at least twice his age had come in to ask if he might delay a payment on some loan. Ali said, 'Old man, don't be sad. Next week, then.' In the car we talked about life here for a young single man. He said, 'We don't have a busy social life here. In the summer the people are in the fields; in the winter they stay at home and make carpets.' He studied English at the local university and travels regularly to the United States.

From the car window, passing through the industrial sites and into the suburbs, you can tell that Konya, which is the sixth largest city in Turkey, is rich. It makes its money from sugar beet and flour-milling. There are no *gecekondu*, Ali told me. It is a clean city, a place that is proud of itself.

He called in at his friends' carpet shop on the high street. There was a rock at the front of the shop, hacked into the shape of an elephant's head with two evil eyes beaded in its face. As I walked in, one of the two brothers who run the place was unpacking his suitcase. He had just been to Milan, and was examining a pair of Italian socks he had bought there. This was Ilhan, the elder of the two. He had just been to a trade fair, and after the socks, he took out a Persian rattle which somebody had given him. Nobody in this shop was wearing a blazer. They were in jeans and T-shirts. Ilhan had lived in England, and his English was fluent.

'This town?' he said. 'This town has changed in the last fifteen years. If you think Konya is full of fundamentalists, you are in fact seeing people who are not religious at all. Mevlana has a great saying: "Konya is like a gold plate full of scorpions."'

Mevlana was the greatest lover in the East, the great mystical poet who inspired the whirling dervishes. Mevlana lived in Konya most of his life, but when the newspapers talk about Konya and the fundamentalist threat, they forget about Mevlana. He was Jalal al-din Rumi, a theologian of the fourteenth century who was born in what is now Iran and came to live in Konya in his maturity. He discovered the ecstasy of religion and described this in some of the most vivid, erotic, spiritual poetry ever known. Much of the poetry was intended to accompany music; much of it was improvised to music and to dance as well – the whirling which symbolized and inspired the trance in which there was selfless adoration of God. Mevlana was a sufi, an Islamic mystic, a man for whom the only thing that counted was a man's love of God. The manner of that communication was personal and versatile, just as there are many ways to love a woman or a man.

Shortly after Ataturk founded the secular republic in 1923, he banned the mystical dervishes. By then, he said, they had become a vehicle of superstition and an enemy to progress. Many groups – and Mevlana's followers constituted only one band – had become politicized under the Ottomans, and corrupted. The Mevlevi were not the most powerful of the *tarikat* religious orders. They were seen as élitist and more urban than most. The Bektashi, historically the most politically powerful sect, had much broader influence, in rural areas and the armed forces. The Bektashi fused Islamic mysticism with ancient Anatolian tradition. They allowed drinking, music and dancing. They were like a parallel society, with their own courts and schools, independent of the orthodox Muslim Ottoman government. The sects, including the Mevlevi, tended to undermine the people's commitment to central authority. They were vehicles of dissent.

Ataturk forbade the Turks to practise as dervishes, and the people were prohibited from praying at the tomb of Mevlana, which is housed under a turquoise dome in Konya within walking distance of the carpet shop. He failed. Mysticism permeates the personality of Turkey even today. It informs the Turks' continuing love of poetry, and of abstraction. Depleted in numbers, the sufi went underground, but they were not exterminated. Today it is still illegal to be a dervish. I had said to Ali that I hoped I would meet a dervish in Konya. He said there were many of them, adding, 'They are the real Lovers.'

We sat down and talked for a while about London. Then, after an hour or so, in walked a most elegant gentleman. He wore matching jacket and trousers in a shade of mushroom-pink and a braided waistcoat beneath his jacket. His black beard was neatly trimmed. His face was thin and tired, but his eyes were full of life, and his bearing was erect, like that of an old soldier. Ilhan whispered, 'This is Hasan. He is a sufi.' I looked at him again through different eyes. A sufi? I would never have imagined he was one.

Hasan sat down and spoke to me in English. He spoke fast, with a mad intensity. I explained why I was in Konya and then I asked him if he was a dervish. He smiled. 'If a man sees Allah, he doesn't say to others that he sees Allah.' I smiled back. He added, 'I am imprisoned within these four walls.' And he clasped his hands to his chest.

'Sufism is a way of Allah. Take the Milky Way. It does not follow the sun, it takes its energy from the real Dervish. It is spinning around *you*. Can you see that?' His face moved hardly at all. It was full of fissures and creases, like an old weathered rock. It was calm, not at all like the tense, strained, alcoholic faces of the young brothers. They clearly thought he was an idiot but would never say so. I recognized a strange fear in them. What if this man really was a dervish?

The dervishes, he said, move with discretion. They are still outlawed. 'But for the last ten years I have never had any problem with the police.'

Hasan was a faith healer. 'I give a guarantee,' he said, beaming. 'Eighty per cent of my patients come with impossible requests, but with Allah's permission I can help. If a man has stomach-ache or a headache, I can ring over the phone – if he has access to one – and tell him where to put his fingers . . .' He raised his hand to his heart and then turned to leave the shop.

Ilhan, a slender man, with experience but not cynicism in the bags under his eyes, watched him walk out of the shop. He thought for a moment. 'Some people go about calling themselves dervishes. I met some last December but their life-style was not real Dervish. They were trying to make money; to impress people somehow. I'm not a dervish. You know – I happen to meet people. I do believe there's an emotional energy: some people can see it and some people can't. I think Hasan sees it . . .'

*

Fevzi Halici believes he sees it. His name means carpet-maker but he does not sell carpets: he sells dervishes, and sees nothing wrong with making money out of them. He is the tourism officer for Konya and his principal work is to organize tours for a band of professional dervishes who perform at festivals and on television. This group is legal. They do not whirl for any religious reason but because they get paid for it. No real dervish will dance in public, or for money. Real *zikir*, which is the name of the whirling ceremony, is forbidden because it breaks the laws concerning political assembly.

Fevzi was also the administrator of the *asik* festival. The two are not disconnected: the *asik* were originally dervishes, itinerant musical monks of mysticism. They remain, generally, men of religion. That day the thin wood-panelled foyer of the Tourism Office was crammed with wandering ballad singers from all over: Azerbaijan, Erzurum, Cyprus. They waited quite aimlessly – you sensed they had been there for hours. Out here, in this confined space, the air smelt of rural men, the warm musk of sheep.

Fevzi was a large, balding, effusive man with big glasses and a clipped grey moustache and a double chin. He has done well. This is the twenty-seventh *asik* festival. In the 1940s there were lots of *asik* in Konya, he said, now there are just three or four. In the office, which was lined with books and gold-plated plaques honouring his contribution to Turkish culture, two of the minstrels were reciting and singing poems: snatches of songs, nothing decipherable. Warming up.

On the bookshelves Fevzi had stacked a number of books that bore his name. There was one in English which was an account of something called the Third International Food Congress, and there was a picture of him with an English cookery writer. Beside the books there was a little sculpture of dervishes whirling. In the middle of the room was Fevzi's large rectangular desk. On it was an old manual typewriter, and just under the lip of the table top, a buzzer which he would press to summon the *asik* from the corridor, a few at a time, to give them a private audition. He had some friends with him, elderly bureaucrats like himself, plump, swinging their prayer-beads, sitting on a long sofa in the office.

As the *asik* trooped in, Fevzi was writing a letter on an old typewriter, so while they sang there was a constant clatter. He smiled and stopped for a moment while a singer lamented the loss of his love, meaning the loss of his God. Fevzi interrupted one song to tell me about a man who puts a needle between his lips so that he cannot articulate a consonant without piercing himself. He is left only with vowels to explain the world – a spiritual discipline, Fevzi explained. One of the men in the room whispered in awe, 'Surely this man is a saint.'

Fevzi returned to his typewriter, caught, it seemed, in the emotion of the moment. He was writing a poem. This tired old administrator was writing a poem in front of an audience. Another *asik* sang:

> A human who covers all his mistakes
> A kind of man who brings an axe to a stone
> A kind of man who can peel a raw egg
> A kind of man who cannot peel an apple.

Fevzi was typing and ignoring this one. Clatter. Clatter.

For the first two years of his life Fevzi was brought by his mother to drink soup at the Mevlana mosque, before it was closed by Ataturk. 'With one ear I listened to the *muezzin*,' he said, 'and with the other to the *ney*. Mevlana had a great effect on me; I have a duty to him.' He spoke with great self-importance and without sentiment. He promoted himself as a man of the new Republic to his peers. 'I call myself a modern sufi, a person who is in step with the time in which he is living. Traditionally, the sufi lived in a convent, separated, but I have adapted to daily life; I wear a tie.' His friends laughed.

'Konya is *not* a religious city,' he continued. 'Konya is a very modern city. Konya is like a walnut. The cover is very hard but inside it is something very different. In Konya there are some fanatics, but they will take you home and give you food.' Again they laughed.

He went on, 'Today in Turkey nobody is a genuine dervish

any more. The people that we call dervishes are performers, actors working in the theatre. That's all. It is merely a reminder of the old days.' But those days were gone. He had become quite sombre. What he meant was that it is over. The dervishes are finished. Turkey has moved on.

Fevzi grew tired of his companions and asked them to leave the room so that he could write. On the way out, passing the minstrels, a man took me aside. 'You know that Fevzi has lost the dervishes?' I said I did not know what he was talking about. 'Oh yes,' he replied. 'The government has taken control of the troupe. They have sacked him.'

In the carpet shop later that day Ilhan was pacing up and down. It was early evening and he was preparing for the night ahead. His hair was slicked back with oil and he was clean-shaven. After he disappeared, Ali arrived and we went to drink. There was only one bar in Konya, not far from the shop. There were some other friends there, and a band playing Greek tunes and Circassian dances: there is a large Circassian population around Konya, and the men put on a fine display of vaulting and jumping. Ali was thinking about two things: money and sex. His father had just been to an auction for land beside a local motorway that could be turned into a gas station. The plot was sold for $1 million. 'It's too much,' Ali said seriously. 'We should be investing in technology.'

As for sex, all these men play a game, according to certain rules, and they found in it nothing to upset their deep and sincere respect for religion. Ali used to play this game, but now he did not have the time. Of all those present he had travelled most widely, and he was proud to tell me, while we drank beer in the small, dark bar, that he had had sex with a Chinese girl.

They all tried to sleep with as many women as possible, but not with Turks, only with foreigners. Ali used to sell carpets because his father wanted him to know what life was like at the coalface. 'I dated three women a week, and about 10 per cent went to bed with me.' On average, they had only two days to seduce the foreigners before they moved on. Most tours spent only a short time in Konya before taking off for the troglodyte monasteries of Cappadocia. 'We tell them dirty jokes, tell them about Turkey, you have to work very hard,' he went on. Ilhan is the best, he said. The highest achiever. 'Did you know that Ilhan is married and has six children? It was an arranged marriage. A traditional marriage.' I was amazed to think of Ilhan with a traditional, veiled wife.

'If you are all so keen on sex,' I said, 'are there many prostitutes in Konya?'

'I don't know,' said Ali. 'I don't use this service.'

By now he was growing disconsolate. 'How can I meet the girls? There are none in the carpet trade.' Ali argued now that his needs required him to leave Konya. He wanted to go to New Orleans. The atmosphere of the bar may have helped to bring on this unhappiness: it was dark, and there was smooching, and by this time a *saz* player was playing jazzy little numbers for lovers to dance to.

Then Ilhan arrived. He said he had had an unsuccessful night. 'If you see anyone let me know,' he shouted. 'I am going home.' Ali smiled.

Yet another kind of lover was Mustafa Arslan, the young man who edited the most radical Islamic newspaper in Turkey. I wanted somebody to come along with me to meet him. Ilhan and the others refused point-blank, but Murat agreed. He ran a carpet shop nearby and he was curious. I was meeting the editor in the hope that he could arrange an audience for me with the most powerful Muslim in Turkey, the man who symbolizes every fear secular Turks have for their future.

Mustafa Arslan had a little office, originally supposed to be somebody's bedroom, in a residential apartment block. There was a large desk, and beside it a cheap sideboard on which stood a fax machine and a pot plant. The carpet was stained and greasy. On the desk were an old manual typewriter and a small, transparent glass kangaroo, presumably used as a paperweight. Suitably enough, a minaret blocked most of the view from the window.

The newspaper is called *Merhaba*, which means hello. Originally it was called *Yarin*, meaning tomorrow, but in 1991 it went colour (Turkey has always led the world in newspaper technology), and it changed its name.

'This is an Islamic paper?' I asked.

'Every newspaper has a policy,' he replied. 'Newspapers take different views. We have one view: we are against the oppression of Muslims.'

Mr Arslan was slow to reveal himself. He wore a cheap shirt and no jacket. He was twenty-six years old. He had a smooth face and did not need to shave every day. 'I do not drink alcohol or smoke, but at the same time I do not pray five times a day. This, of course, makes me sad.' He said this without any visible sadness at all, indeed without any emotion. He spoke with unblinking conviction but without any of the cheap fervour of the born-again evangelist. His newspaper was the largest in Konya with 2,000 readers. He occupied a position of considerable authority locally.

'I'd really like to know whether or not you want Turkey to have an Islamic government, because that is what everybody thinks you want.'

He laughed, but showed signs of edginess. 'Just imagine,' he said, leaning back in his chair, 'that there is an Islamic republic now in Turkey. Many people in Ankara and Istanbul and even in Konya would fight against it . . .'

'But what do *you* want?'

'I want to live according to Islamic rules.'

'Like Iran? Would you like that in Turkey?'

'Iran is a very complicated country. Personally I would wish for something more like Afghanistan, but it is important that the people accept it.'

Murat was surprised. He shook his head in disagreement and became confrontational. 'Why do Muslims treat women as second-class citizens? You must disagree with that.'

'Murat – is that your name? – look. Both men and women are human beings. There are some differences – we cannot say they are second-class – the differences are dictated by nature . . .

No, Islam doesn't treat women badly. Islam doesn't turn them into prostitutes, it reminds them they are human beings. Islam prevents them being objects.' He was trying to be open but Murat felt he was being taunted.

'OK, what about polygamy?' Murat asked.

'It's an Islamic tradition . . .'

'But it's bad for women,' Murat interrupted irritably.

'If you don't have prejudices you will see something deeper behind this.'

'Well, what is there for the woman?'

'There are many rules in Islam that you must follow, and there are some things that are left to your discretion. There are some rules which allow a man to marry three or four wives, but he has to satisfy two women in a sexual way; he has to treat them well; he has to be rich enough. If one woman says, "I don't want to live in this house", he has to have the power to buy her a house. A man needs more than one woman; this is true even in Western culture – there is the mistress; and the prostitute.' He paused. He was neither angry nor defensive.

'These rules are for believers. If you believe then they make sense. You cannot see the existence of God, but we are just following his laws with total obedience. Sometimes even I have my doubts . . .' He smiled for the first time. 'For instance, we are told not to eat pork, but I wonder about it. Did you know that pigs do not experience feelings of jealousy? Did you know that? Perhaps we should all eat pork and this would help us.'

Murat was furious. I said I was grateful for Mr Arslan's time, and raised the point of my visit: could he help me meet the Great Teacher? Yes, he said, he would try. He asked in return if he could have his picture taken with us.

Outside Murat was quiet. 'I find that really worrying,' he said. 'I mean, the guy was so young.'

They printed the photograph the following day under the headline 'Foreigners talk about God'.

Once we had returned to Mevlana's end of town, by the carpet shop and the great mystic's tomb, a parade started. A local conscript had been killed by Kurdish guerrillas in the south-east. It was a funeral march. The military band in red uniform with gold braid and white helmets passed first. Trombones and euphoniums. Everything was out of tune. Behind them the *jandarma* marched a slow step, and a band of civilians followed. The women were wailing and the men were punching the air with their fists. It quickly became a religious moment. The crowd was full of skull-caps and small dark beards. People shouted and wept. Grief is neither meagre nor cheap in Turkey.

The Turks have much to thank religion for: it has given them music. Later that afternoon I was invited by Mustafa, a friend of Ali's, to an underground performance of dervish music. It was impromptu and took place in the cellar of a hat-maker, a man who made the tall felt turbans worn by Islamic clergy. The atmosphere was sweaty and close; the handful of people present sat on the metal hat moulds.

Mustafa had played for a decade in Fevzi's dervish troupe, and not only did he play the *ney*, a double-reeded pipe, which is a symbol of Mevlana, he also made the instrument. According to legend Mevlana invented it, and its voice is the voice of his poetry even today.

It is an instrument that takes many years to master. 'To play even simple things takes five or six months,' Mustafa said. He had wavy black hair and a pointed moustache and in the dimness of the cellar he looked like a magician. 'It's a matter of talent.' Then he stood up and sat down again. 'The *ney* is a holy instrument. Wherever we carry it, we carry it with respect in our arms. There are nine sections symbolizing the nine months it takes to come into the world. We have seven holes in our faces, and it has seven holes.'

Mustafa learned from a sufi teacher, not in a school. When he was at school he used to play the flute and subsequently worked in an iron factory; then the spirit visited him, he said. Now he earned his living from the Ministry of Culture and Tourism. 'I am absolved from it while I play. While I play, I am praying and giving greetings to God.' Secretly, he said, the living leader of the Mevlevi, the Sheikh, visited the players in the orchestra and gave them permission to play by sealing their hats.

Mustafa took his *ney* from its case. He whispered some short phrases to warm it up. To make a noise at all, you must take a big breath and then softly say '*hu*'. This is the secret code word, the abbreviation for Allah.

'The Muslim people know everything,' said one man. 'Not like the people at *Merhaba*. We know *everything* . . . of course, we like to be strong, but we never break hearts. We are humanist, not fanatic. I have many friends, a gypsy friend, and many others from America, from England. Nationalities and religion don't matter.' He spoke rather as if he was drunk. But he was not; he was just burning with enthusiasm. He felt as if he had made sense of his life. The others were less vocal.

Now we settled down while the *ney*-maker started to play. It was beautiful, a sweet voice, like that of a child, and then dark and full of mystery. There were many rhythms, some so finely textured that the sounds, sweet and supple, were like tides. Sometimes it sounded as if it was a woman crying. The great vaulting architecture of Mustafa's improvisation was entirely alien to the Western ear, but it made perfect, unexpected sense. He seemed to be in an ecstasy, expressing himself without reservation or the merest trace of cynicism. I had never heard a man give so freely of himself to others. When he had finished, we all quietly left the room.

The following day I woke to the sound of Lovers. A group of them were standing in the small fenced rose garden in front of Fevzi's office, the office of the Ministry of Culture.

> If someone can write something come to me –
> If someone can know something come to me . . .

The singer was an old man with a little cloth cap and huge coal-black rings around his eyes. His voice was harsh. He was chopping hard at his *saz*, the long-necked lute, and another man joined him and the two of them started a duet. There was a small crowd watching, and everybody was laughing. They started to sing about Ferhat and his girl, star-crossed lovers, a song of old Anatolia. It is the story of a platonic love. Ferhat sees his girl but cannot have her. He goes to the mountains and stays there for ten years. He does not see her but he sings about her all the time. 'Love looks like a sea. It's very big . . .'

Fevzi was in deep rapture. These men had a gift, and he commanded it at his will. They all stopped to clap him as he stepped into the garden in his smart blue suit. Turkish Television had arrived to take his picture, and he stood in front of the lens, beaming with pride. The producer turned to me and said, 'You know, I don't even know why we're here at all, they'll never use it.'

Fevzi then delivered an address to the camera, the spectators and the *asik*. The crowd mainly consisted of off-duty conscript soldiers and lottery-ticket salesmen. They listened carefully to Fevzi and talked only discreetly among themselves. 'This is the start of the *asik bayram*, a great symbol,' he shouted. 'The Lovers come from Cyprus and from Azerbaijan.'

Fevzi grew serious. He raised his hand and took a step forward as if he was about to dance: 'Why do the Lovers have no social insurance?' Everybody clapped. 'The *asik* haven't any social insurance yet they are part of the culture of Anatolia. Some of the oldest *asik* from the thirteenth century are buried in Anatolia; these *asik* live on. But the state does not value their contribution. They find it hard to live . . .'

Fevzi waved his hands for silence but everybody was looking skyward. There had been a drop of rain. 'Look! The government wants to protect a rare bird which is fine; or a turtle, which is good. But the *asik* are like this bird, we have to protect them as well.'

Once the applause had died down, one of the *asik* started to sing.

> Being an *asik* is like a meal you boil in a big bowl
> You will learn in this as it boils . . .

Then people started to drift away. Tonight there would be the first official performance. While the *asik* made their way back to their lodgings, I stopped a remarkable-looking man with a fan beard and sackcloth coat. He was from Erzurum, which is in the east. This was the man who put a needle between his lips. I asked him if he would drink tea with me.

Asik Ali Rahmani was always smiling, and he spoke rather like he sang, as if he has forgotten the crispness of the consonants: his words had the fluid character of vowels. The overwhelming impression he gave was of kindness. This man was humble, gracious and charitable.

'I am fifty-five,' he said, 'but when they ask me I say I am older than my father and younger than my son.' He had the air of a great mystic. He did not elect his vocation to wander all his life in poverty. He had creamy-brown eyes, cool and dispassionate and full of humility. The pupils were black as jet. His head beneath his felt cap was perfectly bald.

'Are you a dervish?'

'When I was small, I hung around the sufi convents. I had friends there. But I started singing instinctively, from the Koran, going from one convent to another. After the convents were closed [now his age became a mystery – this happened in the 1920s – was he seventy? Did he know himself?] I became an *asik* and started to walk.'

A little boy was listening, transfixed by the glutinous language that purred along.

'The dervish leaders are gone now.' He was clenching his fist, embarrassed about talking of himself. On his finger he wore a large ring with an amber stone in a silver setting.

'Why did you become an *asik*?' I asked. He answered with a poem.

> Closer to you than you
> Is God the creator who is very fair
> Your respect is your right
> I swear the beautiful attitude.

He spoke with tremendous rhythm. The loose, liver-spotted skin drew taut around his skull while he sang. He stopped. '*Asik* is the bridge between God and people and also *asik* is beauty.

We just see the beauty that God created and describe it . . . I do not play *saz*. Instead I put a needle between my lips so that I cannot pronounce letters – B, P, M, V, F.' He had an old scar on his lip where he had failed.

The boy said, 'I think it's a kind of miracle.'

'Enough,' he said. 'I do not have a needle.' But there were lots in the carpet shop, so we found one, and he put it between his top and bottom lip. Then he sang again, so gracefully.

> The *asik*, they are looking for God
> If they haven't got love they burn.
> Truth is in destiny and fate.

The sound was indescribable: not singing, something like a moan, but deep, drawn up through his throat. A rough, sad vibration.

Hasan the healer saw me on my way back from the shop. He asked me to join him. He wanted to show me how 'love heals'. Hasan, the dervish, is a shaman. A smooth, double-breasted shaman.

Once I had sat down in his small room, he started to spoon a potion, which looked like Vaseline, into jars. The shop was made up of two adjoining rooms. In the first, which was reception, his brother was repairing a carpet. The inner sanctum, his healing room, was screened from the other room by a kilim hung across the door and was lined with rugs. The walls were draped with gilded fabrics and there was a settle at one end of the room, otherwise it was empty of furniture. There were dozens of jars and the air was heavy with the smell of cinnamon and eucalyptus. I looked again at Hasan who was chatting away while he filled his jars. He was waiting for a patient and he asked me if I had visions. He had thin, splendid features, and generally looked hawkish and solemn. When he asked me about the visions, his whole face relapsed into a knowing smile. Did he see some potential in me? On the one hand, the sufi, but on the other, the pardoner. Behind the knowing smile lurked a sanctimonious leer, and crumbly, bad teeth below a jagged, warty nose.

We sat for a while longer and then I asked him, 'How old are you?'

He seemed upset. 'You ask my age? My donkey age or my soul age? The soul cannot give the number – there are two kinds of age – one is endless. But in my mortal life, Hasan reached the age of twelve.' He was very serious when he said this, and I wondered whether he was mad.

Hasan had led a diverse life. He had lived in Saudi Arabia, Libya and Europe, working as a builder or buying and selling dresses. He had been on the pilgrimage to Mecca three times. The last time he went by plane.

Now we talked about his healing. He explained that people think that it is special herbs that are the secret of his therapy, but, he said, 'I am not under the service of some herbs; they are under my service. The cosmos is created for my honour by Allah; if I am enough for this honour then everything that exists must help me.' He rose, jubilant and ecstatic, clapping his hands wildly and saying, 'Tak-tak-tak – everything is under my service. I can heal one hundred different illnesses. The sun and the moon take energy from me and they have oath to give it back to me – just like Mevlana. I don't advertise; if people know they come to me – one hundred in a year. My system is built on love and energy only.' Hasan was not just saying this; he believed it.

I was still confused about his being twelve years old. 'After twelve years I found my centre. After twelve years I found Mevlana in my dream: there were four caliphs sitting with him, and I kissed his hand and that is where my life started. For thirty-one years I was looking – I spent more than one thousand nights just shaking.'

He was back on the floor, screwing the tops on to bottles of rose-water ointment. There was a bowl full of petals just beside him. He released a big happy sigh and grinned broadly. 'Now let us go to find my patient,' he said.

We walked out of the shop into town. He was making a

house call on a rich jeweller. We walked into the middle of the most fundamentalist part of Konya by the Kapu mosque, a squat grey box in the middle of the bazaar. Hasan feared the militants. 'They tire me. For the energy I spend on ten others, I spend on one fundamentalist.' He refuses now to deal with them. He was obviously nervous – this was a conservative area and people were pouring out of the mosque after evening prayers. We arrived at the jeweller's shop and waited outside for a moment. His client was also nervous: it was as if something underhand was about to happen, as if Hasan was about to hand over a stolen sheep or an illegal revolver (Hasan himself made that joke). The dervish was, in fact, an embarrassment to most of his clients, but they are a superstitious bunch and alert to the much smaller amount he charged for treatment than the local hospital.

The client was a fat man, with rings of jelly belly oozing over the rim of his trousers, and a fat, flat, greasy face. He came to the door but asked us to continue waiting. He did not show us in. He was waiting for the mosque to empty.

Hasan had brought a bag full of his tools: some flasks of ointment, a heat lamp and some Vaseline-type lubricant in a pink tupperware container. He explained, 'He has a blockage in his blood and nervous system. His feet are cold and he feels nothing. This is the last therapy – he is working in Germany and needs five sessions but he does not have time; so I will tell him what to do and sell him enough jars of ointment to do it by himself. If he is good with the recipe, he will have a good result in one month.'

Hasan had an assistant, who was looking distinctly uneasy standing outside the shop. One or two of the people coming out of the mosque pointed across the street – everybody knew Hasan the healer. The assistant, who was wearing a blazer, was in fact a primary school teacher. He turned to me and said, 'I don't like the fanatics – they have no love.'

Hasan added, 'This is the last chance for the jeweller. He has tried many springs and hospitals in Germany. The potion contains fifteen different herbs: for some problems you can drink the lotion, for others it must be rubbed into the skin. I sometimes drink it to show him there is no danger.'

We were still standing on the pavement. 'Is your son a healer as well?' I asked.

He became morose. 'My son has no capacity. I asked him what he wanted to do and he said judo, and then he liked taekwondo. He has no capacity. I am looking for another to succeed me.'

Just then the fat man let us in. He took us upstairs to an abandoned room which was full of builder's rubble and scrap wood. It stank of piss. Hasan refused to work there and insisted that we return to the shop. While we walked back through the bazaar, he continued to complain about his son.

When we arrived at the shop, a boy was sitting in the outer room. Hasan waved him out, and the boy climbed the shallow steps with great difficulty: he had a hideous limp and a face full of hope.

Meanwhile, the fat man was ushered into the main room, the kilim was pulled over the door, and he started to take his clothes off. He peeled off his shirt and stained vest to reveal a yellowing bulk of flesh.

Hasan started to give a running commentary. 'If you see ten people in one month, it makes you happy because they are happy. You must take some of their happiness so that you have more power to help, especially those who have little possibility.' He chuckled.

The fat man lay face down on some old newspapers. His back had not seen daylight for a long time; it was ghostly pale and yellow, as if somebody had rubbed nicotine into it.

Hasan opened a jar of eucalyptus jelly, and his assistant, Ali, beat his fists into the soft, formless mass of the man's back. Hasan started to recite verses from the Koran in Arabic. He stood back from the twitching body and exhaled a huge breath, shouting at Ali to work higher up around the head. Then he let out an extraordinary nasal yelp and became ecstatic, dancing and shaking. It was extremely violent and the fat man on the floor reared up suddenly, his eyes staring in shock. The yelp or whine was like the last breath of a small mammal, a cat perhaps, being slowly strangled, and it was punctuated by a rhythmic snorting. Hasan was swaying from side to side, and his eyes were closed as he squeezed the words out, quivering. His face was taut with concentration. After a while the moan became a quite pleasant sound. The words came out with less pain, the pitch and volume would rise in a manner reminiscent of the sound of a harmonium.

Somebody shouted from the outer room to ask if anybody wanted tea, and Hasan faltered momentarily. He had set up some German spotlights which shed a pink light on the flaccid carcass on the floor. 'It's nice,' he said quite calmly, 'because the material world is at our service.' The lights were tanning lamps.

Next he stood over the patient, holding one of the lamps, and started to jump up and down on his back. He stopped and looked closely at it: there were clusters of tiny red spots all over it. 'You see, this is where I have taken the blood before.' There was some odd bruising around the shoulder-blade. He refused to tell me how he had 'taken' the blood.

Hasan said that the small spots meant that the blood was active, and that the blockage on the back had cleared. In fact the back was bleeding everywhere. All the small spots were growing into tiny droplets of blood. Hasan stood on the bleeding back and said, 'You see, this is the clearing system.' He hung over it, excitedly reporting new clusters of the spots, with the pleasure and eagerness of a banker counting money. He took some blood, he said, some dark red blood, and 'I cleaned it with my private systems'. One lady, he said, had a bad system after a traffic crash: when you touched the body she quivered and twitched but after one three-hour therapy session it was gone. He clapped his hands: 'It was done so.' Another patient could only see double and had one therapy session and one dervish dance and – again he clapped his hands – he was cured. 'It was done so.'

He was puffing all the time. There was a streak of dribble running over his chin. He was sweating. He stood on the fat man's buttocks and pummelled his back, shaking the fat. The man had gone to sleep; then, after a series of violent punches, he woke up with a start. He laughed – a deep, dirty laugh. Hasan, meanwhile, was using every fibre of strength in his slender body to club and beat the man's back. He struck both sides of his belly as if he was shaking cloth out, and then he poked him hard in the ribs, and the man stopped laughing and gasped in pain. Or pleasure.

Hasan cried out, 'He has calcium!' He pointed to circular white patches on his back below the shoulders. All the time he was pummelling. It was disgusting to watch the wobbling flesh. The fat man turned to Hasan: 'You look very weak . . . Allah! Allah!' Hasan was nearly exhausted.

'He is much more comfortable,' he said, like a surgeon. 'The skin is like cotton.' He continued to slap it, like beating a fish, bringing pustules of blood to the surface. 'This is healthy – I can feel it.'

He offered his patient his magic rose-water solution and then, chanting from the Koran, lifted him up with one hand on an ankle and the other on a wrist and swung him around the room. It was extraordinary. The man cried out, 'I feel sick.' He was revolving, by now, at some speed. Hasan shouted back, 'It is of use to your blood.' Then he slowed down and put the man back onto the newspapers.

Hasan ordered his patient to drop his trousers. He peeled them off: they were old and brown and pin-striped with jaundiced yellow innards. They had lost their shape long ago. He took off his long-johns as well. He was breathing loudly and heavily (I was worried he might have a heart attack). Hasan was puffing around the room: 'We must collect the poison from him now.'

The assistant was exhausted. Hasan turned to him: 'It is not easy!' Ahmet, his brother, came to help. He was rubbing a sweet-smelling oil of nutmeg on to the patient's legs, which were like a woman's, with nicely turned ankles. They had clearly done no exercise in many years. 'Look at this body, these legs are very white.' In fact, they were cream. Hasan jabbed his fingers into the man's buttocks and his whole finger disappeared.

He became serious. 'This is a problem.' He shook a foot violently. 'It's getting very warm in this room because of the oil.' As he said this the man looked at him with real concern. Hasan rubbed his hands, looked at me and then pinched my knee. 'You feel warm?' I did within a few seconds. It was not warm; it was hot.

He took a lighter and a strange sphere of glass, like a cup with a lip. He put the flame inside the glass to create a vacuum and then plunged it on to an oily portion of the man's thigh. A welt of skin filled the sphere and then Hasan dragged the vacuum up and down the buttock. He was sitting on the man's back chanting: '*Bismillahirramanirrahim*. The body is eating the oil,' he shouted. The glass popped when he took it off. He was looking happier, no question about that, and he laughed for the first time. We had overcome some hurdle.

Hasan did not pause for breath. No sooner had he laughed than he was jumping up and down on the man's buttocks again, rubbing the balls of his heels into the soft skin. He cracked some ribs and walked down his legs, and then, just as if he was wiping a car windscreen, he rubbed the man's buttocks. 'Look how free – he has some blockage in his buttocks – but now it is easier to work. In Germany they wanted to operate.' The fat man was grunting and snorting. Hasan was punching the buttocks again dementedly. 'My boxing is good,' he said. The fat man groaned, 'You should use a hammer; it would feel the same.'

Quite suddenly Hasan stopped, walked off the patient's body, reached for a cloth and started to rub his hands. It was done. He put his waistcoat back on while the fat man rubbed his bleeding with tissue paper. He did seem happier.

He was due to leave for Germany within days, so Hasan made up a prescription of potions. He explained to his patient that he would have to brew up some special herbs, add honey and rub it in. The fat man complained, 'But this takes too long.'

'You see, he does not want to get well; he wants only to take a pill and go to bed,' Hasan said.

The man backed down. He was told to put black pepper in the ointment and to leave it on all night. Just as he was leaving, the crippled boy returned. Hasan explained that he worked for the post office and was paralysed down half his body. I felt uncomfortable. This boy was not like the fat man; he had a real problem. You could see so much hope in his face. 'I only gave him oil and took some money – enough for my spending,' said Hasan, when he saw him approaching.

'*Abi Guzel*,' the boy said when he saw Hasan. 'Beautiful brother!' He said that the oil was working: his fingers worked more easily; he could turn the telephone dial. 'The energy is moving me and the blood is moving through my muscles,' he said.

'You see,' Hasan told me, 'this boy is like this because of medicine – it was a faulty injection when he was three that paralysed him.' He was touching the boy, who had very withered arms. He sat him down, produced his lighter, and started to draw blood out of the skin with his glass sphere. 'Look,' he said. 'He could feel nothing in his right arm but now he is warmer. Look at the veins; and there are more spots on his upper arm, which means his arms are working.' He rubbed the eucalyptus grease into the withered arms and pointed at all the spots. He said, 'Look! Look! Allah! Allah!' and he started to sing. The boy was singing as well. 'I like to cry,' he said, clearly in some pain. Hasan shouted, 'Let's cry. Open your channels.' He turned to me and said in an aside, 'His mother is dying', and then he continued with the boy. 'He is missing his mother. He has a deep blockage from the missing.' A strange cacophony filled the room as the boy started to cry.

'This cream,' said Hasan, oblivious to the boy's weeping, 'is prepared with heat, the moon and the sun. The body takes it like a friendly army into the bodyland.' He started to sing. 'My voice is opening his soul. Inside there is the blockage of Satan, and the spots are how it is getting free.'

The boy stopped crying and, when Hasan had finished, sat in a corner raising and lowering one of his fingers. He was beaming.

Outside it was dark. I helped him up the steps and out of the shop. He leaned across to shake my hand, and when I felt it, it was cold and weak. In the sky very few stars were visible beneath the cloud.

The following morning I was introduced to the Great Teacher. I made contact at a stationery shop near one of the more functional-looking mosques. There is a palpable sense of high security with these orthodox radicals. The man who ran the shop was working on a new Turkish translation of the Koran. He wore the standard uniform: a light cardigan, a collarless white shirt buttoned around the neck, a tight black beard on his chin. There was a sticker on the door: 'Kafirler Icin Yasasin Cehennem'. 'Non-believers will not go to heaven'. It was only recently, he said, that Turks had been allowed to print Arabic books.

Ataturk's state has always been in a panic over the religious extremists. It has always felt threatened by them. In the early 1990s the Turkish government, mainly to appease international anxiety, repealed articles 163 and 142 of Ataturk's constitution, which banned religious propaganda and communism. Before this it was prohibited to sell radical Islamic works openly. Now the shelves in this shop were full of them. Many were by Abdullah Buyuk, the Great Teacher, the man I was to meet. The shop-owner turned to me and said, 'You know I was a communist as a young man, and then I changed.'

'Why?' I asked.

'This is not the place to discuss it.'

Abdullah Buyuk is one of the legendary imams of Turkey. There are about twenty teachers or *hoca* of his standing in the country. The receptionist at the hotel, when he realized where I was going, said that he disapproved of such people, the extremists who mixed politics and religion. 'Mystics say the law is in the heart, and all religions are equal. But the religious say it must be in the gun.'

The Great Teacher worked in an office in the suburbs of the town, on the edge of an industrial estate, past a maze of small workshops, squat cement buildings producing chicken wire, wheelbarrows and other woodwork.

His office was a long narrow room above an agricultural machinery shop. It was well furnished, and wood-panelled, a tribute to his wealth (or that of his sponsors). A bowl of mint stood in the middle of the glass-topped table. When we arrived, the first thing he said was, 'I do not like the press. Once I gave an interview to the BBC and then a local paper picked up the comments and so I had problems with the government and suddenly everybody wanted to catch me out.' He had called for the restoration of Islamic law in Turkey.

His dark glasses concealed his eyes, but you could feel them fidgeting. The rest of his face remained immobile while he talked. He had a large black-grey beard and a black cloth shirt without a collar. He was militant and intelligent.

He came to Konya in the 1970s having originally lived in Sivas, further east. He was already a famous and uncompromising preacher. 'In Konya people live Islam, that is why I came.' He spoke a very precise, clipped Turkish, neither casual nor intimate. Intellectuals in other cities keep Islam down. But in Konya it is accepted as the proper culture. For this reason there are those who say that Konya is full of fanatics.'

I noticed a smart new fax machine in the corner of the room; and then I caught a sight of Buyuk's stunningly white teeth, revealed briefly while he sucked on a mint. The skin on his face was in perfect condition and you could trace the outline of some very firm pectoral muscles through his shirt. He wore a large jade ring with a clasp on his finger.

Buyuk is an outcast from the church of the Turkish establishment. He is an extremist who has called for an Islamic revolution; he has been a very vocal critic of Ataturk. He has never issued a call to arms, to *jihad*, but there are those who believe that this is his real plan.

He talked about the man in the shop, the former communist. It transpired that he was the editor of Buyuk's magazine, *Ribat*, in which he disseminates his views. This is one source of income, he explained. The magazine sold 20,000 copies in nineteen countries. I saw the point he was making: Muslim clerics are usually paid by the state, but not Buyuk. So how did he live? Some claimed he was paid by some foreign power. Now he was explaining – before I had even asked him – that he could account for his income in other ways.

He said he ran a 'special private school' but would not give any details. I assumed that it was illegal. Over his head was a picture of Medina in a gold frame. There was no portrait of Ataturk in this room.

'Do you feel insulted when people call you a fundamentalist?'

'Yes,' he said – he had been asked this before – 'but Muslims are not angry about this word. People say Muslims are very conservative – it means going back to the beginning, that's all.'

'What about people who say you are the enemy of democracy?'

'The party of Western politics is not a form recognized in Islam – we have no party. Parties divide people, so Islam doesn't like them. It's impossible that a single party can hold Islam – all parties are very bad for Muslims – but if there is one that is good for us, then we say OK.'

'But most Turks do not think that they want an Islamic country.'

'What is Turkey? European? Islamic?' he replied. 'What a pity for the Turkish people that they are born of the Islamic religion: they study like the English; they are sent to jail under old Italian laws; and they are buried according to the rituals of Islam. What a pity! A terrible confusion. The truth, however, is that we are Muslims and we have our book and our prophet Mohammed – these are *our* things. You can borrow from the English if what they have to say is good. But we must live like Muslims because that is what we are.'

He did not shout or show any sort of emotion. He had nothing to prove. He picked up another mint.

'We have no model for Turkey, none of the current models are ideal – Iran, Saudi Arabia – we have the Koran and we want to live like that. That's enough for us. Now, if we took Islam to England and if we said you must like this religion, it would be impossible. But we are Muslims. We can't live with European laws; we have our own laws.'

What has given him strength is his persecution. The state has singled him out for harassment, which has given him almost mythological status. 'Is there any priest in your country who has been imprisoned? Fifty or sixty times I have stood before a judge. In all, I have been in prison for eleven months and fifty-seven days. I was last jailed for preaching about the economic and political system in Turkey. The judge said that I had no right to talk about such things because I had no expertise. You are not an economics expert, he said, you can speak only about prayer.' He had since been prohibited from leaving Turkey – placed, in effect, in internal exile.

He took his glasses off, to reveal eyes of hard black coal which he fixed on me. 'There *is* such a thing as Turkish Islam. This is what we want.' He paused. 'I use the Islamic calendar for praying – what a pity I must use the Christian calendar in the rest of my life . . . Please excuse me now, I must leave you.' He stood up and walked towards the door. 'Please take a mint with you,' which I did, as if obeying an order. And he beckoned me to the door, and I left.

It was time for the theatre. The idea of performance is something that runs deep in Turkey. This show was like a pantomime: all the *asik* on a vast stage in front of a thousand people. It was a leveller: gigolo rubbing shoulders with fundamentalist and would-be dervish. The people, all of them, loved the jokes and the stories. They loved the entertainment.

When I arrived at the theatre, everybody was milling about in darkness. There had been a power cut. The sour stench of locally produced Maltepe cigarettes clouded the foyer. Konya was a wealthy place, but few could afford sweeter-smelling Marlboro cigarettes. There was light after about twenty minutes.

Above the stage there was a huge canvas depicting Ataturk. The irony was inevitable: what he wanted, what he created, what he left behind. He would have loved this – real folk culture – but the religion would have appalled him. He would have ears for the stories but not the mysticism. In this portrait, he was scowling dressed in a dinner jacket.

Somebody went up on stage and drew a red velvet curtain across the picture. The local TV stations (and there were quite a few) stood in front of the stage, shooting when the governor and his retinue arrived. On the stage were tall flower-stands: the Konya Biscuit Makers had presented one bouquet, with long sprays of interwoven fern. Another was from the petrol station for which Ali's uncle had bid $1 million.

Fevzi was sitting with the judges behind a desk to the left of the stage. It was a strange tribunal: how could one compare the Lovers, and by what criterion? Around Fevzi were bowls of carnations. He looked intensely serious.

When everybody was assembled in the hall, Fevzi stood up to welcome an old friend on to the stage to play some music on a *tambur*, a stringed instrument played with a bow, that looks like a gourd and sits vertical between the musician's knees. The strings scraped dreadfully and there was a noisy shuffling of seats. Children started to cry. Fevzi began to talk, but the man continued to play. After a while, with the hall dissolving into noisy pandemonium, the music took on a glutinous serenity and you began to feel that this man, ignored by his audience, was to be treasured: an endangered species unwrapped and on display. He became occasionally distracted from his fingering as he cast long glares across his unhappy audience. The governor was talking now, and when Fevzi saw him inserting a finger into one of his nostrils, he grabbed the microphone and began to speak loudly. The old man with the *tambur* was forced to stop.

Fevzi rose. 'This is a great honour for Konya . . .' He spoke of Ataturk, of struggling to be a Turk; of being able to say, Who is a Turk? These *asik*, he said, were proof of Turkey's wealth. They sat quietly on chairs in a long row that stretched across the stage.

Then Fevzi dipped down beneath the podium and brought out a book. Unnaccountably, it was his book on English cooking. He thrust it before the audience, like an icon. He said, 'This is Turkish culture. We must be proud of it.' He was getting emotional. He turned his attention to the press, and stated three times that Turkish Television had come to the theatre: 'What a privilege!' The few dignitaries present – the chairman of a news agency, a former minister of information – were enough to excite Fevzi's sense of self-importance. In all it took an hour before the *asik* actually started to play.

The *asik* came mainly from the east, from Kars, Erzurum and Adana. There was especially loud applause for a couple from Azerbaijan. The man from Adana looked like a toreador with his white and black shirt and gold braid waistcoat. Most were in suits and ties. There were two women, one in a pale blue dress with a silver and black waistcoat. Another was from Corum, home of the Leblebi nut.

Fevzi had sat down by this stage, and an MC had taken over. He shouted to the audience, 'We live in one country, one beauty – and there it is.' The judging of the *asik* would take three days. The first test was a simple improvisation. You could tell from the start that they fancied Murat Cobanoglu, the most famous of the *asik*, from Kars. He was wearing a kerchief in his breast-pocket, and looked elegant and powerful.

There were jokes between them, and the comedy was good. Cobanoglu was a figure of fun, a stout man with a thick plank of moustache: his *saz* rode on his gut. Fevzi said, picking up the microphone, that he was the father of the *asik*. His fellow-judges were taking notes. Every movement these *asik* made was being judged; it was like watching horse trials.

The contest started. Fevzi shouted out a theme and they had to improvise around it. My next-door neighbours, thinking I was a Turk, kept on turning to me to ask what the *asik* were saying – the words, muffled by the sound system, were very difficult to understand. Some stood alone, without music, to read poems; others shouted above the *saz*. Fevzi, almost beside himself – at one point he was on the verge of tears – stopped them to read out some telegrams. There was a message from the Prime Minister wishing all the best for the festival. It had started to feel like a wedding. Even the hated Social Security minister who refused to pay benefit to the *asik* had sent a message and was applauded.

Now Fevzi asked the *asik* to sing a story based on the word 'Olmedi' – 'He did not die'. One by one, improvising a line or two each, they collectively invented the story of a very handsome prince, who went out one day to hunt a gazelle and became separated from his friends during the chase. He walked on and on. Soon he became tired and rested by a spring. He fell into a deep sleep and dreamed that he saw three dervishes with whom he embarked on a series of adventures in which, by the merest good fortune, he repeatedly managed to avoid death. One day, for instance, he was picking watermelons which were being loaded on to trucks to be taken to market in the city. He rode on the back of the truck, on top of the watermelons. They were not securely stacked and started to roll off the back. He slid on to the road with them, but he survived – much to the hilarious approval of the audience, who could picture the scene clearly in their minds. And so it went on until he caught a simple cold and died.

Then each *asik* gave a solo performance. After a few jolly tunes, the old man from Erzurum took the stage and carefully put a needle between his lips. The audience fell silent. There was no *saz*. They were wondering what to expect from the needle. When he started to sing, they were bewildered. A child sitting behind me was frightened and covered his eyes with his hands. The song was like a deep cry from the pit of the soul – huge and sturdy; hard and painful. Not beautiful, far from it, but intense and entrancing.

It was late when I left the theatre. I never knew who won the prize. I was to leave Konya the following day. I had been invited to join a friend of Ali's for a meal. He said, 'You should come and dance with the dervishes.' He said he had a friend coming from the south-east and that they were proposing to make *cig kofte* and drink *raki*. *Cig kofte* is a speciality of Gaziantep; it is a kebab of raw lamb kneaded with bulgar rice and spices, hot and very tasty. When I arrived back from the theatre, the friend was kneeling over a large plastic bowl full of meat which he had been kneading for a couple of hours.

Then another friend arrived, a dark-skinned Kurd from Van who sold carpets. We went to his shop for the rest of the night. It was bigger, tidier and warmer. He had the television on. There was an American film playing in a Turkish translation, and at first I didn't recognize it. Then I realized it was Francis Ford Coppola's *Rumblefish*. The hat-maker, unshaven, took off his glasses and began to watch. In Konya, I kept on thinking. *Rumblefish* in Konya. He was cutting up the salad with his pocket-knife. They were scrupulously hygienic, frequently stopping to wash their hands and their blades.

I had started to drink, and quickly became drunk. The *cig kofte* were ready and we started to eat. Ali's friend said, 'I have five sons at home, a wife, and I am thirty-nine years old. But I can't stop screwing my friends.' He fell about. Friends, *dostlar*, in Turkish: his mistresses. 'I should not, but I can't resist . . .'

The Kurd said that he had a wife and son in Germany whom he saw rarely. 'Perhaps once a year,' he said. 'Sometimes they come here.' You knew that he was telling a lie. But this is Konya, and people guard their secrets closely. Perhaps he had made a German tourist pregnant. He had a mean face. 'Love and truth,' he said, 'are not good friends.' He smoked imported German cigarettes and wore a torn leather jacket. Was he rich or destitute? Was he clever or stupid? It was not possible to tell. His face was cracked and dirty, and pitted with the scars of boyhood acne. Was he a dervish?

Ali's friend went on to say that the Russians had arrived in Konya. I was surprised that they had bothered. It must have seemed a barren prospect. The Kurd had got in first. There were just two Russian girls in Konya: one was fifteen and the other eighteen. The Kurd said they were virgins when they had arrived. 'They claimed they were anyway, and I had them both one evening – here. Their father asked me to. They came to me for lessons. He wanted me to give my reference to other possible clients. Turkish girls and boys are more expensive.'

By a genuine coincidence, two men suddenly appeared outside

the shop. They were fair-haired and Aryan – clearly Russian – wearing cheap shell suits and training shoes. Who knows, I thought, where they can hide from the scrutiny of the authorities in a place like Konya. They had come to ask the Kurd if he knew of anyone who might be interested in the girls that night. So much for the 'father' – these men were professional pimps. It seemed strange, even then, that he should want to justify the sex by pretending it had parental approval. The Kurd jumped up, and hustled the men out of the shop. Unsure of my reaction, he kept on turning round to look at me. A few minutes later he walked back in. 'Do you want them both for yourself?' Ali's friend went wild with laughter: 'They will give you the saxophone . . .' I laughed, and was suddenly embarrassed. I looked at him, and he poured himself another glass of *raki*.

10

The Zoo

It was not a large zoo, but zoos are few and far between in Turkey. With a collection of 400 animals and a choice location on the banks of the Yesilirmak river that runs through Tokat, it was one of the town's best-loved assets.

So it came as a terrible shock when the townsfolk discovered that their mayor, Ismet Saracoglu, had closed the zoo and ordered the slaughter of many of the animals. The foxes and wolves were said to have been poisoned and some then drowned because the poison was not strong enough; the zoo's single bear was reportedly shot and its three camels sold in segments as meat. The birds and the ducks were sold to poor but sympathetic local families. A pig and a marten were saved by an animal protection society.

'The zoo was an unnecessary luxury and conditions were not good enough to ensure the animals' comfort and safety,' said the mayor at the time. Two of the prize camels had been donated by the former Prime Minister after his successful heart by-pass operation the previous year. His supporters had wanted to slaughter them, but animal rights activists persuaded him to donate them to the zoo instead. The mayor, some local people pointed out, was a member of the Opposition party and they said he was motivated into butchering the camels on political grounds. It was rumoured that he planned a modern abattoir and meat market where the zoo formerly stood.

That was in 1989 – the time of my first visit to Tokat.

Six years later I was returning to visit the local human prison. It is still rare for Westerners to be granted access to Turkish prisons. In an act of unexpected openness I had, however, been given permission. At least, it seemed that I had been given permission.

In all, there are 644 prisons in Turkey. In 1987 inspectors visited all of them, and judged them according to the minimum standards set by the United Nations. None passed. The Turks are justifiably embarrassed by their prisons. When many Westerners think about Turkey, they think first of prisons: barbarous, depraved, inhumane. The film *Midnight Express* was, for millions, a first introduction to the country. It told the story of an American drugs smuggler and his terrifying experiences in an Istanbul jail in the late 1970s. It was exaggerated, but the conditions were largely believable. The American escaped with his life; many Turks, jailed at the time for political crimes, did not.

Keith had never been inside a Turkish prison. He had never been to Tokat. He was a scholar of languages who taught English in Ankara. I had met him through Ersoy, when we had discovered that we had both worked for the *Turkish Daily News*. Keith's students were worried that he was travelling so far east of Ankara. None of them had been so far before. 'They told me I should dress warmly,' he said. He had bought a thick blue coat especially.

The road from Ankara to Tokat is featureless, an endless vista of flat dirt lowlands. Battery chicken farms and brick kilns – long buildings with tall towers – stand like guardians across the landscape. Anatolia is defensive when criticized. It is callous and cruel and does not, when challenged, necessarily see that it should apologize for its periodic brutality. The geography is relentless; the people lead hard lives. They live, for the most part, in isolated small towns and villages spread miles apart across the steppelands. Each town is as anonymous as the next: a tended civic garden, with strings of coloured light-bulbs, hanging precariously from the street lamps; a dusty bus station, where we would stop to water, eat a sesame bread ring, and take on board a handful of peasant farmers heaving huge canvas sacks full of potatoes or rice. Then another few hours in a fug of *arabesk* and thick cigarette smoke, past the sugar refineries of Corum.

And finally to Tokat. The reason for my first visit to this strange town was not connected with the zoo – that was coincidental. I had come to investigate the alleged discovery of what was fêted as a second Ephesus in a neighbouring village. The Turkish papers, pumped up by the local governor, extensively reported the find at Sebastopolis of a well-preserved Roman market town. It seemed a unique asset, something that marked the town apart from its neighbours. It was beside itself with optimism. Those were the gold rush days, but Sebastopolis came and went. The ancient columns stood in the village, unloved, an adjunct to the rough squalor of the modern settlement. The children posed in front of them for our cameras, proudly wearing the imitation shirts of their favourite football teams. The women passed across the old bridge to wash their clothes in the river that flowed beneath the site.

They were no longer serving Sebastopolis cocktails in the local restaurants when we arrived this second time. The tourist rush had not materialized. There was just one lasting monument to the excitement: a four-star hotel on the outskirts of the town. It was as alien to Tokat as the partly excavated Roman bath was to Sebastopolis.

The Turks are good with hotels: this was huge and white, with a sauna and a swimming-pool and shadowed glass and chandeliers. It was a temple of prosperity. When people stood up from their chairs, they politely moved them back to their original site. The dust and the noise were outside. This was the future in a bubble, with American rap on the public address system. Not far away, the farmers still lived in breeze-block houses with flat mud roofs.

Tokat was once a great trading town. For more than 2,000 years it was a stopover for caravans travelling along the Silk Road to Antioch or Aleppo. The Seljuks endowed the town with some architecture of great and enduring quality, like the thirteenth-century Hidirlik bridge which straddles the Yesilirmak river at the western entrance to the town. It also enjoyed some vicarious fame from the nearby town of Zile. Here in AD 47 Julius Caesar is said to have stood on the ramparts of the castle and boasted, 'Veni! Vidi! Vici!' after defeating the king of Pontus.

In the bar of the hotel we met a plump guide from the Tourist Office, called Erdogan, who emerged almost as soon as we had left the reception desk, offered us a drink and then asked if we were enthusiastic about railways. 'I am a great enthusiast,' he said. 'I have, in fact, just written a TV commercial about the Tokat railroad. This is a rich town in the heart, and it is the most Turkish town.' He was sitting beside the manager, a fatter man with a moustache and a large chunky gold bracelet and signet rings studded with diamonds on two fingers. Neither of them was drinking alcohol. One could sense the reserve.

'I like clean places, I don't like dirty places,' said Erdogan. 'The future smells good.'

'Tokat is a crossroads,' said the manager. 'People stop on their way . . .'

The guide interrupted. 'Tokat is a good place for factory workers to come and breathe one hundred per cent oxygen. Other attractions include canoeing up the Yesilirmak river.' He was a small man with a perfectly round face and a shiny forehead.

We were talking in a frosted glass booth by the hotel bar while others played backgammon. Taking us into his confidence, Erdogan said he was a Jew, descended from those who fled Spain in the fifteenth century to the sanctuary of Anatolia. The manager was shocked. Erdogan looked at him. 'I am a human being. There is no problem. Just the struggle to survive.'

'What do people in Tokat do?' I asked the manager.

'They do trade,' he said without looking up. Then he left, but the tourist guide remained. 'Do you know France?' he asked in a confidential whisper. 'I used to work in a restaurant in France.' And then he stood up and walked away.

The following morning we telephoned the governor. He should

have been told of our permission to visit the prison. He was out. The hotel manager then called the town hall. He was suspicious – why were we so interested in the police and prisons of Tokat? 'There is very little crime in this town,' he had told us the night before. Eyeing us with disdain, he spoke to an official at the governor's office. 'Spies?' he said over the phone, thinking we were not listening. 'Tourists, I think. At least, they said they were tourists. They talked to me last night about the unspoilt traditions of Turkey . . .'

The assistant police commissioner called back later. 'OK, they can come – but not for a week. Tomorrow is Republic Day and then it is a weekend holiday.'

Republic Day – we had both forgotten, although the bunting had already gone up in the hotel. This is an important day in Turkey, a day on which the nation reminds itself of its nationalism. The day on which Ataturk declared the territorial integrity of Anatolia. 'Maybe,' the manager said with some satisfaction, 'they are studying your papers . . .'

Then, unexpectedly, the governor himself called the hotel on his car phone. No, he said, he could not see us. The manager put the receiver down before I could reach it. What could we do, I asked him. He shrugged. Where could we find the governor? Perhaps we could ask him in person? We only needed to know that he had our permission. It was *official*, we explained. From the government. The wreath-laying, he finally said. Probably he would be at the wreath-laying.

We went into town and found the main square where a few stand-up bouquets on metal stands were perched along its perimeter; schoolchildren with white ruffs and black smocks were milling and chirruping under the trees around it. We went into the town hall to seek some information and the governor's secretary agreed to see us. We met him in his office, a room upstairs; there was no paper on the desk and he was literally twiddling his thumbs. 'Tokat does not like strangers; the mayor doesn't like strangers. You are wasting your time here.' He refused to find out whether any permission had arrived from Ankara or not. 'It is not my responsibility.'

We stood around downstairs in the lobby, considering options. At the bottom of the stairs, Keith noticed, there was a pool of congealed blood on the floor. It did not seem surprising at the time. The atmosphere in this cold, concrete building was openly hostile. We stood there as dozens of bureaucrats whizzed between offices, carrying old dog-eared files, trying to finish up their business before the start of the holiday. When we tried to flag one of them down, they just stared and moved on, quickening their pace.

We tried the secretary again. This time he simply shook his head to each question we asked. From the secretary's office, you could see children playing with flags on the square; the holiday was descending. There was no joy on their scrubbed faces, no enthusiasm, just ritual obedience. At noon, all government offices would be closed until the following week. For the secretary, it was therefore simply a question of stalling us, keeping us away from his boss. Why was he so unhelpful?

We regrouped on the steps outside the Governorate. We examined the square: and realized for the first time that there was no noise – except for the children – around it at all. No traffic, no birdsong. Nothing. People were whispering. It could have been a funeral. After a while a young man from the Office of Population and Census came out and joined us – an emissary, we suspected, from the secretary, trying to establish our real motive. This bureaucrat asked many questions: Are you married? Are you a soldier? We said nothing.

The square was filling up with people. Young boys dressed up as military policemen with the letters AZIZ stencilled in white on their green helmets stood guard around it. The average Turkish soldier has an aura of dispensability: ragged uniform and scuffed boots. But not these smart men. There was still no sign of the governor.

From the steps there was a broad view of Tokat, flanked by a single craggy mountain and some green hills. There was no notable geography; it had the air of a small Tyrolean town, but none of the charm. There were the baths, with their onion domes covered in glass, like huge warts. There was a large, lifeless statue of Ataturk in the square.

The dignitaries started to arrive, jostling in front of the statue, enjoying their status. There were soldiers in ceremonial uniform, and civil servants in pressed suits and polished shoes. We joined a crowd of ordinary people looking on from the edge of the square. Keith approached a policeman and asked him if he would tell us when the governor arrived. He said that he normally worked behind a desk. He was in charge of immigration into Tokat. I looked surprised. 'No, not that,' he said. 'We have a lot of Afghan refugees, that's all.'

The ceremony started. The first of the bouquets was placed in front of the statue. A man on a lectern read off the names of those presenting the flowers. It was rather like a school prize-giving, but conducted in silence.

As the first wreaths were presented by the police and the agricultural faculty at the new university, I saw the governor. I assumed it was him. There was a gang of bodyguards to-ing and fro-ing behind him. He stood in the middle of a row of VIPs that stretched across the square, facing the statue. The military bandsmen in white helmets and gold plaid were playing, and little girls wearing red sashes were waving Turkish flags. The music was impossibly out of tune. The dignitaries remained, however, at attention and impeccably serious.

The townspeople and street urchins cackled and swooned at the precision of the band's marching, then went quiet as the wreath of the *Muftuluk*, the local Muslim hierarchy, was placed before Ataturk. The children were surprisingly disrespectful: they noisily mimicked the dreadful trumpet playing.

The immigration officer came across and tapped Keith on the shoulder, pointing to the governor. But just as he opened his mouth, a plain-clothes policeman approached him and said something in his ear. He turned his back on us and walked off.

Keith and I started to barge our way through the crowd towards the governor. A senior soldier wearing a ceremonial sword was standing next to him. He saw us approaching and rubbed his scabbard like an old pirate. We continued to edge forward. When the ceremony finished, the VIPs quickly moved off towards their waiting cars. I could see the governor making towards a black Mercedes whose door was being held open by a chauffeur. We broke into a run, and the governor, turning his head and seeing us, quickened his pace. He was walking very briskly. Just as we came within shouting distance, two vast bodyguards stood in our way and brought us to a halt. They said nothing. A civilian in a brown suit came panting up behind us and said, 'Stay, you can see him in his office.' The governor drove off. We turned and asked the man, who was sweating, who he was. He said, 'He will be back in ten minutes,' and then he ran off. Keith was furious. A secret policeman sent to keep us away. The governor had flown.

We returned to the hotel. I called Ankara.

'Does anybody know we are here?' I asked.

'Yes, the chief prosecutor.'

So we called him. He was just on his way out of the office for the holiday. 'Welcome to Tokat,' he said. 'I am sure you will like it here. Please call the prison governor if you wish to visit today. I will arrange it. Go this afternoon if you like.'

The jail in Tokat was a closed prison, which meant it was only for the most dangerous criminals. It had ninety-six residents, men and women. None of these were political prisoners – at least, this is what we were told. Turkey maintains that its population of political prisoners is rapidly dwindling. Many human rights campaigners are sceptical about this claim.

The Republic Day holiday is the highlight of the convicts' calendar. It is the one day of the year on which relatives may visit for more than a few minutes, and in privacy. Normally they may only talk through grilles in windows. But during this holiday they could walk out in the garden together.

The prison was on the banks of the Yesilirmak, not far from where the town zoo once stood. The road petered out into mud by the gates. When we arrived, a queue of relatives was waiting outside, arguing with the guards.

It was a small place, formerly a school-house. They had clumsily built some new breeze-block wings on to the old buildings. The walls were topped with chicken wire. There was a rickety watchtower from which a boy soldier looked longingly down at the town. There were spotlights, but they were small: big enough to light a small night-club, but not to patrol a perimeter fence. This was not a prison that took the prospect of escape seriously.

The young *jandarma* on the gate let us through without any sign of surprise. To one side of the yard there was a small rose garden, with a bench. Otherwise it was concrete. The entrance to the main block was up some steps by the cook-house. The governor's office was the first door you encountered. The place smelt like a school: the walls were painted china gloss and they were damp with the moisture of so many confined bodies. It was stiflingly hot.

The governor expected us to ask him immediately about torture in his prison. So when we arrived, he was tense. It was a tiny office. A television showing a football match was playing on a shelf above his desk. On a coffee table by the door there were a number of potted plants wrapped in tinsel paper. This is the traditional gift Turks give when a colleague moves job, becomes engaged or has a baby. He must have been a recent arrival. He was tense, but he was bored. He was rolling a pen up and down on his blotting-pad when we were shown in. He wore a grey shiny suit and a tie with a little gold clip. He had a squashed flat face with grey hair swept to one side. His appearance was oddly immaculate in this environment.

A colleague came in, introducing himself as the prosecutor. He sat down and, while we all watched, curled a strand of greasy black hair around his finger and flicked it across his bald head like a piece of string. He looked like a monk. The bald patch was almost perfectly circular, like a tonsure. The two men could not have been more different. The prosecutor's collar was unbuttoned, and his tie loose.

The governor was impatient. It was his day off.

'How long have you worked in prisons?' Keith asked.

'I like working with people,' he said. He had been in the service for twenty years. 'Everything has changed. I mean, the people have changed.' He had worked all over the country, most recently in the southern port town of Samsun. 'There was a lot of theft in Samsun, and here there is a lot of murder. People change . . .'

Samsun is a big town. 'How big was the prison there?'

'Six hundred.' The monk flashed a glance.

Six hundred. What had he done to be sent to Tokat?

Now he ordered tea. You sensed something delicate in this man: a hesitancy, a vulnerability. His tie-pin shone from his shirt, the brightest thing in the room. Did this suggest he was proud, or vain, or self-conscious? He was still waiting. I asked if we could see the prison.

They had rehearsed this. The governor lifted up his blotter and produced a copy of our permission: 'The directive we have received states explicitly that we are to receive you and meet with you . . .' We agreed. 'It does not state that we are to take you inside the prison.'

'But this is the point of our visit,' I said.

'I would, of course, like you to see it – we have nothing to hide – but I do not have permission.'

There was a pause. The monk burst in: 'You damn people! You don't even recognize our right to *live*. This is a closed prison, and we have to adhere to these rules; there is a directive and we have to abide by it.'

The governor, alarmed by his colleague's anger, said, 'We have nothing to hide – I mean it sincerely. I believe the police in Britain use truncheons. Well, there is nothing like that here. There are fifty-seven employees here, and there is no individual with a gun except me. When people come in, they leave their weapons here.' He slammed his hand on top of his desk. 'Perhaps I can bring people in and you can ask questions . . .'

The monk cut in: 'Mostly you people are interested in torture and hanging – but even when it did happen, it didn't happen in this prison.'

The governor stood up and changed the subject. 'Let me show you the kitchen.'

It was outside the main block from which we had just been barred. There were large metal bowls lying on the floor and two large men tending to the cauldrons of porridge: one was a murderer and had been in the jail for twenty-four years. There was a pancake of salt on top of a tree stump by the door. 'It keeps the flies away,' said the murderer.

'The people here are unfortunates,' said the governor, ignoring him. 'That's the way we describe them.'

We asked to go back to the office to review the exact wording of the permission. Both officers were becoming tetchy. We all re-read the permission. It stated, quite explicitly, that we had authority to *meet with the people in/at the prison of Tokat.* In Turkish the suffix 'at' also means 'in'. We argued 'in', meaning inside; they argued 'at', meaning outside. We spent half an hour debating Turkish grammar. Keith was an expert.

The monk grew angry. 'Now wait, just a minute, you do not tolerate us.' A short silence: 'I do not mean you personally, but in general.'

Keith, however, sensed danger. We said that we would leave them to their holiday and return the following day.

Outside the gates, most of the families had left. But there were a couple of hard-looking men lolling against the crumbling wall. They said, 'Do you want to drink tea?' when we passed.

There was a tea-house close to the prison. Across the river were the modern quarters of the local garrison – sandy-coloured – and behind them bare hills; horse and traps filed past carrying bricks, and old men in bobble-hats.

One of the men explained that his brother was a murderer. The killing, over a land dispute, was in the market at Erbaa, an hour away from Tokat. 'My brother's a bit of a thug; he can fight; he likes it and he can draw a gun just like that,' he said. 'But this is a blood feud – a matter of honour. My brother is mad, but I'm even more mad, and my two other brothers even more crazy. The other family know we kill them . . .' You did not doubt his word. He had a dark, creased face, with the texture of tree bark.

His brother had killed a member of another family, shooting him five times at point-blank range because he had cursed his mother. He was sentenced to sixteen years. 'We are pleased. We taught them a lesson, and now my brother has a good position in the prison, he makes tablecloths.' Both, however, had been refused access to see him. Apparently they had not applied in advance. They were both very angry. They felt they had been conned by the governor who promised that all relatives would be allowed in on the holiday.

This was an intense conversation in the afternoon sunshine, sitting in the little garden outside the tea-house. Giant yellow-headed dandelions were growing out of the paving stones. Across the river, I noticed, there were several old Anatolian town-houses next to the garrison compound, with their top-heavy second storey, now warping, in rich violet and canary-yellow pastels, hidden behind clumps of poplar. The river, when you looked at it closely, was nothing more than a dirty stream. Workmen were building a retaining wall. In the middle of the garden was a fountain, a strange ornament for Tokat. But it did not work and was badly chipped.

The second man was a travelling salesman who sold jumpers. He scolded his younger relative for talking about blood feuds. 'You must think this is backwards,' he said to us. 'In the east there are blood feuds. Not here. In the east there is no night life. There is a disco in Tokat.'

The first man turned to him. 'We have our own way. If somebody sleeps with your women, you divorce them; here we kill them – that's our way.'

'What are you doing here?' the jumper man asked.

We explained that we had come to see the prison. 'Would you like us to visit your relative – in the prison, I mean?'

'Why not?' his brother said. He gave us the details.

On the way back into town we saw a sign for a newspaper, the *Tokat Meydan*. This blood feud sounded interesting: perhaps the local press would know more. Perhaps it would also know what really happened to the old zoo.

The newspaper office was on the second floor of a rancid-smelling and grubby bazaar block on one side of the main square. All these buildings are the same wherever you go in

Turkey: bald concrete apartment blocks that spread like a rash across the country during the 1950s and 1960s. There was a toy shop in the corner with a promotion in the window for pencils and rubbers and a variety of small plastic handguns.

In the office a man was sitting behind a desk. Above it were some Koranic scrolls but no picture of Ataturk. He was in his thirties, with a flat, fat face and a wiry black moustache. His name was Mete, and he said he was an electrician and edited the newspaper in his spare time. He was overjoyed to see us. 'The zoo! The zoo! Of course, well . . . the zoo wasn't closed because of the weather, let me tell you that, although the winters do come quite hard here, it's true. Perhaps they emptied the zoo because we already have enough animals – foxes and wolves.' He fell about laughing. 'But it's true we don't have camels any more. We used to, we used to, when Tokat was at the crossroads of the Silk Road. There were camels then.' He was still laughing.

'You know there are some special people who have come from Tokat. There are some very, very rich businessmen from here – one's a ship-owner; one's a trader, and a jeweller. They all live in Istanbul, of course. The armed forces commander is from Tokat; the head of the constitutional court; and a world-famous cartoonist.' He shouted to his secretary to bring him a book of cartoons. He showed us a picture of Prince Charles, who had once visited the town, scaling a tower to rescue Rapunzel. Instead of rope, he was climbing up her long, blonde pubic hairs. 'You see? You see?' Mete said, still laughing.

'Please, please, you must see my pictures.' He opened his drawer and produced a thick stack of photographs. 'Here, look, there is a general overview of the industrial estate. Do you see? And here. You see – some people arrested for forging money.' The notes were laid out in bundles on a table and the men hung their heads in shame.

'Now look at this.' It was a picture of an odd-looking man with a square head standing next to a small wooden box, which had a bucket on its head, and little legs. 'The inventor,' said

Mete. 'This is a robot.' He fingered the picture. 'He's poor and ignorant but he creates a robot.'

'A robot?' I said.

'Yes, a robot,' Mete replied.

'What kind of robot?'

'Look, here is the article.' On an inside page of the newspaper there was the same picture of the square-headed man. The headline read: PRIMARY SCHOOL GRADUATE WAITS FOR ATTENTION AS AN INVENTOR. The article reported that a twenty-three-year-old villager, a father of three, had constructed a robot which could see through hills and fire weapons at a range of 500 metres. The machine, it continued, had been successfully tested in front of the sceptical reporter. For the purpose of this experiment, the inventor had used a toy gun and caps rather than the rifle with real bullets for which it was intended. This inventor lived near Erbaa, not far from the feuding families.

When we returned to the hotel, the manager asked us to keep out of the way. The lobby was out of bounds, as was the bar. The Republic Day reception was underway and we were not invited. We asked if we could have tickets. He said he would ask, but he doubted it. We were told we would have to eat in the breakfast room, if we wanted food. Downstairs all the richest Turks in Tokat were gathering: there was a rock band and a cocktail pianist playing Edith Piaf. Outside the hotel the ordinary people were celebrating: a procession of cars went by with lights flashing, trailing huge portraits of Ataturk.

We were not the only displaced guests in the breakfast room. When Keith and I arrived, a man was talking angrily about the presence of *yabanci* – foreigners – in Tokat. He did not mean Europeans. He meant other Turks.

The food was dreadful – the *sis* kebab was not cooked and it was cold. At another table there was a party of riotously drunk visiting businessmen. One shouted, 'In Istanbul you can do anything, anything!'

That night, Keith and I, intrigued by the increasingly brutal character of the town that was supposed to be home to the purest Turk, decided to seek a different insight. We paid a visit to the whore-house. In most ways Tokat felt like a frontier town – there were guns, and there was the whore-house. Every Turkish town has one. They are legal. Tokat's was on the outskirts, hidden among some trees. It looked like a café, but there were only men queuing outside. It was next to some slum houses, and for a moment I stood watching the rising column of foul-smelling smoke belch out of the chimney. What where they using for firewood? Tyres? This was a poor province.

There was a whore-house. And there was a night watchman. In Turkey they are called *bekci* and they wear a uniform, a dirty brown version of the green that the police constable wears. The night watchman, the great romantic figure of nineteenth-century fiction – the anonymous, hopeless, useless by-product of society, imbecilic, clueless, illiterate, and powerless, beyond hope. The caricature of the night watchman is one thing the Turks share with the Western Europeans.

This particular night watchman had a little office just outside the main door of the brothel. The men had to file past it. The regulars peered in to say hello. There was little in the room, just a couple of chairs and a desk on which there was a telephone and a radio on which the watchman was listening to a military band play 'Captain America'. The walls were painted pink. We asked if we could spend some time with him, and he seemed glad of our company. No Europeans had come to this brothel before.

There were seven or eight whores, the night watchman said, and they changed by the minute. They got up at midday, and then they ate, had a bath and waited until the men came. He was dubious about our motives. He said, 'I do not think you want to have any girls. But are you spies? From the police?'

I said, 'Why should the police be interested? This is legal.'

He nodded.

The madam walked in, in slippers, with a man in tow. He had slimy skin which made him glisten. 'I couldn't find other work,' she told us, warming herself by the stove. 'I had to do it.' She was exhausted. Her companion, the pimp, said that he was not pleased either. He was not really the boss: 'No, that's a woman somewhere in Izmir.' The highest tax-payer in Turkey was said to be an Armenian madam in Istanbul.

'It's a bad thing according to society,' said the pimp. 'But it needs it.' He was wearing dirty green socks. 'In Tokat, the people don't mind it.'

'So what goes on?' asked Keith.

They looked strangely at him. 'Whips and tying-up are not allowed here,' said the woman. 'It is like a supermarket, just normal dress. They have a test two days a week and every two months they have an Aids test. People who want to can use contraceptives – if they are foreigners, they have to.'

Of course, they don't have foreigners. 'None at all,' said the night watchman. 'There are no tourists here at all.'

The night watchman had a simple job: he checked that none of the punters was carrying weapons, that none had come to mutilate the women. We asked him why somebody would carry a weapon, and he faltered. To think about why, to acknowledge the possibility that a local man would be capable of injuring a woman, was painful for him.

'There is the possibility,' he said. 'We do find weapons sometimes and then I notify the police station, but,' he added quickly, 'there are no sex murders in Tokat. There is nobody who would so pervert the customs and traditions of our society.' Our attention was diverted by a squall of noise outside the door. A party of customers was leaving the building, smoking, chattering and zipping up. A second group passed by the door: young, well-to-do young men in blazers and cavalry twills.

'What about religion?' Keith asked. 'Isn't this all rather immoral?'

The watchman replied, 'Islam is a religion which encompasses many things. We're not in a position to make pronouncements. We are just officials. In England, I believe, there are homosexuals – two men getting together. There is group sex in the West. We see that in the films. Compared to the West, this place is good. In this society, it's a man and a woman. Two people in one room.'

The pimp was standing by the stove. He wore a large red signet ring. 'In Turkey, one man can have lots of women,' he said, smiling. 'We know about these things . . .' The watchman looked across, squirming. The pimp went on, 'I'm married, you know. Live in Tokat. I don't know about the other places but Tokat is a beautiful place – farmers, a mixed place . . .'

'Have you had any famous people in here?' I asked.

'I have not seen any famous people in the brothel,' replied the watchman officiously. 'There is no entertainment here. This is a public place but it is a place only for sex. If they wanted music, then they would need a different licence.' The watchman was married too, but his wife did not know he worked here. 'I tell her that I am patrolling around the power station.' The pimp laughed.

More men poured out, swinging their prayer beads and zipping up. Early evening was approaching and the place was beginning to get busy. Some of the men were embarrassed as they showed their ID cards to the watchman.

The pimp wanted to show us around, so we stood in the queue for a while. The other men were surprised but said nothing. The girls (few of them were actually girls, most were middle-aged women) sat on grey secretarial chairs, in T-shirts and leggings, behind a large window. The men filed past the window and pointed at the one they wanted, then they bought a token from the cashier. Each woman held a coloured token which marked the price per minute. There was no smiling on either side of the window. Most of the men had not showered; the women's make-up, where it existed, was smudged on their lips. I understood that they outlawed kissing, but it looked as if this rule was routinely ignored. There was only one light in the middle of the room, on the women's side of the glass: a pink bulb without a shade.

Some of the men were clearly frightened by the women on the other side, and left before their money was taken at the turnstile. There was no embarrassment. When he saw us, one man said, 'Tourists, you go first!' The pimp was slouching around, dragging his slippers along the ground.

We went back into the watchman's room. The pimp had asked us to stay a while longer because the whores wanted to talk to us. 'They rarely meet a foreigner,' he said.

Outside the room there was laughter. One man poked his head around the door and shouted, 'I came, I saw, I conquered, and then, 'I came and then I went.' The watchman was now listening to the football on his orange radio, which had a large bandage wrapped around it.

Suddenly the laughter became shouting. There was a fight. The watchman stood up and went outside. 'Keep it quiet, will you? What's your problem?'

'This mad dog took the woman I had chosen,' a man replied.

'And then he cursed me, behind my back,' said another. 'He is from some bloody eastern town. He has no good manners.'

'Whatever city he's from,' said the watchman, 'he's a child of our nation and you should not fight each other.' They walked off.

There was a long period of embarrassing silence. The watchman could think of nothing to say to us. He pointed at the wall and was about to open his mouth, but then thought better of it and looked away. Finally I asked him what he did while he was on duty. He scratched his head and touched his walkie-talkie – I thought he was going to call HQ and report our presence – then opened the single drawer of his desk, and very carefully took out a thick book. There was a bookmark a good way into it, but not a single crease on the spine. He was a careful reader.

Remembrance of Things Past by Marcel Proust. In an Anatolian whore-house.

It was in a Turkish translation. 'The tea cake,' he said. 'I love the smell of the tea cakes.' He looked at us. 'This is about a family; it's a series of two books in one novel with an introduction, a story and a conclusion.' He was telling us because he assumed we had not read it. 'It is a very fine book. But it is not my favourite. My favourite,' he said, 'is Charles Dickens.' He had recently read *A Tale of Two Cities*.

The night watchman had been to school. First he wanted to become a teacher, but he changed his mind and tried to become a policeman. Unfortunately he was too late for the police; he was too old for the entrance exams. He could not find another job as a teacher, so he was forced to become a night watchman. 'Now I am studying on the Open University to become a manager. But it is difficult to succeed when you are born without money,' he said. Turkey had failed this man.

He walked over to Keith and took his hands, saying, 'God made the fingers a different size.' He pulled each of Keith's fingers to demonstrate. 'He makes rich and poor.' And then he sat down. 'Is it any different in England?'

Every so often his walkie-talkie exploded, and his sergeant asked, 'Number seven-eight-zero, is everything OK?' He looked at it, lingering over an answer, knowing that he should say, 'Well, sir, I have two foreigners sitting in my office!' But each time, replied, 'Yes, it's OK.'

He turned and said, 'It won't be the same for my children. I have three, you know and they are all studying. One is studying health, and another tourism. And the last is studying English. You know, I would really have liked to work in public relations. I think I am a good communicator.' The pimp walked in with a couple of the women. The watchman stopped.

One of them had come from Mersin just ten days before. She was married and had two children. She had been a prostitute for three years and she was twenty-nine, although she looked older. 'Of course, it's a good living, but I don't enjoy it. They understand, my friends. They know.' Her black hair was put up in an untidy bun; she was thin and her face was fleshy and pale, as if she was a drunk. She had some simple gold bracelets on her thin arms, and she wore her wedding band. She had pink plastic slippers on her feet. 'We keep Turkey free,' she said, 'like a safety valve.' She had had thirty men that night. 'It's all simple sex, not whips.'

The other woman was younger, from the east. She had the tight eyes of a Caucasian Turk and thick, pancaked make-up which did not fully mask her pitted complexion. Her dry hair was peroxide-blonde. She wore long gold earrings and velvet pantaloons, like an Ottoman whore. She had been on the game for only three or four months. She was much more alive than the first, who spoke slowly and seemed miserable. The younger girl, who perhaps was only nineteen, was full of optimism. 'I won't be doing this for long,' she said. 'It's only to earn a little money.' For the older woman, it had become a way of life. The younger girl was divorced. Her husband had given her nothing. 'I will get a house, get a business and I'll leave.' The watchman laughed with unexpected cruelty.

'There's a stigma,' the older woman interrupted. 'You can't escape it. You are at odds with society. You get bad eyes from the women. That's the way it is.'

'We are not really allowed outside the brothel because it is considered dangerous,' the younger one added. 'But sometimes,' she looked at the pimp, smiling, 'sometimes I walk around town with dark glasses on.'

'I don't think about it,' she went on, jangling a dozen gold bracelets on her forearm. She looked down at the floor. 'I'll be a housewife with a family.' She had had forty-five men that night. Sometimes, in a twelve-hour shift, she had as many as sixty. 'It's very tiring,' she said with a sigh.

She insisted that we see her room in the whore-house and we went past the glass window and down a corridor. Some of the girls lived here; others lived in town. On the doors of the rooms there were shower curtains, and through them there was a red haze. Each room was lit by a single pink light-bulb. In the young girl's room, which was also where she received her clients, the walls were bright blue. It was clean and neatly organized. There was a poster on the wall – a photograph of a field of red poppies. It was torn at the edges. 'I take this with me to each of the brothels,' she said. 'I think it's nice.'

The following morning we returned to the prison. The governor was on his own, behind his desk, reading an ultra-nationalist newspaper. He was distracted by something and seemed much less antagonistic than the previous day.

'How was the Republic Day cocktail party?' Keith asked as

we sat down. Outside, you could hear a hubbub of noise from the relatives waiting to see the inmates, arguing with the *jandarma*. The queue was longer today.

'I don't know. I didn't go.'

'Oh?'

'No, I was not invited.' He looked up. 'I am an outsider.' He stood up to close the window. The headline on the front page of his newspaper reported a government corruption scandal. He said, 'You give something and you expect something in return. Turkey's biggest problem is economic: if that was solved – the corruption, I mean – there would be no more bad luck, no more injustice.' I knew that this was a privilege. He was trusting us. He was trusting our discretion. Perhaps he didn't care any more.

He looked out of the window, his hands clasped behind his head, leaning back on his hard little wooden chair. 'The pensions by the sea in Mersin were better than the four-star hotels here. Do you know that? One day I couldn't find yoghurt in this town – just ordinary yoghurt. I mean, I'm from Kayseri and there you can buy it everywhere. Tokat is so backward. You know they have set up a university, so maybe – in thirty years – things will improve. Maybe. But this place is so full of ignorance. Bloody ignorance.

'I'm a foreigner here and I only come from Kayseri, 200 kilometres away. This is a closed box; there is no investment; the economy's weak. Tokat is on its own.' He stopped and smiled, embarrassed perhaps by his own bitterness. Nobody likes to admit that they have lost control of their lives. He slowed down. 'They are planning to build a new prison, but for ten years at least we'll have to work here in this old place. Slowly, slowly in Turkey – that's what I mean. I'm trying to get out – 600 people were in my last prison and then I was appointed here. It was politics and I had to go, that was the end of it. Hardly promotion. Everything was better in Mersin. The vehicles and the tools were better.' He pointed at the ceiling of his office. 'Look!' The ceiling was made of rotten planks with holes in them. 'But it is the government who appoint the prison governors. Perhaps somebody close to a politician was given my job. I have no politics. This is Turkey; it is bad.'

This confession was entirely unexpected. But he smiled. Perhaps he felt better. 'You know, they cut my salary when I came here. The rent here is one million lire. In Mersin there was no rent. But they cut my wages by 150,000 lire. My wife doesn't work. We have no money. I don't even have enough to pay for cigarettes. I earn 2,500,000 lire. You know that is as much as a *bekci* [a watchman]? Did you know that?' I was shocked. A doctor gets five million and a teacher four million. The prosecutor earns seven million. A prison governor on such low wages. No wonder the Turkish prison system has problems.

He said he wanted to change things in the prison. He said he wanted to make them better. 'But everything is done in Ankara. I think it's wrong. If I am to administer this place, then I have to have laws to allow me to do it. I should have the authority. When Ankara administers everything it cripples the service. I can't do anything here without asking Ankara. And the people here, the prison officers, they can't think for themselves. There are forty who work for me. They don't know how to think.'

The governor then invited his chief prison officer to join us. The chief had been in Tokat for twenty years. He was a big fat man with three red stars on his blue tunic.

'Oh yes,' he said, 'how did I come to work in the prison?' He looked at the governor, who nodded him on. 'The land on which I was farming wasn't sufficient.' He had green eyes and a bulky moustache. His Turkish was very poor, barely intelligible. 'We had to pass the exam to join; I passed. I went to primary school . . .'

The governor interrupted, 'Now, of course, most of the people go to secondary school. And there are schools in Ankara for the warders to improve them.'

I turned to the chief and asked, 'Why are there so many murders in Tokat?' The fat man's tunic tightened around his waist; he was wearing a cardigan underneath it and a little black tie. 'Well, we've got the town of Erbaa – there is a blood feud there and most of the murders are committed there – but there were many more twenty years ago. The consciousness has been raised. In twenty years a lot has changed – there were no private toilets, TV or radio in the prison then – and there were 500 people crammed into this tiny place. Now they have a toilet. They have hot water showers and bunk beds. There is an emphasis placed on cleanliness. Those who wish to wash in the morning can, but everyone has to wash at least once a week. We make them go – this is a result of our beliefs, you see.'

The governor said, 'Four years ago it would not have been possible for you to come. There might have been misunderstandings between us.'

The chief added, 'Oh yes, there is no torture here – people here are respected as people.' The prisoners had lessons after breakfast and then they could play ball in the garden or work. They ate at 4.30 in the afternoon and then they went to bed.

'We have good food as well,' said the chief. 'Once a month the men get fish.'

The governor turned to us. 'They eat better than I do; they are eating potatoes and macaroni this evening and I will be joining them in order to keep my expenses down.' After a short pause he added, 'Last year one prisoner was due for release but he didn't want to go home. He felt the people here were his family and his life here was good. There is all sorts of food. In the prison shop there is cola at just 1,600 lire. The canteen makes quite a profit, I should say. Everything is cheaper in prison – tea is only 100 lire; outside it is 1,000. We even have a doctor in here; I can't always afford an operation myself but in the prison they can have one.'

The chief agreed. 'People get arrested in the winter because it's warm in the prison. When it is spring they leave.'

At this point the prosecutor and another man, the prison teacher, came into the office. The chief continued. He said the people of Tokat tend to murder rather than anything else: 50 per cent of those in the jail were killers. Only four were there for rape, and four for robbery. One was convicted of extortion and one for wounding with a knife.

Were there any crimes that one might associate with a modern town, like serial sex crimes? The prosecutor became stern. 'Ninety per cent of the sex crimes are between men and women; 10 per cent may be men and men, but I've only heard of one incident where a man has raped another man. The aim of our rapist is to marry, you see. There are times when people just want to satisfy their lust but more than 60 per cent have the aim of marrying. Say a man took a woman, and the woman wanted it a bit, but she is too young, the man has to go to prison. That's the law: you go to prison for under-age sex.' He rubbed his hand across his head. 'If a man has kidnapped a woman, and then he marries her, and that is approved of by the parents, then it's OK. But if they divorce within five years then he is arrested for kidnapping. I think it's unfair. Of course, I could not say such things in court or I would be considered biased.' He paused. 'There is, of course, wife-beating but it doesn't get reported because women tend to accept it in families of lower culture.'

The teacher added, 'The wife expects it in the evening. That hasn't changed.'

The governor said, 'Look, in Tokat – in Turkey, in fact – it is all one-on-one sex. There are no psychopaths here. There was one man I believe who raped a nine-year-old girl and he received fifteen years –'

'Yes,' interrupted the teacher, 'but I reckon that wasn't proved. He raped a nine-year-old and then he was arrested three years later. Somebody simply said that was the guy when they saw him in the market. There are no mental people in this prison because if they were mental they wouldn't be here. If there was a psychopath we would send him to a hospital. There are some suspected psychopaths, like Zeki who was a criminal – he had a criminal face-type according to the system of the Italian criminologists. He wouldn't look one in the eye, and he pushed a tea cup very violently. He shot his father dead when he was twenty-five.'

The prosecutor, embarrassed and outraged, said, 'I don't accept the theory of the criminal face – the beard, the scarred face – there are facial types that conform to crimes but not everybody does it. Do they?' He frowned at the teacher and slapped his hand on the table. 'We have nobody here who killed more than one person. There are blood feuds, that's all.'

Keith and I asked if we could meet the man involved in the Erbaa shooting. We explained we had met his two relatives.

The three of them looked at each other, then the governor pressed the bell on his desk and in came a warder.

'Tea?' he asked.

'No, please bring in Telli,' the governor said.

'We don't know why this feud started,' said the prosecutor. 'A family kills one man and then another. This is ignorance.'

'They don't consider what they are doing,' the governor said. 'In some places feudalism still survives. You probably cannot understand how strong family links are in our society. That has been destroyed in the West.'

The chief came in with a lean young man. He stood to attention by the governor.

'Tell us why you are here,' the governor ordered.

'Well, sir, the other side killed my brother. They didn't accept that he had become village headman. They met him by chance – it wasn't planned – there wasn't an argument. They just shot him. On 4 March last year I met the other family by chance in the market – they drew their guns and I shot the uncle. Two people were killed and one injured. I am a high-school graduate.'

'Are you sorry for it?' asked the governor.

'We're not for this sort of thing and we don't want this; we're sorry. There was a moving of the heart, with honour at the centre of it. For us honour is everything, it's a matter of respect, protecting rights. The families haven't made friends; they stand apart from each other.'

'Do you like the prison?'

'There are very good things although of course the sweetest thing is freedom. There is TV in the cells.'

The prosecutor looked at the convict. 'He is a good prisoner. He has won our confidence because he is sorry for his crime.'

'Can we talk to him on his own?' I asked.

'No. We know who you are,' said the prosecutor. 'You know Amnesty International.'

'Of course they do,' said the teacher.

'Well, it is against Turkey and cannot be trusted. You all make things up.'

'Have you ever tried to escape?' I asked.

'No!' The convict laughed. 'Even if there were no *jandarma*, I would not try to escape.'

'It's comfortable here,' said the governor. 'Why should they try and escape?' He motioned to the convict, 'You can go now.'

When he had gone, the governor said, 'I suppose you might like to ask about political prisoners.'

'Do *you* think it's right that there should be any?' Keith asked.

'Everyone has laws and people who contravene them go to prison. We have thought crimes, yes, but they are misunderstood abroad. The point is simple. These subversives are not merely writing things, they are trying to destroy the fabric of our society. No other country would accept it. Somebody kills with a gun, somebody tries to kill the country with a pen, and there's no difference between the two.'

This met with approval from the monk prosecutor. 'There were lots of people like that in our prisons. They were trying to destroy the thoughts of the country. If you have a pen, you don't have the right to insult me or my country. It's not the thought that is punished but the attempt to create an uprising, trying to destroy the country.

'You have not felt the terror of these people. Well, I have, and when you have, you remember it. I studied law in Ankara during the anarchy and street-fighting of the 1970s. I made not a single friend. I talked to nobody. It was dangerous and frightening. Students were being shot. There are a lot like me: people who studied and have no friends. We do not forget.'

He stood up. 'I think we have fulfilled our duty now, and I

must leave.' The teacher stood up too to follow him out. But the governor said, 'We must show them the canteen – all the goods the prisoners can have.'

He took us to the shop. It was a little room with shelves running along each wall, and they were well stocked. There were belts and hair tonic, soap and sweets, shaving foam and bags of flour. The governor was animated when we stepped inside. 'You can get yoghurt and Marlboro,' he said. 'Our men want for nothing.'

The cashier was a murderer. 'I killed someone when I intervened in a fight. They gave me fifteen years.'

The prosecutor, leaning against a shelf, said casually, 'You could have saved yourself without the killing,' And then he laughed.

The governor called in briefly at his office before we left the prison. While he was there, Telli came in again.

'Sir, I have some relatives outside the walls who are being told that they are not allowed in. Sir, originally you said that it could be cousins as well as brothers and sisters . . .'

'Yes, well, I have changed my mind,' said the governor, rummaging for something in one of his drawers.

'But sir, they have come a long way.'

'I told you who could come today to enjoy the privilege!' Telli clasped his hands together, pleadingly. 'We cannot make exceptions.' He smiled broadly as Telli left the room, and he flicked his wrist hard, as if he were slapping somebody.

He walked out of the prison with us. He was going home to spend the rest of the day with his family. The other two had disappeared. 'We will be at home today, maybe just to watch the television. I cannot afford to take the family out for a meal.'

Once we had gone outside through the little gate, he pulled some dark glasses out of his jacket pocket and put them on. It was a cold day, but the sun was bright and the air was clear. The crowd outside the gate had grown again, and it was loud. One or two people were shouting hysterically at the guards to be allowed in. In a few minutes the holiday would be over and the special visiting concessions ended for another year. The governor walked through the crowd, ignoring the shouting. 'For the sake of Allah!' cried one man as he passed. 'Please, please. I have come so far. Please tell them to let me in.'

The governor was wearing a smart silvery suit and a starched shirt. He made everything else seem drab and dirty. He made the people standing in the queue seem like a rabble: unshaven, in flat caps and stained trousers. He was heading towards an apartment building on the other side of the river. And when we reached the bridge, he turned to shake our hands.

He was as much a prisoner as those he was guarding.

Keith wanted to go back to the prison gate, to talk to some of those waiting and find out why they were being excluded. When we arrived back, we could see the prosecutor talking to a soldier. We approached the pair. The prosecutor had not seen us.

'Sir, I was only telling them that they could not come in because the exact time for their visit had not come up,' said the soldier.

'Look, they are human beings just like you, treat them with some respect.'

Then he turned around and saw us. He walked into the jail, looking back at us with a strange, haunted expression.

11

The Robot

We took a *dolmus* from Tokat to Erbaa, driving through the sugar-beet plantations and the poplar trees. There were no sharp edges to the landscape, as if somebody had draped a dirty brown blanket across it. For miles and miles, just dirt and poplar trees.

The road into Erbaa was lined with brick kilns. It was a poor town – you could see light through the breeze-block walls of some of the houses. Thirty-five thousand people lived here. 'It's about the same size as Tunbridge Wells,' Keith remarked.

In the town centre there were shops selling concrete and there was a grain market. Circassian firs and silver birches lined the high street. Everybody on the bus had heard of the robot. We asked the driver if he knew the village in which the inventor lived. He said he would take us there.

When the *dolmus* pulled up in the village square – hardly a square: it was a ragged circular space of mud and stones – the place was deserted. But one by one, people came from the surrounding houses. After a few moments, when the driver had explained to the villagers why we were there, they opened the mosque to call the inventor, who was called Huseyin. He was not in his house. Nobody knew where he was. One man went into the mosque to make an announcement across the public address system but walked out, scratching his head. It didn't work.

It was a warm afternoon; the sun dipped in and out of the square, casting long shadows over the houses. Women were axing wood on one side in front of a row of warped two-storey wood and mud houses: not hovels – these were the homes of working peasant farmers.

'He could be looking for friends in other villages,' said one man.

'No, he does not have friends in other villages,' said another. 'He has no reason to go.'

One of the old men beckoned to us to go into the tea house. We sat outside on metal-framed chairs with torn red vinyl seats – the sort you might expect to find in a government office – set out on the dirt. There were chickens pecking around our feet.

An old man leaned across and said, 'Zeki is a clever boy – he's the next one.'

There was a radio in the tea house. As they served the tea, it played the theme tune to *Once Upon a Time in the West.* Keith had brought a copy of the Tokat *Meydan,* and when the villagers saw it, they all crowded around him and asked him to read it out. The old man said that Huseyin had made alarms for cars. 'I can see a proper use for that,' he said. 'He takes the pieces and he builds it but he can't do everything because he can't afford the components. He started four or five years ago. First he made an electric mousetrap; then an electric cradle for putting children to sleep; then he made a house alarm . . .' He tailed off as a slightly built man with huge eyebrows that joined in a tuft above his nose came running across the square. It was Huseyin. He arrived breathless and full of apologies. He did not ask us who we were. Just: 'Welcome! Welcome!'

He took us to his house, around the corner from the tea house. He lived with his family in two rooms. The whole family slept in one bedroom, two children in one bed, their parents in another. Everything smelt of animals: warm and slightly sour. We sat on the bed, which was covered in a multi-coloured quilt. There were a dozen green crushed-velvet cushions on it. It was also the family sofa. Outside in the hall several women were kneading dough in huge bowls. There was very little space in the bedroom. It was crammed with villagers.

Huseyin said, 'I've invented a remote gun and a lamp which lights by air. Wondrous things!' He pointed up to the roof and continued, speaking very quickly, 'And an electric cradle, which I saw in a dream.'

The bedroom was also his workshop. Against one wall there was a cupboard in which he kept his tools – a soldering iron and some screwdrivers. 'You see, I have this television' – an old Soviet set, sitting on top of the cupboard – 'and I take all the components from it to make my inventions. I can only make one at a time and then when it is made I have to undo it, so that I have components for the next. I cannot afford to buy new ones.' Above the old television was a picture of pilgrims at Mecca printed on a cheap green carpet.

Keith showed him his picture in the newspaper, and one of his illiterate neighbours looked at it and said, 'This is an English newspaper?' Huseyin was delighted with the picture. He took the newspaper and stood on the bed, showing it to the assembled crowd.

'My latest invention,' he continued, 'is destroyed because nobody was interested in it. The town council showed no interest in the robot. They didn't give me any money; I don't have a financial position.' He was suddenly quite glum.

He opened the doors of the cupboard to reveal the skeleton of the disembodied robot: a wooden box with a few straggling wires, and a plastic bucket cut in half for its head. Poking through two eye-holes cut out of the bucket, he proposed to install cameras to take photographs. If an enemy was sighted, the machine would report it to a base station. Above the eye-sights were little eyebrows that he had painted on to the blue plastic head. 'It could see for ten kilometres and it could detect movement by radio.' He shrugged his shoulders. 'I've got nothing that works at the moment. It would cost too much to put it together again. It would take a week.'

'Did it really see so far?' I asked.

Huseyin looked at me. 'Of course,' he said.

'How did you become so interested in inventing?'

'I was watching a programme about the Japanese – you know, they were making these machines. And I thought, "Well, if they can do it, why not me?" I prayed and then I started to have the dreams. This was about five years ago.'

He looked on a shelf and produced a file which he showed to

us. It contained his personal papers. He had trained to be an electrician and had attended a course in Izmir, graduating with good marks. He worked in Izmir for a year. He had only had a primary school education and he was proud of his qualifications. He was probably the only person in the village who had travelled so far outside it.

'A month before I went on the course I was married. My wife stayed here, and she didn't interfere in my departure—'

'He is a democrat,' shouted one of the villagers.

'So I came back when I had finished. But the work here is hard. Mainly I am a farmer now.'

'What about the dreams?' Keith asked.

'It was information, it could have been from God, and I would write it down. My dreams are not much of a dream but all about technology; the technical knowledge comes from God. It was the picture of the robot; it was visible—'

A boy said, 'It was a black and white dream—'

'I get the dreams and they developed into other ones – my brain is set up and the ideas come to me. The first thing I made was a voice computer, where you speak and it writes.'

This baffled many in the room.

'What kind of thing is that?' said one old man.

'Anyway, it does not exist any more,' he went on. 'Then I made the mousetrap—'

The villagers warmed to this and one interrupted him: 'When the mouse entered the trap, a light would show. It killed it and then it disposed of it. There were needles, which electrocuted it – and after it died the table moved around and another mouse was allowed in.'

While the man was talking, Huseyin brought out a little black box from the cupboard, which had a small bulb on the top. 'You see, the mouse makes a circuit when it touches the needle and the lamp lights up,' he said. 'The machine could take four mice. I killed fifteen or twenty with it. The light was there to inform me that a mouse was killed – I knew then that my guest had arrived.' There was lots of laughter. As a demonstration, he connected his box to a battery and the bulb flashed on.

'After the mousetrap was the child's cradle. When the baby cried it would rock automatically, and when the thing detected wetness it would send out a signal. So it didn't need a mother. The father would do.'

He had diligently patented each invention with the Erbaa notary. But so far he had not been able to sell any of them. Nobody was prepared to believe that they could work.

'The governor is constantly against me. What did he say about the mousetrap? He said, "We have no mice because we have killed them all with a bait of poisoned wheat." I said, "So the mice eat the wheat and then fall into a stream, and that is no good if you are drinking it." And then the cradle. The governor said there was no need for it. He said a mother can rock the cradle with her foot. I said it would be good for orphanages and hospitals. Finally they agreed to inform Ankara. But there was no news. Eventually, an official told me, "Look – you're a primary school graduate; and we're not interested."'

He was very angry, impotently waving his fists in the air. 'You know, a lot of – oh, what is the word, the old scientists with gold – oh yes, the alchemists and philosophers and Edison were not taught at university. They were born with their genius from birth.'

Once there was some official interest. He invented a machine which could weigh lorries by measuring the air pressure beneath them. The local chamber of commerce was intrigued. 'They said they would get a report from a university. But it never came, I went to the Turkish Chamber of Commerce and they said, "Well, you must publicize it. Have an exhibition." But how can I? I mean . . . and then some senior officials came to the village – the governor and the director of the Tokat professional school. They said, "You are just a primary school graduate. No good at all." Now I am complaining about the government because they don't help me and they should. One of the officials said, "You should go to a foreign country, get your passport. Nobody is going to be interested in you in Turkey." People like you, they said, they don't stay in Turkey. Well, of course, I would like to, but I have no money.' He stopped for a moment.

'And there is another problem. I am not thinking of a new project at the moment. It is to do with the dreams. I do not get them often any more. Even if I did, what could I do? I do not have enough to build another robot.'

His identity card gave his age as twenty-three. But he was probably in his thirties. It was normal in the villages for parents not to register their children until they were seven or eight, so that their conscription into military service would be delayed. That way they would work their fittest years on the family land. He was very, very poor: the poorest in the village, said the others sympathetically. His land produced few crops. He did not even make five million lire a year. 'And all that goes on the children,' he said. In his spare time he repaired the televisions and refrigerators of the other villagers. But he did not have a fridge of his own.

By now the crowd was beginning to disperse out of the house. I was flicking through his file. I noticed that there was a letter from the Turkish Electricity Company. He had written asking for a job. He received a reply – six months later – telling him that he would need to apply through the state employment agency. There was another letter from the public relations department of the Prime Ministry saying that his request for assistance was being looked into. It concluded: 'Very best wishes.'

There was also an editorial from the local Erbaa paper: 'The children are the future of this country . . . he has achieved some experiments . . . he has applied to the local governor's office, but he is told that he does not have sufficient education. He needs help. No inventor was convincing at the first stage. He has always been rejected by society – that has been true since the beginning of the world. We believe things should be done to help this young person and people should be found who believe in him. If there is anyone who is interested we hope they will be able to help him.'

One old man then asked us, 'Are these inventions useful, are they usual?'

Another asked, 'Is it possible?'

They did not expect an answer. We could not have given one.

It was growing dark and it was time we left. One of the boys offered us a lift back on his tractor. He said he was going into town. We said goodbye to Huseyin.

Our tractor driver said nothing for the first few minutes of the bumpy journey. Then he turned in his seat and asked, 'What God do you worship? Did you know that in Norway – or maybe it's Sweden – they see a cow and they stop and worship? Sometimes they worship the sun.'

Later on – we had all laughed about the Swedish sun worshippers – I asked him where the village of the blood feud was.

'Blood feud?' he said. 'We don't have blood feuds.'

'But what about the Tellis? We met one of the boys in prison in Tokat.'

'Oh yes . . . the Tellis. I went to school with him. He was a nice enough fellow, I suppose . . . but if someone kills your brother then he should move away from these parts otherwise he will be killed. I don't know what I would do. But I could kill even though I know it's wrong.' The tractor jumped over the potholes until it came to a halt at the top of a hill on the outskirts of Erbaa.

'Do you know where we can find the village of the Tellis?'

'Yes,' he said. 'It's just over there.'

Girls with jet hair and blue eyes were walking with washing along the banks of the dried river-bed. It was a more prosperous village than Huseyin's. There were brick buildings and a telephone. We found the headman's house on the other side of the river-bed past the school, which had a Turkish flag flying from a tall pole: one of the girls pointed it out to us. The two-storeyed house, with a wooden balustrade, was painted egg-shell blue. Women wearing purple head-scarves and pink and white shirts were leaning on it. Outside children were playing with light-bulb filaments which had been discarded in the river-bed.

We walked into the house. Some villagers were gathered in the sitting-room and they invited us to sit with them on the floor on soft rectangular cushions. They were all watching the television, a children's show with the pop star Baris Manco. He was talking to an old man who had thirteen grandchildren. 'The key to old age is no drinking and no smoking,' said the man. The villagers all laughed. None of them was smoking.

We were not sure how to approach them. Keith and I talked about it in English first. How would they react if we asked them about the feud? It would embarrass them, probably. We did not know which side we were with.

'We heard that there has been a blood feud in the village?' Keith asked as casually as he could. The men all turned. They were suspicious. One of them said, 'They killed a man and those men went to prison. That's all.' They turned back to the television.

A woman was reading a poem: 'How happy are the people in the country where we live . . .'

'The land here is good land,' said one of the men, 'for growing tobacco and for wines. We grow sugar beet and corn.'

And then the headman came in, wearing a little bobble hat, a brown cardigan and big plastic knee-caps on his frayed trousers. The man we had met in prison was his son.

'We have to make an effort, it is not so easy now that Halis is gone.' Halis's wife lived in his house. The old man said that Halis was one of twenty children. He changed his mind: 'More than twenty.' He could not remember accurately. 'But for now let me talk about the telephones. There are two in this village. I have one and it easily calls outside the local area. It easily finds the other place.' His face scrunched into a grin. 'We live in the same village as the Polats, but we are down here and they are up there. We do not want to talk of them; they are our enemies. They are the ones who are responsible for sending Halis to prison.' At that moment one of the women brought a young girl into the room. It was Halis's daughter. There was a lot of laughing. The little girl was taken out.

'Now we must eat,' said the headman with a grand gesture. 'Halis will be the last,' he said. 'Thank God there will be nothing again like that. We have peace in the village now.'

Food came in: fresh french beans, grapes, potatoes and spring onions.

One of the other men said, 'The Polats, we hate them, they killed two of his sons.' He pointed to the headman, and the old man shook his head miserably. 'They are dead – one twenty-five; the other thirty. One was killed on the road; the other in the city. But you must know that the bad people have gone; and they have been killed. So there is no more gossip. There will be peace.'

The other man was angry. The memory was still fresh for him. 'One boy was killed after being insulted. The Polats refused to let him pass through the woods on his way to the village. He had committed no crime. They insulted him and then they killed him. The Polat killers went to prison. You see, we, the Telli, are like a shoal of fish, and they are small in number. The Polats came here after us. We came here during the war of liberation when the Armenians left the village; they came fifteen years after us – the state sent them here because the nation was becoming more populated. They wanted to appoint the headman. They didn't want a Telli *mukhtar* – that was the reason for all the killing.'

The old man weighed in. 'We do not want any more bad things. Only good things. This fight is over now. We only want to work. We all worship in the same mosque.'

The others went quiet. Keith asked them if they were friendly with any other villages, like the one in which Huseyin lived.

'Where is that?' said a younger man.

'It is on the other side of the valley,' said the headman. It could have just as well been Istanbul. 'We don't go out of here. We're happy here, our life is good. Who wants to go to Istanbul? Not us. If you're working, then everywhere is Istanbul. If you sit around, then everywhere is bad.' They were all smiling again now.

'What will you do now?' he asked.

'Well, we are thinking we might go and visit the Polats,' I said. There was consternation.

'But who will take you?' asked one of the men with real concern.

'We can find our own way,' Keith said politely.

'It is dangerous. They are not good people.'

Then we left for the top half of the village, back across the dried river-bed. Asses were moving across the rickety concrete bridge past a small playground.

An old woman with gold teeth came up to us outside the school. 'Do you know Halis?' she asked. 'You don't look to have come from around here. Are you from Tokat? Is he all right?'

Children were playing on oil drums in the dry stream. Out of the bed grew some thick-trunked trees with leaves like those of maple. We walked up past the graveyard. Both Polats and Tellis were buried there. There were a few headstones, but mostly there were just pieces of wood marking simple graves. The sticks had special metal caps on to protect them from the rain. Further up the hill we passed a tea house and asked inside if there was anyone who could introduce us to the Polats. People looked at us oddly and none said a word. We continued upwards until, on a little hill overlooking the house of the Telli headman, we found a second tea house. And this time, when we asked for the Polats, we were asked which one we wanted to speak to.

The first thing we noticed about the Polats was their poverty. The children, and most of the men, wore rubber shoes and some were wearing worn-out flip-flops. The Tellis must have taken all the best land when they first arrived. There were no telephones up here. A dozen men were sitting around in the tea shop with nothing to do, too bored even to play backgammon or to talk. A small boy was wandering around with a wooden bow and arrow. One of the Polat elders asked us to sit with him. He ordered some chairs from inside the shop, and a table, and these were set down on the mud outside. For some reason it was colder here, and the weather was closing in. The sky was darker and there was the very real prospect of rain.

When we sat down, the elder said, 'The feud is finished. We

came here one hundred years ago from Malatya. We are called the Akpolat.'

A lot of men, bored and expressionless, were surrounding us now. It was uncomfortable. The old man continued to talk. 'The trouble was caused by a young man called Akif. He was one of our family, and it was one of our family who finally killed him. He killed the Telli boys. Akif was not an ordinary man. I mean – he looked around him, some of the faces were hardening – 'he was a man God created. How can we know what kind of man he was?'

The little yard was full of Polats now. We were sitting down; they were standing, blotting out the sun. 'I think Akif went mad after the Tellis killed his son. They stabbed him forty times. We don't know why.' The Tellis had not told us that.

'Nobody speaks the truth,' said one old man, looking fiercely at the elder sitting beside us. 'They talk about peace. But there is no peace. Akif is dead, and now we have no more heroes.'

The elder said, 'Why does it happen? It's a small place for so many murders – it is because of ignorance – have you heard of educated people killing others?'

'Some things should not be said,' warned a young man.

'We wanted peace, we always wanted peace,' said another.

The young man turned to him with hostility. 'It is only finished when the guilty party emigrates or dies.'

One of Akif's relatives spoke now, slowly. His feet were thickly encrusted with mud. I could not tell if he was wearing any shoes. 'From a young age Akif was never still; he stabbed people and he hounded men; he fought with police. How do I know why he was like this?'

A young man serving tea walked through the sombre crowd and said, 'I'd like a better life; we'd like to live as human beings; we want to be everything by the heart. I don't want to live here.' People looked at him with pride. 'I have seen Istanbul, as a soldier. I would like to live there.' The elder stood up and walked quietly through the crowd into the tea house. A number of people were arguing with each other, jabbing with their fingers. Keith nudged me. It was time to leave.

'Halis will die when they release him from prison!' a youth shouted. Keith and I stood up and started to walk away. Few noticed, except the boy serving tea who ran across and said, 'It was nice to meet you.'

We were waiting for the bus in Erbaa. In the office the ticket collector said, 'These bloody shootings. They happen all the time.' He took us to the front of the shop and pointed to a number of sharp dents in the metalwork beneath the windows. 'Those were from the bullets they fired last year. And there has been another shooting this year. Tak! Tak! Tak! They shoot each other in the market, and in the street. Tak! Tak! Tak! Just like that.'

12

For You, My Father

Before being
In the town on the coast,
The small river
Did not pass in front of the house.
The lake was far away
And could not be seen.
For the first time in my life
I didn't enter the sea
I didn't eat fish
But
I could smell moss.

This poem was written by a Turkish policeman called Babur. I met him in Sivas, in November, as the Anatolian winter was deepening. The city was caught up in a corruption scandal and the new government had turned on it. The town's biggest factory was said to be full of malingerers, political appointees. It had become news in the national papers. There was talk of old religious feuds fermenting, feuds that had, in the tragic and not so distant past, cost hundreds of lives. The town was in the grip of the worst recession it could remember. It was half the size it had been twenty years before. A million had left to seek their fortunes in the western cities. And most had failed. Sivas was fragile, defensive.

I had never met a Turkish policeman to talk to. Several years ago I watched an officer shoot his gun into a crowd of protesters during a rally in Istanbul. He killed one man. I can remember how the bullet drilled a neat hole dead in the centre of the demonstrator's forehead. There was very little blood: a little fountain erupted from the wound and then nothing. The following year I was attacked by a gang of policemen during another demonstration in the Kurdish city of Diyarbakir. They tried to beat me with a baby's cradle, which was broken and had been abandoned by the side of a road. I started to run away and then I tripped and fell on to the tarmac. They kicked me.

I was surprised when the Turkish government agreed to let me meet a policeman. I wanted to spend a few days with an officer. When we arrived, we did not know which policeman they would nominate.

The hotel had direct-dial phones, an affable cosiness, and three gold clocks above the reception desk showing the time for London, Sivas and Riyadh. Once there were a lot of Arab traders passing through, the manager said. But now the carpet was tattered. Keith and I had tea in the foyer and then I wandered out into town – just a short stroll up from the hotel – to buy a copy of the local paper. The main story concerned two attempted suicides. A local driver had had an argument with his family and had tried to overdose on aspirin. A second man had shot himself. Another big news story disclosed that Sivas schoolchildren would be able to drink milk for free at school because the local governor had arranged it. Seven thousand other poor people would get free coal.

A columnist in the newspaper complained that Sivas had a problem with suicides. It had a large and consistent number. Why? the writer asked. Was it because of poverty? Was it because of some epidemic mental illness? Was it because of the overhanging cliff on the edge of the city? He concluded: access to the cliff's edge should be made more difficult. This would dissuade people. But a psychiatrist writing in another article warned that putting chicken-wire up to stop the depressed jumping off the cliff would not end the problem.

Sivas was once a glorious place to live. Pompey came here after he had taken the city from Mithradates and was greatly impressed. Sivas, he wrote, was the richest of Mithradates' treasure-houses. Sivas was also a key market on the Silk Road and the capital of three Anatolian states. It was from here that Ataturk first ruled his young – and then illegal – Republic. When we visited, there were only 778,100 people living in the city; 1.7 million had migrated westwards.

That night an exhibition of photography was to be opened by the governor. The pictures had been taken by a trainee psychiatrist who doubled as a local art teacher. We were invited to attend. 'Our deputy chief of police would like to meet you,' an official had said. 'He has invited you for dinner afterwards.'

'What is his name?' Keith asked.

'Babur,' the official said. 'You know – Babur is the name of a great Mogul emperor.'

The exhibit was full when we arrived. People were gathered on the steps outside in the dark. Then the governor came. His car drew up at the foot of the steps, surrounded by the blinking blue lights of security vehicles. He stood on a step and delivered a speech about the structure of the arts in Sivas, how it was a tribute to the Republic. He came up the steps afterwards and glanced quickly at a couple of the photographs, then charged out and jumped back into the car.

The psychiatrist was standing next to him. 'As soon as I can I am leaving Sivas,' he said to me, watching as the governor's car drove away. Then there was a cocktail party: people sipped dark cherry juice laced with alcohol – rum or gin? The flavour was indistinct. A teacher of some sort said loudly in the middle of the small gallery, 'Civilizations rise and set in the Middle East and those civilizations are always attacked by other countries. Turkey is like a living museum – a cradle of civilizations. It is still a virgin land – so little has been excavated. Peasants are digging things up all the time.' An architect joined him. 'The mosaic of Turkey is being destroyed; my friends!' He spoke now to the whole room. 'My friends! This is not to be welcomed. Local customs of hospitality are being lost. The idea of just entering a house without knocking is being lost.'

It was a gloomy picture of Turkey that emerged from the photographs. Black and white. Craggy old men, unshaven, sitting on stools staring blankly into space, as if they had no opinions. The title of that portrait was *Yorumsuz*, which means, 'No Comment'. There was a colour portrait of a beautiful girl, erotic, very Turkish, with a thick red gloss of lipstick on her lips, called 'Stillness'.

The official found us in the gallery and said it was time to leave for dinner. We were taken to the only classy restaurant in the town, in the buildings of an old caravanserai. Babur was standing at the entrance waiting for us. It was difficult to see him clearly in the dark, but there was no mistaking his demeanour. He was a tall man, serious and well-disciplined. His entrance was like that of a *pasha* – all the others in the restaurant stood to attention. They followed him in a line as he made his way to the table, and later they brought gifts of fruit, on huge trays, some peeled and sculpted to look like flowers. Babur seemed embarrassed rather than flattered by the attention. He stood in the centre of the room, his brown eyes grim beneath his green cap. He seemed lost for a moment, then he looked at his hand and saw his walkie-talkie. He made quickly for the table and put the machine under a napkin. Then he took off his cap and smiled.

Initially he said very little; the conversation was slow and stilted. But the mood changed after an hour or so. By then the waiter had recharged the flagon of *raki*, and we were drinking it like water. I had gone – my words were slurred – and Babur started to talk. 'I used to watch old television programmes about the British police and would see people saying that they didn't trust them, which surprised me, I must say,' he said.

The waiter came over. Babur said he would have trout – grilled, not fried. 'This is too rich,' he said. People were still coming up to him with gifts: baskets of fruit.

'Do you know I write poetry?' he said.

'No . . . I had no idea at all. I mean, it's not every policeman, is it?' Keith replied.

'Well, I am a poet. Have you heard of Nazim Hikmet, one of our greatest poets? A beautiful poet.'

'Oh yes,' said Keith. We were both astounded. Nazim Hikmet, modern Turkey's finest poet, was a lifelong communist who had been forced into exile because of his politics. He died in the 1960s and there is still a government ban on the return of his body to Turkey. There must be very few such senior policemen who would dare to support him. But there were probably very few senior policemen who considered themselves poets.

'He shouldn't have been banned,' Babur said. 'By the way, do you know of the actor Genco Erkal?'

'Yes, I do,' I replied. Another prominent left-wing artist.

'Please ask him to come to Sivas. He has a new play – readings by Hikmet.'

'There would be no audience here,' I said as a joke.

'I would come,' he replied.

The following morning a car arrived at the hotel to take us to the police headquarters. On the wall of Babur's office there was a montage of dead people, and newspaper cuttings designed to illuminate the dangers of reckless driving. Babur had painted it himself. The room was otherwise unremarkable: a large desk, a handful of police manuals in a bookcase, a couple of pot plants, a queue of petitioners outside the door.

Babur was pleased to see us and he wanted to tell us the good news, striding around the office as he talked. The night-watchman system was being phased out, it had been recently announced. There would be more policemen patrolling on the beat. 'Sivas is a quiet town,' he said. 'Little serious crime.'

On his desk was a copy of *Turkiye*, which in the light of everything he had said the night before seemed oddly out of place. This is the most traditional newspaper in Turkey. But perhaps he was expected by his peers to be reading something of this sort. Sivas was a very conservative town. The Islamic Welfare Party was consistently top of the polls.

A woman came in to plead for a green passport: she was a doctor and wanted to visit America, but her family would not give her permission. Babur agreed to help her. 'It is important that we meet with other peoples. Then we will not lose touch with our Turkishness. More than anything, I hate ignorance,' he said.

Before Sivas Babur was a traffic policeman in Istanbul, a senior one in charge of publicity and road safety education. He talked of these days with great fondness: 'I would have them back if I could.' He had saved one of the pamphlets, and found it in a cabinet behind his desk. There was a painting of an imaginary town, a dreamland: the roads were clean and lined with trees and green grass; the cars were clean, and the detached houses clinker-built, with shiny roofs.

He found other pamphlets, all carefully folded: there was one which taught people how to deal with foreign drivers on the road. They used to drop these, attached to little parachutes, from helicopters on to the streets in Istanbul. Babur borrowed many of his ideas from a German brochure he had once seen. 'Children in England, I think, are taught about road safety by a Green Giant?' he asked. We nodded. 'Here they learn their conduct with a duck.' And he pointed to a little cartoon duck and laughed.

We were due to take a tour of local police stations and meet some of his staff in headquarters. 'Do you know about democracy in Turkey?' He looked down at us from his desk. 'Democracy – it is a lovely word. Full of light. But now we have politicians like children who think they are democrats. There is corruption. I think appointing your friends to office is very wrong.'

There was a new scandal: it had been discovered that 900 people were working at the massive iron and steel plant just outside the town. The factory actually only required about half of this number to do the job. The rest were given work by political and family patrons as a favour. One newspaper article claimed that more roadsweepers than engineers were employed by the plant. In Turkey this is called *torpil*, an important concept. It is not bribery in the conventional sense, which involves money. It is nepotism – the use of influence to win jobs for friends and relatives. Turks do not like discussing it: even the Turkish newspapers are uncomfortable writing about it. The chest-beating over the iron and steel plant was unusual. Perhaps the Turks were tiring of corruption. 'There is little *torpil* in the police,' said Babur, 'but it is good someone is doing something at the iron and steel works.'

He told us to return to the hotel and wait for him there. He would join us later. Outside his office there was a large mural and a bust of Ataturk on a pedestal in the middle distance. In front of that familiar face a large policeman was standing to attention, holding an automatic machine-gun; there were others wearing riot helmets and carrying pistols. No suicides were reported in the local paper that day. Instead, it was disclosed that a man had been arrested for trying to escape the province with a false passport. He had hoped to flee Turkey altogether.

Later Babur came to the hotel. He was alone. 'We know each other now,' he said. 'I want to talk to you as friends. I want to talk.' So we went up to the coffee bar.

'I became a poet when I was very young,' Babur said. 'I write about love and life. I mean, I am only an amateur – of course. I would like to spend more time with it. Sometimes I send the poems to one of the newspapers – *Cumhuriyet* mostly – but I do not use my real name. There was a competition one year and I was commended . . .'

He grew up in the Black Sea port of Trabzon but there was some undisclosed family problem and he and his brother were sent to a boarding school in Istanbul. At fifteen he went to the police academy, the only place, he said, which offered food and an education. His brother became an army doctor. The previous year he had been given his discharge. Babur said that he had been freed. He wished that he too could leave.

'You know, at first, my dream was to be an actor. I wanted so much to study at the conservatory. But there was no money. An actor – imagine! When I was fifteen, I remember that the police were respected. It was not bad then to be a policeman. And I grew to like it.'

He was sixteen when he met his first artist. It made a lasting impression. The artist was an American photographer who worked for *Time Life*. 'Once I asked him to come to my home in Istanbul and I asked him, "What do you think is the best Turkish tradition?" And he replied, "Taking your shoes off."' He laughed again. 'You see, we are very clean people. The most expensive buildings in the Topkapi palace are the *hamam* and the toilets. I may be wrong, but at the same time they were building the Versailles palace and there are no toilets there.'

He was talking and talking, and enjoying himself. Every so often he paused and changed the course of his thought. 'My father was eight in the Russian war in 1893 when they invaded Trabzon. He can remember the Ottomans. He was there in Trabzon when Ataturk landed. A friend of his was killed – by Ataturk himself. My father used to say that if Ataturk killed, it meant the man was against the Republic and democracy. That was how far his love extended. My father remembered that time well – they are our teachers. I think they were our examples – they worked hard, very hard. They taught us freedom, and Turkey is now free.

'Do you read?' he asked with sudden urgency. 'Do you read books? My favourite is the *Tale of Two Cities* by Dickens. It is set against the background of the French Revolution. It was such hard times but it was such soft love. And you know about *Crime and Punishment* by Dostoevsky? Remember Sonia? Remember that love? Pure love.' Then he said that he would have to leave us. He would see us again the following day, but he had to go to a wedding. He was full of apologies.

He had a strange face: ordinary features, correctly proportioned, but they shone with cleanliness. They were ruddy, as if they had been scrubbed. Even the insides of his ears had a sheen. The few hairs that remained on his head were carefully combed across it. Nothing about his face was accidental.

After Babur left, Keith and I walked around the corner to a small apartment block to find the local representative of the human rights association: I had been given the address in Ankara. Here we observed fear for the first time in Sivas. This lawyer was frightened. He sat behind a large wooden desk in a small office with dirty yellow walls. His desk was clear and he was doing nothing when we arrived. He had an exhausted face, with the sinews of his cheeks visible, stretched across the bone, and a sagging yellow bag under each hollow eye socket. It was difficult to tell his age, but I thought he was in his sixties.

'The truth,' he said, 'is that I don't know it any more. Torture? Abuse? There are students they detain and they claim torture. But when they leave the police station, the doctors always say that there has been no torture. We cannot say that this is the truth. A truth perhaps. Whenever people are questioned, they get knocked around. I haven't seen any incidence of torture against people here. But in general when people are detained they are questioned for a long time with blindfolds and held in confined spaces. This is not done by educated people. Unfortunately victims are not allowed to sleep. The blindfolds are there to ensure that the questioners are not known – particularly if they are political police.' He said it again: 'Political police.' He was wearing a pin-striped suit which was badly stained. 'You see, nobody trusts the association any more. It is known as a left-wing group but even the left-wingers do not come to us any more. I think they believe we work for the state. I have resigned in any case.' He did not say why.

'Upstairs in this building there are some students. They write for a magazine called *The Struggle*. Sometimes they are arrested.' I had heard of this magazine in Istanbul; it was an underground newspaper for the militant left.

'Your files?' Keith asked. 'Can we see your files?'

'We do not have any files. I have resigned. I told you that.' He was frightened. Perhaps of us. 'It has wrecked my life and my business, but the police treat me as kindly as they can.' He looked out of the window and then towards us. 'They have never tried to close down the Sivas branch. Some people accused me of not working hard enough, but our powers were limited and no members of the association are allowed into prison. We feared the closure of the branch. In general, people don't look favourably on the work we do. This is our fault. It is a conservative neighbourhood. There have been no threats against me; but people are a bit reserved.'

And then we left. 'Please, I wish I could have been more help,' he said.

Keith and I went upstairs to the room occupied by the magazine correspondent. The place was very run down. There were some pieces of card on the walls on which had been stuck small passport-size photographs of dozens of men and women, most of them young; some of the women wore their hair in schoolgirl buns, and frilly-collared school-girl blouses. Above the pictures was the word 'Martyrs'. All these people had been killed since 1991. There were two new pictures – deaths in the previous fortnight. One or two had died in Sivas but the majority had been shot in Istanbul or Ankara. Some had died in prison. They were members of the outlawed Marxist radical terrorist organization Dev-Sol – the Revolutionary Way. There was some Dev-Sol literature in the shelves by the door, and a stack of old magazines. The current edition described how the two most recently killed had fought for freedom against the state. There was nothing from Sivas in the magazine. There was a boy in the room, probably about twelve years old, and nobody else. He said, 'The correspondent is not here.' So we took a copy of the magazine and left.

On the ground floor of the block there was a bookshop with Turkish translations of Lenin, Marx and Castro on the shelves and photographs of Yilmaz Guney, the radical film-maker, for sale. There were postcards of blank-faced Turkish peasants, with stanzas from Hikmet poems underneath. On the door there was a poster advertising a play at the local student theatre: 'The Memoirs of a Criminal Lawyer: A Black Comedy.'

There was a lot of poetry for sale. In modern Turkey poets are usually left-wing, sometimes communists, protesting. Under the Ottomans poets were members of the élite that governed the Empire, part of the establishment and among the most influential members of society. I was surprised that a place like Sivas would tolerate a shop like this. Poetry today polarizes society: the new poetry is the champion of fairness and of integrity, of liberal values. It is the enemy of the old order: the rigid social hierarchy, the *torpil*, the sleepiness, the fatalism.

The shopkeeper, a young man with a goatee beard, said that his father was a poet. He offered tea in a nearby café, the Halikarnas, named after a left-wing writer who had been internally exiled to the seaside town of Bodrum and then called himself after the narcissistic god. The young man had trained to be an actor at the Istanbul conservatory, as Babur wished he could have done, but he returned to Sivas during the street fighting of the late 1970s to help his parents. He was not a militant, he said, but was caught in one battle. He was shot through the hands and in the shoulder by right-wing gunmen. His father was shot eleven times. 'He still has a bullet in his buttock,' he said. Seven years ago his father had a stroke and now he could not speak. The conservatory would not take him back, so he never graduated. There were many Turks whose lives were disrupted by the fighting. It victimized ordinary people and turned them into radicals, right as well as left. He had been working in the bookshop since 1980. In the beginning the army used to burn their books. Things had improved recently, he said, but they were still harassed by the police.

The shopkeeper had greased back brown hair and hazelnut eyes and was wearing cowboy boots. There was a painting on the wall beside him of a girl behind a gate, with a red and yellow face, all enclosed in a psychedelic purple border. 'I like the IRA,' he said. 'Fighting for freedom.' He waved across the room. 'You should meet my friend.' He pointed at a man sitting on the other side whose face was dark and shrivelled like the surface of a prune. He spent a decade in prison and was released in 1990. 'He was tortured.' He looked at us but did not come over to the table.

Two seats from him was a man in a smart blue suit, wearing a tie. He was pretending to read the newspaper, but it was obvious to everyone that he was a policeman. 'You can tell,' said the shopkeeper. Ten days ago, he went on, some students had been beaten up and others arrested because they had books by Dev-Sol in their possession. Nobody knew what had happened to them. The literature was in fact legal in Turkey, but the police still harass those who flaunt it openly. Sivas has a long history of dissent. It was the home of the first Dev-Sol martyrs, who died in fighting in the early 1970s and became home to Nazim Hikmet. He was internally exiled for a time to a small town in the province called Zara. On the one hand, there was the history of Sivas as the first city of Ataturk's young Republic; on the other, this alternative history of dissent.

In the newspaper the following day there was another report of a suicide. A man had hanged himself inside a barn. The doctors attributed this to depression. The paper also disclosed that the local council was to give free circumcisions to those who could not afford it. That is real poverty.

We met Babur early to begin our tour of Sivas. He sat in the front of the police car. 'Sivas has some unusual characteristics,' he remarked. 'Both in Sivas and in Turkey there hasn't been a noticeable increase in the number of suicides. But some days you can notice an increase.' We passed a police compound where 150 families lived behind barbed-wire walls. Next along was a small hill of earth, almost a dune, with sandy dust swirling along the kerb. There were a few saplings planted in the eroded soil and a sign: 'The Black Sea Forest'.

'Ah yes,' he said, 'I did this with some of my friends from the Black Sea. We did it with our wives and children. But we couldn't find so many trees . . .' We drove on. 'Yes, the suicides. I mean, mainly it is the young students. It seems to be the subject of love that is most often responsible. When we look at the reasons, it seems to go in that kind of order. The next main area is a lack of success at work. There are economic problems here.'

We passed empty red apartments. The builders had simply stopped working a while back. Nobody seemed to know what had happened. Babur said how important family relations were and how this would help bring down the suicide rate. He was worried that Western culture encouraged suicide. 'Turkey shouldn't adopt Western culture,' he said. 'In the West, unfortunately, eighteen-year-olds are able to leave home and they get lost.' There were not the trees of Tokat, which was greener. Sivas was on a more exposed plain. 'Here those who cannot support themselves receive help from their parents.' Above the high street there were some banners. One said: 'The villager is the *efendi* of the nation.' 'The police,' said Babur, 'are a separate community in the town.'

We drove into the suburbs. There were some old wooden houses, but mostly it was new building – straight up and down, cheap, with little iron balconies. There were children playing football in the road. Babur said, 'I am very interested in old historical buildings. I'm very sad that so many cities have lost their historical characteristics. It makes me very sad to see how we have been losing these places in recent times here.' He told the driver to stop the car and we watched some workmen smashing the walls of an old house with long hammers. 'When I see that I am sad.'

We arrived at the oldest police station in Sivas, in the poorest area of town. It was a tiny place. By the side of the entrance there was a small wooden pavilion on a terrace so that, as Babur put it, 'People can sit and discuss.' Around the edge of the terrace there were rows of old paint and fuel tins filled with earth and small flowers. Keith and I started to walk towards the door but stopped after a moment and looked around. Babur was kneeling by a can, touching one of the perfumed orange blooms. He turned and snapped it off the stem, and he gave it to Keith. 'I don't know the names of these flowers,' he said. There were plants everywhere. In the foyer there were large oil drums stuffed with flowers. It was an old, cold concrete building, with no carpet on the floor. It stank of piss.

The station was named after Osman Nuri Gezmen, who was the most famous policeman in Sivas. There was a picture of him in the foyer – fat-faced – and the dates 1926–1973. Babur explained that he was 'very successful in relations with the public. There were some financial difficulties in setting up the station – but Gezmen had the building erected with the help of the people. He died of a heart attack, and it was the desire of the citizens that the station should be named after him.' There was a quote below the photograph engraved on a metal plaque: 'He who serves the people is he who is shown respect.' Beneath that stood a young policeman holding an orange-flower. I looked around the room. All the policemen were holding small orange-flowers.

We were directed into the station chief's office. He had a few black teeth in his fat mouth. In one corner of the room there was a fish tank, burbling, filled with an exotic variety of strange tropical fish, with golden bodies and black tails. The chief asked us to sit on chairs next to it.

Babur motioned to him to talk. He was sitting behind the chief's desk, fingering the blotting-pad. The chief sat on a hard wooden chair by the door. 'There are 50,000 people in this area but there is not much crime. We try to help the citizen. There is nothing being looked into at the moment in this police station. Nothing at all.' A constable came in with tea and biscuits. A small tray of butter shortbreads. He passed around a bottle of bright lime-green cologne.

The police chief continued, 'The most recent event was a quarrel between two families. We sent that to court – there were insults and a minor assault but the court set them free. In the last nine months there have been eighty-five events. There are no unsolved crimes. There are car thefts and woundings, and child kidnapping – a girl was kidnapped for marriage. That's all. And the suicides. There have been six of those.' He was pointing to a wipe-clean chart on the wall which listed all the crimes and he filled in with a pencil.

'Kidnapping?' Keith asked.

'Well, not exactly. Mostly it is by mutual consent. We understand it is love, but the families report it as kidnapping – they do not want their daughter to be married and lose her virginity, so they report it as kidnapping. It's a poor area.'

'Have there been any political crimes?' I asked.

'Nothing against the constitution. It is quite a religious area.' He paused. 'There are eighteen police here. You could argue that it is too many. Things are easier for us now. In the early days – twenty years ago – we didn't have walkie-talkies. Even in Izmir – a big city – there were only twenty vehicles. Of course,' he hesitated, 'there was a bad time during the 1970s when incidents increased. But this was because of social events and they disrupted relations between us and the people.'

Babur, who had said nothing, then looked at the chief. 'I was head of operations in Izmir for a while during those days. Twice we were involved in armed fighting but we were able to arrest people without using weapons. Once, four police officers were wounded. We were in the position of being able to wound members of the public. We could have done that. But it is very hard to kill people.'

There was silence in the room.

'In the UK and in America – maybe if it had happened in Britain, maybe you would have killed. We watched American training films and in America they can say halt and then they can fire. It was a very difficult situation, one doesn't forget after twenty years, it's as if we are still living in that situation.'

I waited a moment and then said, 'Have you ever killed anyone?'

'That was the situation, that's all,' he replied. He looked tired. He stood up to leave.

The chief said, 'We like people; fish – everything. We like all people.'

We were back in the car before we spoke again. Keith broke the silence. 'I wonder . . .' he said. 'We hoped that you would show us around the Ataturk museum.'

'I don't have much time, but you are my friends.'

We walked quickly around the building, an old school-house where the original Sivas Congress that first declared Turkey a Republic was held. He took us into the classroom in which the meeting had been convened. Delegates sat behind old wooden school desks and debated. The room had been preserved exactly as it was. On each desk there was a photograph of those who attended – some with turbans, others with the fez, and others bare-headed. Ataturk sat at the front behind the teacher's broader desk. There were cabinets at the back filled with old memorabilia of the Congress: teapots and milk jugs. On the walls were more photographs. There was one of Ataturk lying asleep on the snow, wrapped in a great coat. 'This Is Being A Soldier', the caption read.

'This is the most important place because we live with this history. Really it is moving to think that such important decisions were taken in such a noble, undecorated place,' Babur said.

Ataturk's bedroom next to the schoolroom had been preserved, with its lacy bedclothes and great iron bedstead. 'This is moving and I always bring my guests to this room. They are all affected and some have tears in their eyes. It is a very important part of our history.' He came here once or twice a year, and yet he still stopped and stared. In the cupboards, cutlery once used by Ataturk was displayed. There was a plate and a water jug, an ugly thing with hand-painted pink and yellow flowers curling around its body.

In the neighbouring room there was a telephone: an old field telephone with cloth-like flex and a wind-up handle. It played a recording of Ataturk giving what has become known as his eleventh speech. It was an unexpectedly shrill voice that called the Turks to arms.

'One of the ministers came here a while ago and he cried when he heard it,' Babur said. It was true: there was something moving about hearing the voice of a man after all the statues. In the next room there was an amazing collection of bric-à-brac – old 78-rpm recordings of the national anthem, pendants from local sporting clubs protesting their love of Ataturk. And everywhere there were pictures of him: at Harbiye military school in 1902, when he was a fat kid with a thin, boyish moustache; the elegant Ataturk with a long French cigarette-holder. This was another world: civilized, progressive and beautiful. There were many beautiful things in these rooms.

Outside on the street Babur stood by the police Renault for a moment. 'I would like to see you tonight if you are free. I will pick you up. Perhaps we can go to see some belly-dancers.' He clambered into the passenger seat and reached for his seat-belt.

'Babur,' I asked, 'we were told we had permission to see the police cells.' To see, in other words, who was in them. The headquarters building had special cells for political suspects.

'No,' he said, 'you have been refused permission.' And then the car moved off.

We had our own plans. We wanted to visit the iron and steel factory. The crackdown on corruption by the national government was, according to the newspapers, going to start here. Three hundred political appointees would be sacked. This was a war against *torpil*. The city was uneasy about this. In the restaurants people talked about it. Sivas was frightened of more unemployment.

When it was first built, the factory was heralded as the city's saviour. It would provide jobs and work for local businesses. It was half an hour away on the road to Kayseri: a vast steel building on an empty plain. A lifeless area. In its shadow were some peasant villages: mud houses, children without shoes. Outside the huge building there were dozens of men in blue uniforms lolling around. The receptionist showed us into the office of the technical director. We had no appointment, but nobody was busy. The technical director came in after a few moments. He had mad, tufty hair, which stood at oily angles to his scalp. His chair was a violent rainbow of colours: red and yellow. It was a big room in chaos.

'Why have you come?' the man asked in English. He seemed friendly. 'Oh, it doesn't matter. Everything here is OK. We have waited for five years but now the plant is working. The rolling mill is operational. We have no technical problems; we are just waiting for the scrap metal to arrive.'

'So you have not yet made any steel?' Keith asked.

'No.'

'But you have a thousand workers?'

'Yes – and about that you cannot ask me anything. I am not a politician.'

'Why is the plant here – in Sivas, I mean?'

'No comment,' he smiled, and lit a cigarette. 'This is a political thing. Could have been anywhere.'

'But the steel is useful for Turkey,' Keith commented.

'Not really – we are making it all for the Chinese.'

'Where are the machines from? They are from Turkey?'

'No, from Britain, Japan and Belgium.'

'I see,' said Keith.

'Look, I am very tired now and I would like you to leave.' He did seem tired. His feet were on top of a stack of files on his desk, and he was scratching his ear. His eyes were bloodshot, and he was unshaven.

There was a fish tank in the office, with some fluorescent fish with tall spines swimming about. 'Actually, this is a minimal plant and we only need about forty people to run this factory. We don't need any unskilled at all. We just get scrap in and process it.' He lit another cigarette.

The whole place was miraculously quiet. His windows were open and the office was opposite the plant. But there were no machines grinding or whirring. There was nobody talking. You could see people outside the window, just sitting.

'A lot of people are unemployed. Everybody wants work but can't find it. Maybe there are people working for work's sake.'

'Is this *torpil*?' Keith asked.

'To get into work everybody relies on other people. Every new government changes and they want their friends. We only need skilled people and we don't find them here in Sivas. The bosses say that the newspapers are wrong. But *they* are wrong. We only need a few people. You can see bloody *torpil* everywhere in Turkey. I only want to make the place damn well work. Don't ask me any more. Only technical questions.'

He swung his feet on to the floor and walked in front of his desk, pulling at his hair. He asked us to promise that we would not name him. 'Oh God, I don't suppose it matters.' He lit another cigarette. 'This is supposed to be modern industry that is going to modernize Turkey. But I can't fire anybody without permission from Ankara. The roadsweepers are appointed in Ankara. All job applications go through Ankara, and if you know someone then you will get the job. You know, we talk about this all the time, but nothing happens.' Even the secretary, who had come in to take our tea cups, laughed at the talk of roadsweepers being appointed in Ankara. 'But it is serious,' said the manager. 'It is like a disease holding people back. In Japan the people work hard. In Sivas, they sit and listen. Why do you care anyway, it is not such an interesting town?' He stopped. 'Go on, I don't know who you are. Will you just go now?'

His secretary, in a state of great excitement, organized a driver for us back into town. 'There are lots of drivers,' she said, and then she laughed a little.

The driver was full of chat. 'How many people are there . . . who just, well, sit around doing nothing? I mean, nothing at all?' asked Keith, who was in the front seat.

'Oh yes,' said the driver.

'No, how many?'

'Well, yes, a few. But I'm safe. You see, I'm the manager's driver. My job is not through *torpil*. I have no relations at the factory and I don't know the director-general. You have to know him, you see, to get a job. It's no use knowing one of the staff.'

'Did anyone get their job by paying a bribe?'

He looked at Keith. 'I live here.' He stared at the road. 'Turkey is at a crossroads. You see, we have to enter a new era – the person who deserves it should get the job. The plant is the new Turkey but the old has already taken it over.'

The driver dropped us at the hotel, and we found a message from Babur. It said that we should meet him at his friend's shop around the corner.

The shop was full of furniture – armless sofas covered in polythene sheeting, and odd items such as children's bicycles hanging by rope from the rafters. We told Babur's friend, the owner, that we had just been to the iron and steel plant.

'I am really surprised there is so much corruption,' I said. As he was Babur's friend, I thought he would be like Babur. He had another friend in the shop and said, 'Talk to him, for God's sake. He works there.'

The friend said, 'Well, they say they're going to sack them. But none have gone. You know the plant was supposed to save Sivas. Corruption, filthy corruption. The politicians . . .'

'It is a disease which is killing this country,' interrupted the owner, who was short and fat. 'I'm telling you, the only solution is for a firm hand. This democracy just encourages the filth. The left, the filth. It's time for a new, firm politics to clean up.'

It was dark in the shop and we felt cold, sitting on cellophane sofa wrapping. He had a customer so he wandered off, returning a few minutes later. 'Where were we?'

'Well, actually, I know this is sensitive but . . . I was just interested in bribes. I thought everybody was up to it. I mean, don't people – you know – sometimes bribe the police?' It was sensitive, and I sat quite still. The television was on in the office, which was at the other side of the shop. You could hear a man's voice reading the news.

Babur's friend laughed. 'Well, what do you think? Ninety per cent of the police take bribes . . . If the richest man does it, why should the poorest man not do it? Everybody knows these filthy politicians take money.' He looked at his friend, who was laughing as well. 'They come to me for furniture. I don't give them money. Maybe a chair, you know, if they will get a friend out of jail or if you are drunk and you want to avoid prosecution. Everybody does it. Not always money – maybe a meal, perhaps.'

'So many policemen?' I said.

'Not all. Probably Babur is the only exception. He is an honest man. I know that he must find it difficult on his salary. They don't earn much. But he was in the other day and he actually bought some furniture. He bought it on hire-purchase. I do it with politicians – you know, give them something for a favour. It is normal.' If Babur was a good man, then he must be a lonely one to keep such perverse company. 'Yes,' he declared, 'I am fascist. Look at the Turks today. All they are good for is instant luxury. We can eat, sleep and drink. That's it. Look at *Tan*.' He picked up his copy of the downmarket newspaper, full of naked girls. 'We have to go back – the Middle Ages was cleaner and less dirty. The Imperialists, the Americans, are responsible for everything.' He continued, 'The Japanese come here to research laziness – Did you know that?' The TV in the office was broadcasting a soft-porn movie. We could just make out from our corner of the room the silhouettes of a man and a woman embraced in dubbed passion; the groans, exaggerated for effect, by the Turkish voices. 'A bloody disgrace . . .'

Suddenly Babur pushed open the door to the shop. He was wearing a grey suit. We went to the Castle *gazino*, the only night-club in Sivas. There was a curtain erected across the back of the hall where the women could sit, but we arrived early and Babur was allowed to sit there. It was a large, dusty, wooden auditorium.

'The music is too loud near the front,' he said. He ordered whisky and *raki*. His friend drank both. The musicians were already at work: the *ut* (an ancestor of the lute), a violin, two drummers. The music was loud, played through amplifiers, but it was warm and husky, and full of rapture. The audience was small, but after a few minutes the belly-dancers came on to the small stage, and then jangled their way between the tables, too fat for wild acrobatics. Babur leaned across when one passed, and gave her a note. She pinned it to her glittery brassière so that it rested on her cleavage. After a while, as others gave her money, the notes hung in one long tail from her breasts.

More people were arriving. The place was becoming warmer and smokier. Babur was smiling. He was happy. We were smothered in a thick syrup of tawdry romance and the atmosphere was sensual, even exotic. The coloured lights above the stage blended into the dark wood, and behind the net curtains, which were like a mist, the dancers became young, beautiful women.

Some young people were sitting at a table behind us. I remembered one face from the Halikarnas café. They got up to dance with their arms outstretched and their fingers clicking, circling one another. They motioned to us to join them. Babur was joking from his chair, feeling stiff in his suit, his walkie-talkie hidden under his napkin.

The sweat gleaming on our faces, we sat down to eat: goat's cheese and chopped liver, deep-fried in flour and spices, green beans in olive oil, honeycomb, strained yoghurt and mint. And then, after the grill, the fruit: mountains of watermelon and honeydew melon, apples, bananas, oranges.

Babur was talking about justice. 'At least,' he said, 'Turkey is not like a Latin American country.' Turkey could have become one. That was true.

'Oh, come on,' said the shop-owner, 'we should not talk of these things. These people,' he pointed at us, 'are young.'

Babur leaned across the table. 'Have you heard of the poet Ataol Behramoglu? I think he is a fine poet.'

'Yes, yes, I have,' I replied, and then after a moment's pause, 'You know that there is a bookshop in Sivas which stocks some of his work?'

'No, but you must tell me where. That is a surprise to me.'

'It was to me.'

'You know, I don't care who is left-wing or right. There is already too much of that.' He was drunk. His friend was shocked.

Babur summoned one of the waiters over to the table and requested a song. 'Livaneli, please,' he said. Livaneli is one of Turkey's best singers, and one of its most liberal. The orchestra played a favourite song, and the students behind us clapped and started to dance again. This time Babur joined them. Would it have made any difference if they had known he was a policeman?

There was a break after the song, and after a few moments one of the students started to sing. It was another Livaneli song, about peace. The whole room was silent. She sang a verse and then others began to join her, until the whole room was with her, Babur amongst the loudest.

The following morning we returned to meet Babur at the police station. He had promised the night before to introduce us to some other senior officers. The head of the smuggling division came in first. There was not much going on: a few false passports, a little gun-running. Babur was wandering around the room checking his plants. He had asked for a Nescafé, which was provided in a sachet on the saucer of a cup of hot water. He was watering a plant with the water.

'Occasionally we get some tourist trying to smuggle some antiquity out of the country,' said the head of the smuggling division. 'I don't know, they go to Ararat for six months hunting for Noah's Ark and stuff like that.'

'He used to be a primary school teacher,' said Babur, looking up from one of the plants.

The head of the CID joined us. A university professor had been murdered. A worker from Austria had been killed. The police found out that he had been killed by an angry coach driver after he asked to be dropped between official stops. 'The man just threw him out of the bus and he died when he hit the road.'

There was a third man in the room, who looked coldly at Babur, by now back behind his desk. This man, Babur said, was responsible for the political police. He was slumped on a chair in the corner, almost hidden from our view by a large straggly pot plant in an old jerry can. He took a penknife from his pocket and started to trim the dead branches. He was wearing a tight blue suit, which was uncomfortable even to look at. His eyelids were deformed. They covered half his eyes, like dark hoods.

'Are there many political problems?' I asked.

'There isn't any politics here now. We just collect information now, that's all.' He was nipping at the side of a branch with his knife, worrying Babur with his vandalism. I noticed that he had very small feet. 'The Baha'is are here, though, and we investigate them . . . there are the Alevi but they are very good and we don't investigate them. There are no problems.'

Baha'i. I had no idea: Baha'is in Sivas – and a political threat.

'Did you ever think of becoming a Muslim?' he asked me. 'Are you circumcised? You see,' said this weasel man, 'we do not trust the British. Your police – they have shaken us. We thought they were the font of human rights.' He clicked his penknife closed.

'What do you say to all those people who complain about the political police?' I asked.

'People complain sometimes about wrongful treatment but there is usually nothing wrong. There have been no complaints about ill-treatment while people have been in the police station.' He was nearly shouting now. 'Maybe in *other* places but not here.' He stood up to leave. The two others, who wore uniforms, saluted Babur as they left, but the political policeman only glanced at him and then turned quickly into the corridor.

Babur stood up to close the door. 'There was an incidence of police corruption and . . . the person was dismissed. He was judged by the courts and was sentenced.' His brown eyes were focused sharply on us, austere and stern. 'The policeman was arrested and then released but he told a friend about it and the friend told us, and when we were able to confirm it we went into action.' He sat down. 'I have been sincere with you.' Keith was examining a metal badge on his desk. It was a plaque of some sort, with Ottoman words engraved on the surface. 'This is what they used to wear on police helmets,' Babur said. 'It says Security Police Official. It is a genuine antique.'

Then he opened a drawer and produced a few sheets of paper. 'Poems,' he said. 'I looked them out for you.' And then he started to read one. It was entitled '*Ozlem*', which means 'Longing'.

> It was as if the coasts had become distant
> Shared coasts can no longer be heard
> The spring of longing overflowed
> The happy echoes were silenced.

He read slowly, with precise diction. He held the piece of paper in both hands, like the wheel of a car.

> In truth the sleeplessness of the sandy beaches
> Is like the waterlessness of the Sea . . .
> Doors will open to the neighbour
> Curtains cannot stay closed.
> There's no way to avoid a greeting
> And hands will join together only if they stretch out.

In truth not peeling a fruit
Is like not hearing a scream
The flower of the olive branch is bound to open
Even were the meadows of longing to fade
The doves of freedom are bound to fly
Even were the obstacle a miracle
In truth like snow falling on the equator
Or a springtime at the Poles.

He stopped and looked straight ahead, past Keith and me, at the empty whitewashed wall at the end of the office. It was snowing outside. The first snow of the winter.

We stopped at the Turkish Airlines ticket office on the way back from the police station. The computer system had crashed. Nothing could be done, a young girl told us. So we waited for a while. It suddenly occurred to Keith that we should try to call the magazine office and see if the correspondent was there. The girl offered us her phone, as a gesture. Keith nodded his head when the telephone was answered. He meant: there was someone else in the office this time. Keith explained who we were and then put down the receiver. He turned round. 'My God, they've arrested the correspondent. There was a woman, she said we should go quickly. Perhaps we could help . . .'

At the magazine a young woman was sitting behind the desk and a baby was sleeping on the sofa. She said that she was assistant to the correspondent. She said that he had just been arrested. 'I asked you to come when you called. I thought you might be able to intervene or something with the police.' A boy about sixteen years old came in, and the baby woke up. The boy opened a small carton of sour cherry juice and the baby drank it thirstily through a straw. She smiled at the two of them and then said that the correspondent had been been arrested because he had been involved in some protest against the Board of Higher Education, which is a widely hated institution, and a political vehicle. 'Look, I'm sorry, I forgot to ask. You must be thirsty. Let me offer tea.' She asked the young boy to go downstairs and ask the concierge for some tea. The correspondent was covering the demonstration for the magazine. But he was arrested before he arrived. His name, she said, was on a blacklist. The police said he was a suspect terrorist. Neither his lawyer nor his family had been allowed to see him.

'I am very worried for him,' she said. She wore a ragged blue and green jumper and her hair was tied back in a fading violet hairband. She had a fresh, pretty face, and she looked younger than she was – twenty-six. But she was painfully thin: her cheek-bones jutted out under her pale flesh. Her skin was the colour of parchment. She looked as if she had not been out of doors for weeks.

She had been working for the magazine for seven months. She had studied sociology at the local university and since graduating had chosen to be unemployed. Her father was a teacher and her mother a civil servant. She had been arrested twice. Once she was sent to prison for two days for faxing to the Istanbul offices of the magazine a report that eleven people had been arrested in Sivas. Police raided the office just as she was doing so and they claimed she was a terrorist. The second time, she was arrested for trying to send a message to other correspondents around the country. The message was one of support for Dev-Sol militants.

'Does the magazine support Dev-Sol?' I asked.

'No – that would be illegal. But we look warmly on it.' Above her desk was a picture of a man lying under a prison bed, smiling.

The boy returned, shaking his head. 'They will not bring tea because they say we are communists.' She was not bitter: this was not the first time.

Behind the boy came an old man in a dirty trenchcoat. She continued talking. 'The police rarely inform families of arrests. But we try to keep a list. We keep a list of all those who have been tortured as well and . . .' The old man interrupted her. 'My daughter and son-in-law were taken at the beginning of the last academic year – he was studying engineering and the other training to be a doctor – they were taken for questioning and then they were tortured, and taken to the state security court in

Kayseri where they were held for three months and then they were released. They have been held again – yesterday. It is the beginning of the term and if they miss this then they will be out of the university.' He was close to tears. 'They say that these children are members of Dev-Sol; that they are terrorists. But they have never been violent.'

His coat was too large. Underneath he was of slight build, with thick hands and a round, hairy face – a farmer, judging from his boots. He kept the coat on because it was cold in the office. There was no heating. The baby was giggling because the young boy was pulling faces at him.

'No, no, they did not torture my daughter,' the man said. 'Only my son – they used the electric and a fire hose with water in the cells, and electric on the fingers.' He was crying. 'I believe they will be released because they haven't done anything wrong but two of their years of education have been wasted and they are pushed to become anarchists – in Turkey and in Sivas the police are the terrorists. In Sivas the bastards have arrested sixty people for political reasons and they have all been freed. For God's sake, what do I do? I am just a farmer. This is not my world. Politics. Bloody politics.' The old man asked for paper and a pencil, and then clumsily spread the sheet on a low coffee table next to the sofa. The baby came up to the table and snatched at the pencil. He shooed the child away, and it cried. His mother smiled. He was trying to write his name but he could not write properly. He said that he wanted to make a list for us of all the people who had been arrested and then released. His children were arrested the day before we arrived in Sivas, and he had still not been allowed to see them. They were being held in Sivas prison. The old man said that he had been to the prosecutor who promised to let him see them within the next few days. They might be held in custody for months, simply because the local courts had such a backlog of cases.

The correspondent's assistant said that the students had been arrested for attending the funeral of a Dev-Sol activist. This was several months ago. They were arrested and then released and then for no apparent reason a large number of them were rearrested. She was also at the funeral (she was breast-feeding the big blue-eyed baby while she talked) but she was not arrested – she went to the village the day before and did not give her identity to the *jandarma*. They thought she was a villager, a fact which obviously pleased her.

The old man kept on crying, great tears of frustration. 'I am a father, I have two children. I found it hard to make my children study – I found it hard.' She handed him a tissue. 'I can't find my rights. I can't seek them because I'm frightened. Yes, me, a man with many years – I am frightened.'

The woman kissed the baby on the crown of its head when he had finished with the breast. 'You see, they fight a war against us. We have no alternative but to fight back,' she said, gently putting the baby back on to the floor.

'But why is there any need for violence?' the old man asked miserably.

'We must support the armed struggle. It is the only way.' She smiled.

'You must not say you support the armed struggle,' he said. And she looked at him, but did not reply.

'What will you achieve?' I asked her.

'We want a people's revolution, a popular democratic revolution. It is wrong to think that just because the Soviet model has collapsed, communism is not the ideal. Take China. There is a good deal of literature. This will help you understand.' She was not trying to insult me. She was trying to teach me.

'Have you ever read the magazine?' I asked the old man, and he laughed for the first time. The baby sat on the coffee table in the middle of the room, playing with the carton of juice and pointing at the people around him, shooting them with his finger.

Dev-Sol has shot a number of innocent civilians over the years. It is the most dangerous and unpredictable of the Turkish terrorist organizations. It is a Marxist group, but its aims are unclear. It has assassinated British and American businessmen in Istanbul, chosen at random, because it wants to scare off foreign investors. This way they will overthrow the government.

'I did not know they shot a British man,' the woman said.

'But if they did, there must have been a reason. Let me telephone the Istanbul office and ask if they know about it.' She made a call but the line was engaged. That was what she said.

On one of the walls there was a photograph of a beautiful dark-haired girl beneath the words 'We will not forget Seker'. An architecture student, she had been killed in Istanbul earlier that year. Her death had achieved nothing except the extinction of her life.

The old man was still busy writing his list. He said he was going to send it to the press so that it could be published. 'I am going to send it to the Prime Minister and to the Interior Minister.' He had written across the bottom of the first sheet of paper: 'THE SIVAS POLICE ARE MAKING INNOCENT PEOPLE INTO TERRORISTS.'

We did not see Babur again. He was busy when we tried to call him. Perhaps he knew of our visit to the magazine and considered us a liability. We wanted to ask him about the students. Some weeks later, Keith wrote to him at the police station. He never received a reply.

13

'The World is Like an Egg'

Babur's Sivas was disintegrating: an illusion of harmony. His political officer had mentioned the Baha'i and the Alevis. How were they faring?

Sivas had a large number of Alevi residents. The Alevis are the biggest religious minority in Turkey – perhaps as many as 30 per cent of the population. There are no official figures. The Alevis are the Turkish Shi'ites. Like the Shi'ites of Iran, they believe that the leadership of the Islamic community belongs to the line of Ali, Muhammad's son-in-law. They reject all the leaders, or Caliphs, historically nominated by the Sunni Muslims, who believe that they should be appointed according to their ability. Where the Sunnis believe in communal consensus, the Shi'ites advocate authoritarian government.

The Turkish Alevis are suspected and despised by orthodox Sunni Turks. Not only are they feared as Iranian fifth columnists – the agents of Islamic revolution – they are also reviled as heretics. They have been ruthlessly suppressed. It was only in the 1960s that their existence as a minority was even recognized. The Sunni have invented a mythology in which the Alevis are said to indulge in wild living, orgies, the killing of children, the beheading of chickens. Shamanism. It is true that the Turkish Alevis are a heterodox people. They have, historically, embraced ancient Anatolian religious customs and old mystic cultures. Today's Alevis are the descendants of the old mystical sects – the Bektashi most significantly. They have always tended to be in opposition: the Sunni have always controlled the institutions of government. In the modern Republic, they are the liberals, generally supporters of left-wing politics. Many writers and artists are, by birth, Alevi. The patron saint of Turkish poets, Pir Sultan Abdal, was born in Sivas. He was a Bektashi.

Periodically in Turkey the Sunni and the Alevis fight each other. During the late 1960s and 1970s the fighting in some towns threatened to divide communities as finally as in Nicosia or Beirut. Sivas has a dark history of religious intolerance. In late 1979 one long battle cost 110 lives. People still remember the Alevi insurrection of the 1920s in which hundreds were slaughtered by the army of the new Republic.

It was not difficult to find the Alevis. They lived in a ghetto on the edge of the city. It was emptier than it used to be. In the 1970s, before the fighting started again, 20,000 Alevis were packed in there. Many have since left but the circumstances of those who remain have not changed. They are supposed to live in peace; but the peace is an informal apartheid.

There was a tea shop on the main street of the ghetto and it was full of unemployed men passing the time. There was a mischievous chemist called Ali who said, 'The Alevis came to Sivas in 1270, but we are still oppressed in Turkey.' He brought us some tea. 'You know these men all around here are frightened by you. They whisper, "Are they police spies?" This is so fragile.' He laughed. 'If the Alevis are accused of spreading bad propaganda about community relations they will be punished.'

It was warm in the shop, which had a tall wood-burning stove in the middle. Men played cards on most of the table. 'We all live in the one area. Perhaps there are 150 houses now,' said the chemist. 'We are like the blacks in South Africa.' He was being outspoken, and some of those who had gathered around our table to listen looked at him very grimly. The apartheid may not be legal but it is institutional. Alevis find they cannot work as public servants. 'There are no Alevis who have been successful applying for stalls in the main market. I opened a shop here and at first they didn't give me a licence. I appealed to the court and I got the licence from the court but it's forbidden for an Alevi to have a shop outside this area.'

The Alevis, unlike the Sunni, do not forbid alcohol. 'There

were four or five restaurants which served beer but these have now been closed by the town council,' said the chemist. In Sivas, the Alevis are also banned from performing public religious rituals. 'So we have to do it secretly.'

A second man said, 'Sometimes people get arrested. They sit and play cards and then the police come and arrest them.'

This repression has driven many of the young Alevis into sympathy with the radical left. One of the young boys at the table had been arrested two months previously for attending the funeral of a left-wing terrorist. 'I was tortured in the police station,' he said. He spoke with unquenched hatred.

There are those who say that if there had been no Kurdish rebellion there would have been fighting between the Alevi and the Sunni. That would have threatened the integrity of the whole country. There are Alevis everywhere in Turkey, many more than people think.

'Don't stir things!' said an old man to the chemist from another table. 'We feel a part of Turkey, because we support the state – you know, we pay taxes.'

'But the state doesn't look so kindly on us,' said a second. 'We look different, perhaps that is part of the problem.'

'No,' said a third, 'we don't look different.' There is no difference. Maybe they looked wilder, and their clothes older. They spend less time at the barber, judging from the length of their moustaches. Perhaps there is no barber in the quarter.

We wanted to speak to the community leader, the *dede*, and one of the men offered to take us to him. He was in the *saz* house, which is where they made the instruments. The *dede* was said to be a fine musician himself. The shop smelt of glue. He was pleased to see us, and insisted we go with him to his home. We drove through the quarter, past the prison and into a block of newish apartments, perhaps ten years old, and compared to the rest of the Alevi accommodation, in good shape. But it was very, very cold. He said that the heating had not worked for some time. The residents had complained to the town council, but nobody had been to fix the boiler.

We sat in the sitting-room, and he asked us if we would like to drink coffee. He had a jar of Nescafé next to the television. It is expensive in Turkey; a luxury. He found it difficult to bend his fingers around the jar and carry it into the kitchen – it was that cold. Next to the coffee was an empty bottle of Ballantine's Scotch whisky. As he served us the coffee in prim little cups and saucers, he said, 'With the Alevis, the first act of worship is to love people; in our politics Ataturk is number one; our prophet is the holy Muhammad; our sect is Alevi and our Imam is Imam Jafa the Just.' He was a curious-looking man with matted black hair flat on his head – it was real hair, but it lay flat as if somebody had taken a mallet to it. He wore a pin-striped suit jacket over a brown zip-up cardigan.

'But there are some problems?' I said. 'You are not allowed to worship in Sivas?'

'*Cem* is our prayer. It means gathering. It is not conducted in a mosque – we believe that every house is a mosque. We are not obliged to face Mecca. Unfortunately it is forbidden in Turkey. The Sunni say that it is wrong. In Turkey there are many minorities – we hope that with the new government, with its democracy and human rights, this will be over.' He punctuated the sentence with a weak smile. 'We have fought each other. But I think people have begun to see that we are of the same religion, of the same God, the same Koran. Very recently with human rights our complaints have begun to be heard. At last heavy oppression has begun to lighten.

'When I was a boy there was a conflict of ideas and we discussed this through dialogue, but in 1979 one hundred died – a fight between the left and the right. The oppression does not come from the law but from the religious. Indeed, there are even Alevi ministers in the government now.' There was one: the Minister of Justice. 'There is not much discrimination with this new government. But, of course, we cannot get to the European level in an instant. The police do not know we worship in our houses.'

Ismail was first a farmer, and then an iron ore miner, now he is retired, playing the *saz*. 'Ten years ago we used to be second-class citizens, that really was the case. It is better now, but the balance is not totally righted. We would be pleased if we were allowed to build our own places to worship.'

He stood up and started to walk towards the Nescafé jar again. He obviously intended to offer us another drink.

I said to him, 'Do you know that there are Baha'i in Sivas?'

'Yes,' he replied suspiciously.

'Do they have any problems?'

'I don't know and I don't care,' he said with growing hostility. 'We don't like them at all. They are Arabs and pagans.' He put the Nescafé down by the television and sat back in his chair. He did not offer us another cup.

How to find the Baha'i? Not an easy task. We went to the left-wing café, the Halikarnas. I asked one man quietly if he knew where they lived. I was whispering because I worried that the request could cause offence in here as well. 'Yes, sometimes they come to the bar. Some of them teach in the university. Medicine. They are doctors,' he said. 'They realize the consciousness of the people and they try to oppose injustice and they go to prison. They are our friends.' A little later we were given a name. The last Baha'i in Central Asia?

Arnold Toynbee wrote once that the Baha'i were about as well known in the world as the Christians were to Romans in the second century AD. Keith and I knew very little of them when we set off for the university hospital on the outskirts of the city. What could they have done to have upset Babur's policemen?

I had heard of the Baha'i before. A cult? A religion from Persia? Once I had interviewed the jazz trumpeter, Dizzy Gillespie, in Istanbul. He wore a piece of rock in a golden clasp on a chain around his neck. He said he was a Baha'i and that the stone was chipped off a holy mountain in Iran. But that was all. Keith knew Iran – he even spoke Farsi – but he knew nothing about the Baha'i.

The cold was intensifying. The taxi took us past the industrial suburbs, dozens of small workshops and oily garages. Icicles were hanging off the eaves of some of the sheds. Boys were kicking a football down the side of the road. They wore only rubber shoes.

The taxi driver was full of talk. He told us about the latest outrage in the city: how two boys had tried to sell a woman and had been tricked into selling her to a police officer. 'Can you believe it?' he said. 'They would certainly be caught for such a crime. They must have realized.' The car turned into the avenue that led up to the hospital. The newspaper was open on Keith's knee. The lead story was headlined 'In Autumn, The Leaves Are In Place'. We were some way outside the city. From the hospital, you could see right across the plain, past the dirty smoke rising above the city, to the Karkasla mountains, clean white cones of rock. 'Winter falls very suddenly,' said the taxi driver.

The hospital was brand-new, not even fully fitted. The newspaper explained that one old man had waited fifteen days for it to open, camped outside, despite the temperatures. He could not pay for his treatment, so the director of the hospital had agreed to operate for free. Outside there were some thin terraces of foliage and some skeletal bushes planted in the central reservation of the access road, which snapped backwards and forwards in the wind. No shelter from the cold.

We asked where we could find the Information desk. The doorman shook his head. 'No idea.' We asked a doctor. 'Second floor,' he said, and walked on.

At Information, we asked a woman for the Baha'i doctor. 'He's gone to America. They've all gone to America.' It seemed that they had been driven out of town. But then we asked another doctor. 'Umm . . .' he was thinking. 'Baha'i . . . not easy. They have a difficult time over here.' But he did remember one doctor, and so we telephoned him. A woman answered the phone. She invited us to meet her at the family apartment.

The door was opened by a woman of unexpected beauty, with resonant blue eyes, as if they were filled with turquoise water. Her child – there was a girl behind her – was the same: exquisite. They were smiling broadly, and the little girl said in perfect American English, 'Hi! Come on in!' It was a spacious apartment, very comfortably furnished, more luxurious than anything we had encountered since we arrived in Sivas. But there was nothing indulgent about the room. Everything had a purpose: the books, for instance, were all educational, for children and for teachers.

The mother, who spoke only a little English, asked us to sit down. The girl, I noticed, was wearing chunky pink trainers on her feet. Her T-shirt carried a logo for Charlie Brown. Just a normal American kid. They both sat down with us. The mother was a woman of great self-assurance. She looked at us and said, 'Have you come to find out about the Baha'i?'

'Well, I suppose we have,' Keith replied. 'You see, we have been in Sivas for a few days . . .' And then he explained to her what had happened: Babur, the arrests. 'They told us that you suffered as well . . .'

'Let me tell you about our faith,' she said. She gave us booklets in English which explained, and she provided a commentary.

The Baha'i believe that an Iranian scholar and a man of social standing called Husayn-Ali is a prophet. He lived between 1817 and 1892 and proclaimed that he was the messenger of God in the 1860s. He claimed that God, speaking through him, urged mankind to put aside dogma in favour of reason in organizing its affairs; that human beings should embrace science rather than be frightened of it; that they should recognize the importance of education and intellectual integrity. He preached the equality of women, the sanctity of the environment. He urged peace in the world, and taught that all religions shared a common ancestry and should recognize it. It was a religion of enlightened democracy.

In his lifetime, Husayn-Ali was viciously persecuted, along with his followers, by the Iranians, who viewed them as a threat to civil order and as heretics. Thousands were killed: some were blown from cannon mouths, others led to their executions with burning candles inserted into open wounds. The prophet, renamed Baha'u'llah, was imprisoned for a long period and then exiled first to Iraq, then Turkey and finally Palestine. Once he had declared himself the Messenger, he wrote to all the world's heads of state asking them to consider his revelations. Not one replied.

But the Baha'i have been persistent in the face of scepticism, and today they are one of the fastest-growing religions in the world with around five million members. They are also one of the richest and best educated. The emphasis on education and science and logic has proved attractive to the intelligent middle classes. So too has the emphasis on building an international sense of community, and the denial of nationalism. Many Baha'is are professionals; many are also stateless people, driven from their homes.

'There were many things that told of his coming,' our hostess said. 'The world should have been expecting him.' She had a smile on her face, a fixed radiance. 'According to our law we have to pray once a day, and have to fast for nineteen days in March. For the Baha'i there are nineteen months to the year and nineteen days to the month,' she said. There was a chart on the wall: the official calendar. Today was *Bedi* 148. 'Of course we use the ordinary calendar most of the time.'

It was designed as a practical religion. 'You pray three times a day, whenever is convenient, and you should read some verses everyday. Alcohol is forbidden; cigarettes are not advised; you are allowed to eat pork; and you can marry outside the faith. The Baha'i believe in the equality of women, and you are expected to wear what is the norm in the country you are living.' She was born a Turk from Izmir, and her husband, who was not at home, was a Kurd from the east. She was among the earliest converts in Turkey.

'My parents accepted it when I was at high school, we really didn't have much difficulty, but because it was something new – well, we always explain what's going on because we get lots of reactions, some are really positive . . .' She did not stop smiling as she changed the subject: 'In Baha'i sins are forgivable but if you don't educate your children that is not – and you should educate the girl first, above the boy.'

'How did your parents learn about it?' I asked.

'They were converted by a neighbour in Izmir. My mother knows the Koran very well – she shows the verses which talk about Baha'i.' Her father was an expert on control-testing for cotton exports, a university graduate. She taught gynaecology and women's medicine. She said that there were one hundred Baha'i in Sivas, which surprised me.

I asked the little girl if she would show me her ID card. All Turks have to identify their religion. I wondered what it would say. It did in fact identify her as a Baha'i, which is unlikely to be an advantage. By law, all children have to study the Koran at school. For a girl of ten, she took an astonishingly mature view: 'This is the way I look at it: all religions are one – Islam is a very holy religion – but there is no pressure on me at all. My friends have taken it very well – all my friends know that I am a Baha'i. There are people who say, "Don't talk about it." But I like to remember that Turkey is a free country.'

Her mother said that the local Baha'i had been given permission to hold a meeting in the town's cultural centre in a few weeks. 'We have invited all the brass – the governor, the police chief – we are going to explain that we are no danger to the society. Anyway, we have permission.'

There had been arrests. Two years previously, some Baha'i were taken in an outlying village. They were interrogated but then released. 'The behaviour of the police was a bit ugly, but they were not tortured,' said the mother. 'We are respectful of local laws.'

She paused. 'More recently, there was a meeting in Sivas for about forty Iranian refugees and my husband went along. Somebody gave the police the wrong information. The police came and arrested all of them. They did release the children but they behaved very badly in front of them – we tell our children to respect the police but they see this bad behaviour and now they refuse to. My husband stayed until morning in the cells but he was released the next day, after the prosecutor said there was no evidence that he was trying to damage the state.

'After that we decided to promote ourselves so that people do not misunderstand. We have to explain to the officials – the governor is quite an enlightened character. The old police chief was a fanatical Muslim and he tried to stop us getting an office in the town. We went to court, and the court said it was OK, but they have kept it closed on a technical point.'

It is a very organized religion: summer conferences in Turkey and in America, and special schools for the children. It even has its own universities.

At this point the housekeeper came in. She was a local Turk from Sivas, a peasant. Thinking that she must find it difficult working for such employers, I was embarrassed for her. She saw my confusion and said, 'Don't worry. I am a Baha'i.' Our hostess added, 'Some of our people are from poor families – some are very poor – we give them money to buy bread. Even some of the Alevi have joined us. There is one Alevi leader and one Sunni *hoca* with us, and they love each other now.'

Once Baha'u'llah himself passed through Sivas. There was a picture of him on the television set. She looked at it: 'We will have a little peace by the year 2000, because it has been promised to us.'

The housekeeper sat down and smiled. 'Baha'i is the real world religion. It correctly predicted the collapse of the Berlin wall as a step for world union.' She had been converted by the doctor. Now her husband and her six children were all of the faith. They became friends because the old lady had come to this house to help cure a problem that her husband had with his hand: and as they dealt with this problem, with massaging and other tricks, they became close. 'We are Alevis, you see. My husband believed that this was the Prophet who had returned to the world. He was so excited. Now ten years later, without any pressure, I am a Baha'i.'

Life has not been easy for the doctor. She has been investigated by the Council for Higher Education because she had attended a Baha'i conference; but the case was dropped. 'In my teaching I reveal nothing of the religion.' She avoided the charge because she was able to tell the Council that during the 1920s a Swiss

Baha'i called Albert Frel had written to Ataturk himself about the religion and explained it to him. They produced this letter and the Council let them go.

'The world is like an egg,' she said. 'This is a time where the egg goes bad and its contents are used to feed the chick. Like that, we are feeding a new world. There is hope.'

Seven months later, 2 July 1993. Thirty-five people were killed after Islamic radicals burned a hotel in the central Anatolian town of Sivas. The extremists were protesting against the publication of an unauthorized translation of the *Satanic Verses* by British author Salman Rushdie. It was the worst outbreak of religious violence for decades. The translator of the *Satanic Verses*, Turkish journalist Aziz Nesin, was staying at the hotel while he attended a left-wing cultural festival in the city. Many of those who died were poets and artists.

The festival was held to celebrate the work of an Alevi poet, Pir Sultan Abdal. A statue of the artist was destroyed by the Sunni demonstrators. So too was a statue of Ataturk. The riot was in part provoked by a speech made by Mr Nesin in which he said he was an atheist and that religion should adapt to modern times. He also asked why it was necessary to obey books written thousands of years ago.

Shortly after noon prayers, a crowd of people waving their fists and chanting Islamic slogans attacked the festival. The crowd turned on the hotel in which participants were staying and stoned it, set fire to cars outside it and shouted for the 'devil Nesin'. After eight hours, some radicals managed to gain entry to the hotel and set fire to the lobby. Fumes from synthetic materials were responsible for most of the deaths.

The Interior Minister, Mehmet Gazioglu, was quoted as saying, 'By standing against public beliefs and making inflammatory statements, Nesin provoked the attack in Sivas.' Police were blamed for not acting fast enough to prevent the fire. Senior officers refused to comment on allegations that policemen had been actively encouraging the rioters.

14

The Magic Fish

'There is much about this province that is special, unique. Recently, for example, we had a psychopath,' said the newspaper editor excitedly. 'Yes, yes. Two children were killed by a man who also killed their aunt. He raped the aunt, you see, and the children saw him. The mother of the children was in Istanbul, but the children wanted to stay with the aunt. The man knocked at the door late at night – he didn't know the children were there. Then he knocked the woman out and raped her. The children were watching television. They didn't know why their aunt didn't answer their calls. They started screaming when they found her and so they were both killed with a cable and then he – the man, I mean – chopped them up with a knife – well, he didn't cut their heads off, that's true. He did the same with the aunt, locked the house and went out.

'For two days nobody knew what had happened. The kids, obviously, were not at school. Neighbours could see that the house was locked but people thought they had all gone to Istanbul. Their grandfather, who was in Istanbul, phoned the house and got no answer. He phoned the murderer himself to ask if he knew where the children were. Could he have a look at the house and check all was well, the grandfather asked. The psychopath's father then telephoned the police and they found the bodies but it wasn't known who killed them.

'A year later they arrested the guy and then he confessed; it was right in the centre of Sivas. And there was a huge reaction among the people. People felt terror – it was the way I reacted. The people wanted to kill him. They caught him because when they suspected him they sent a woman police officer to him and he tried to kill her too. We don't know if he murdered others. Maybe.'

The editor of *Hurdogan*, the Sivas local newspaper, was telling us what made the province different, what it had to offer. This murder, he said, had a grave effect on the town. There were calls for a return to a better religious life. Most people believed that it was an act of God, inspired as some evidence of their collective wickedness. The editor said, 'Some thought it was proof of urban degeneration. But others thought it was normal: if I fall, for instance, into great financial problems and get into a depression, maybe I could become a psychopath . . .'

He set up this newspaper with his family's money. It was his dream – to be a pressman. He was young and slim and quite intense. By night, he worked as a computer operator.

'God is very involved with Sivas. He sent a meteor to the town. I took the photos for seventy-seven television companies, including CNN. It fell over a village, but nobody died. It came down on open land. That meteor was in my house for days – it weighed forty kilograms. It was examined in various ways – bits were even taken to Japan. We could hear it land even in Sivas, a huge explosion, heard for hundreds of kilometres round about, and the local villagers thought a plane had crashed. People were very frightened. The next day the governor went to the scene with some geologists. They told me it was a meteor, and the villagers said that it was raining stones. But, according to the scientists – and I am not a superstitious sort of man so I believe the scientists – it had hit a rain cloud, hardened and kept its shape when it landed.

'Well, those are special things. Now . . . let me think of others. Because there are many . . .' He was thinking. 'Yes, yes, the fish. You see, we have curative waters and the fish live in the intolerably hot water when they should not.' He held up a photograph which showed him crouching in a pool surrounded by tiny black fish. Not a natural pool, more like a swimming-pool. 'If you put them in cold water they live, but if you put them back in the hot they die. There is a proverb: the big fish eat the small fish; but here it is different, the small fish eat the big fish. There are also snakes in the water which can cure snake bites. In 1976 somebody came from London who was bitten by a snake. She went to the pool and a small serpent came out of the water and wrapped itself around the wound, and I was there, and her wound started to go white. Incredible!'

The editor told us the name of the village nearest to the miracle pools. We walked through town to the bus station, past the ruins of the Buraciye *medrese* which dates to the thirteenth century. In the courtyard of the Sifhaiye *medrese* there were some small souvenir shops. It was bitterly cold and few of them had any electricity. It was early afternoon and already dark. In the carpet shops they were selling postcards of Christian icons taken from Russian Orthodox churches.

The town petered out abruptly. The last building was the bus station, and beyond it the low, dusty dunes of the steppelands. There were shops advertising tickets to England and Holland. It was a filthy place. Men sold rotten cabbages from wooden barrows; scrap men passed by in traps drawn by mangy horses.

Opposite was the Ulu mosque. Inside it was low and dark, a forest of arches which dated to the twelfth century. It was silent except for the ticking of a grandfather clock. There was a classroom just outside the entrance, and on a blackboard the teacher had written:

'Six Descriptions of God:
That He Exists.
That He Does Not Begin.
That He is Eternal.
That He is One.
There is Nobody like Him.
That He exists by Himself.'

One of the boys came towards us, and then his teacher, who had a beard like a stiff brush, shooed us away from the door.

While we were travelling to Kangal, the town nearest the fish, Keith looked out at the brown world through which we were passing.

'Anatolia is romantic, don't you think?' he asked.

'Not here. I think here it is hard, unforgiving land.'

After an hour, we reached Kangal. Concrete houses with hay bales on the roof for insulation and warmth. Even in the bus people were shivering. There was one old taxi in the market square. We asked the driver to take us to the fish and he was delighted. Thirty minutes later, down winding tracks, we came to Kavak.

On the journey I had looked for water: rivers or streams. But there was nothing. There were no dry river-beds or springs. The place seemed to be waterless. Kavak was hidden at the bottom of a small, steep valley. It was surrounded by a thicket of trees. The first thing we noticed was the mist: hot, damp fog that hovered half-way up the trees. It looked like steam. We could hear the water rushing just yards from where we stood although the fog was so dense that you could not immediately see it. When we walked closer, we saw a shallow river coursing over a stony bed. There were some buildings on the other side across a small wooden bridge. We asked the taxi to wait. We had no idea what we would find. All around the river and the buildings street-lamps cast a sweet orange shadow. We found the office and then the manager's room. He was very helpful, saying that more than 10,000 people each year visited the spring in the hope that it would cure them. 'It is easily the biggest tourist attraction in the area,' he added. Everywhere – in his office, in the corridor – there was a strange, sweet smell, like mown grass. His office was lined with photographs. Each showed a person covered in tiny black fish. They were repulsive. These people had terrible psoriasis, with a scaly caricature of skin.

The manager had been here for six years. The miracle, he said, had been discovered in 1964. 'The fish came with the spring – a shepherd found it. His sheep were ill and he washed them in the water and they had scabies and they were cured – and that was just with the water, not the fish. Before 1988 local people used to come for the day. But now the whole world has heard of it – it has been on CNN.' In 1988 the spring was officially opened as a healing centre. 'It is the only one of its kind in the world. Doctors and psychiatrists come. The water has antiseptic qualities – this is proved by medical science. But why? Nobody can tell. Why there should be these magical fish as well, nobody knows. It is a miracle of God; it is God's wisdom. Fish are not supposed to be able to live in waters of 30 degrees, but this is thirty-seven degrees and the water is very rich in minerals. And on top of that, the small fish eat the big fish in April and May when the water cools down.'

He explained that there were three types of fish in the water, each a different size. They performed different functions. The *delici* fish had a very fine mouth; the *pansuman*'s is wide; and the *imici* have normal-shaped mouths. The *delici* opened up the wound; the *imici* cleaned it; and the *pansuman* closed it. A person with psoriasis – and the condition has to be psoriasis, the fish will not touch the body otherwise – simply walked into the pool and waited for them. After a time, shoals of the tiny fish grazed on the bad skin, drawing blood, and then eventually they left it. Why they come and go like this has not been explained. Nor have the snakes who live in the river-bed and swim into the pools only when somebody with a snake bite is there. How they detect this is a great mystery. But it works. The manager said that sufferers reported a near 100 per cent clear-up rate after the fish or snake treatment. 'The snakes only really come in the summer – they go back to their nests in the streams. They are between sixty and seventy centimetres long, and they suck at wounds.' On the wall there was a picture of some lime-green snakes on a woman's leg; it made me feel quite nauseous.

'This is a holy place and alcohol is forbidden here. When people are here for healing, they eat greens, and are not supposed to drink fizzy drinks. It's not holy like . . . you know, it can't be explained. There is no proof that it is a holy place. It's holy because the fish are a miracle.'

The manager used to work as an accountant. Originally, he said, he was trained to work with metal. He invited us to have a look around the facilities. One of his boys was our guide. We stopped by the river on our way to the pools. The boy leaned down to wash his hands with sand on a bank, and then he spotted a snake in the smoking water. He shouted to us and pointed. All I saw was a flicker of light beneath a stone.

Men were lounging around the side of the pool, trailing their feet into the warm water and talking, as they would in the *hamam*. The pool was like a swimming-pool, tiled around the edges. It was open to the river at one end. There was no permanent roof: polythene sheeting was secured to the walls. During the summer, when it was hot, I assumed that the pool was open to the elements. Walking into this room was like walking into a cloud. It was hot, and unbelievably humid.

We walked to the side of the pool and could see the people more clearly. There were about a dozen men in the water (the women were in a neighbouring building). In one corner, hundreds – perhaps thousands – of minute fish were swarming around one man's face. He heard us walk in, lifted his face out of the water, and turned to reveal a terrible mask of disease. His whole face was bleeding. The fish were biting into it. He smiled and waved at us: 'Welcome!'

'*Gecmis olsun*,' said Keith. 'Get well soon.'

The people here have tried everything to heal themselves, but conventional medicine has failed them. So, in their agony, they have turned to the fish.

There was a Spaniard who had been in Kavak for seventeen days. He was nearly at the end of his course of treatment. He had first learnt of the existence of the place during a Spanish television programme on the unexplained and supernatural. There were no fish on him when we arrived, and he looked healthier than the rest. 'It is working,' he said. 'The pain is much less.'

There was a Turk next to him, who had also first seen Kavak on the television. He had then spoken to his grocer, who suffered from the disease too. The grocer urgently recommended the fish. He had visited the place, and afterwards his condition went into remission. 'A miracle,' the man said. 'He told me it was a miracle, and to be honest, when you have had it as long as I have – twenty years – you are ready to try anything.'

I asked them what it felt like with the fish nibbling your skin.

A young man in his early thirties swam across to us and said, 'You can feel the fish biting. It feels like an electric shock. Then you bleed – they come and they open up your wounds.'

A middle-aged Turkish man suffering from some bone disease was scratching at himself. 'You know, people come from America. They come to make themselves beautiful.' He spent six hours a day in the water. 'The fish are my friends. I am not frightened of them.'

Although the men were nervous of the snakes, they were relying on what they had been told: the snakes would appear only if somebody with a snake bite climbed into the water.

'Has anyone seen a snake?' I asked them.

'No,' said the Spaniard.

The Turk with the bleeding head said, 'This is the power which God gives. This came to Turkey. It's a grace which God gives this nation above others. To show that we are chosen people. The whole world can benefit from us.'

A young man walked into the room and stood beside us. He was studying science at the university in Ankara and had brought his father, the man with the bleeding head, for a week's cure. He was quite harsh and scientific.

'What do you think?' I asked. 'Is this real? These fish?'

'They believe it. So it's real. They believe it and they get better.'

The young man in the water shouted, 'It's not psychological.'

'According to my idea, you have to believe something – people believe – that's all,' said the student.

Keith and I decided not to go into the water although they were encouraging us to do so. It was strange and inexplicable. The boy who was guiding us said, 'They sent scientists, I think from England, to see if the fish worked, and they concluded – though they didn't know why – that it worked.'

Perhaps there is no explanation. Perhaps this really was a miracle. Keith and I made our way back to the bus depot in Kangal. It was freezing by now, and dark. We waited in a tea room where a group of Iraqi refugees were playing pool, trying to cadge cigarettes off sympathetic local Turks. They were runaway soldiers, conscripts who had fled shortly after the Gulf War. Keith was pleased. He spoke good Arabic and he talked to them for a while. We exchanged cigarettes. They did not want to discuss the past. The Turks had granted them temporary asylum while they applied for permanent residence elsewhere. They hoped to go to Canada. Some had been in Kangal for more than a year. They smiled, but they did not disguise their despair. Kangal was not a place in which you would live by choice. In many ways it was real Anatolia: rustic, basic, bare and functional, simple and unpretentious.

The Iraqis were cold and miserable. They waited there most days, said the tea shop owner; just waiting for their letters of residence. They had no money, no jobs. The Turkish authorities would not allow them to work. They were allowed to live. That was all. 'They talk about Canada. But most will not make it there. They will stay here until the government throws them out.'

One of the Iraqis asserted, 'Soon we will be going. I am told that my permission will come in the next month. Yes, I know,' he said to a friend, 'they told me this before, but this time I have a good feeling.'

15

The Watermelon Man

The war began at Van.

At the entrance to the town there was a banner which flew on a metal frame above the high street. It quoted from Ataturk: 'Those who have no civilization are doomed to live under the feet of those who do.' Van calls itself a city. It has the infrastructure of a city: shopping malls, wide boulevards, little parks. But it is in fact a village in the adolescence of development, grown wealthy because of its participation in the booming trade in Iranian opium. Like every large town in eastern Turkey, Van is ugly, filthy and idle. It is uncomfortable with strangers, suspicious of their purpose, silently shocked by their rudeness. But it tolerates foreigners because it needs their money. It is not an easy place to keep a low profile.

The war had deteriorated since I was last here. The BBC reported the day before we arrived that forty-five had been killed in the fighting between the Turkish army and the Kurdish guerrillas. The army said that all the fatalities were guerrillas; the Kurds said they were all soldiers. Who knows the truth? This war has been raging, on and off, for hundreds of years. It is one of the murkiest, most impenetrable disputes on earth. But in the last few years it has reached a new intensity.

The Kurds are among the oldest tribes of the Middle East. There are Kurds living in Syria, Iraq, Iran, Central Asia and Turkey. They number perhaps as many as twenty million. Twelve million live in what is now called Turkey. They have no homeland. They live as a dispossessed people in other people's countries. In northern Iraq they launched a campaign for independence in the 1950s. The Arabs reacted by trying to exterminate them. In the late 1980s Saddam Hussein dropped chemical bombs and killed thousands. After the 1991 Gulf War the Kurds, protected by the Western allies, finally achieved self-rule in the north. But for how long?

In Turkey, the Kurds do not even have autonomy. Only recently have they been able to speak their language without fear of arrest, or publish newspapers in their own language. There are now members of the Turkish General Assembly who openly advertise their Kurdishness.

These concessions were not easy for the Turks. For many years Kurds were officially classified as 'mountain Turks'. Ataturk feared that to acknowledge the ethnic diversity of those who lived within his Republic would provoke nationalist uprising and tear it apart. This possibility haunts the modern Turkish establishment. But the Turks were finally forced to act because fighting in the south-east reached such a pitch that they needed to win friends among the Kurds. But the fighting persisted, and worsened. There is evidence of military desperation: evidence that the Turkish military is organizing death squads to murder Kurdish activists – even members of the Turkish parliament. By the time I arrived in Van, more than fifty-three members of a legal Kurdish political party had died in mysterious circumstances. Not one of the murders had been solved.

Thc fighting started in earnest in 1984 when a group of Marxist students founded the PKK, the Kurdish Workers' Party. It wanted independence from Turkey. The Syrians and the Iranians put some money into it, but it was not a popular uprising. Most Kurdish farmers resented it for bringing the Turkish army in such large numbers to the border regions. By the late 1980s the insurgency was enjoying broader popular support. Villages were razed by the dozen; the villagers were being brutalized by the army; there was mass migration to overcrowded local cities. The army alienated ordinary Kurds.

There had been another development: the PKK had taken to kidnapping foreigners who visited the region. By the time we arrived, the heavy artillery was making its way into the south-east, and travel into the area was vigorously discouraged. We were not being foolhardy. I had friends there who had offered to ensure our safe passage.

We were the only foreigners to disembark at Van airport. It was a small place, full of military policemen. Until quite recently, tourists used to come through this yellow terminal. Van has a huge lake, famously blue, in which people could fish for *dareka* – the only species that can live in the heavy water – and swim, or around which they could walk. Steamers used to ply across this little sea, which covers 1,300 square miles, and stop at the islands, with their churches painted with frescoes.

The area is littered with ancient monuments. Thousands of years before the Kurds, Van was capital of the Urartu nation, one of the great states of ancient Anatolia, with possessions as far away as modern Armenia and Iran. After the collapse of that civilization in the seventh century BC, the kingdom of Armenia grew up. The presence of Armenians in the city was ended, quite finally, during the First World War when they were massacred by the soldiers of the Ottoman sultan.

We emerged from the airport into the sunshine and the arms of a dozen screaming taxi drivers. Van does not change: the new city (built after the massacres) has a potent sense of dereliction about it: its buildings have no past to speak of. It is a present-tense city; a place of the here and now. The old Armenian city which was levelled by the Ottoman soldiers is a mile or two away, on the edge of the lake. Nobody chooses to live on such an enormous graveyard.

Most of the Kurds arrived in Van in the 1950s – many, like Massoud's family, from northern Iran. Massoud's family migrated to Van from a village on the border. For centuries, bundles of unrefined opium poppies have floated on rafts from Iran into Turkey, to be shipped on to Europe. The village had become one of the largest heroin trading posts in the world. Massoud's parents, however, left before it reached the peak of its prosperity, and were not involved in the trade. Instead, they had gone into tourism. There was some other industry in Van – a famous sausage factory and a sugar-cube factory – but tourism was the most lucrative business.

Massoud's carpet shop was off the central square. Massoud is an unusual man: he lives in Europe for much of the year and returns to Van during the summer season when he sells carpets and other baubles to the tourists. This year had been the worst he could remember: there had been virtually no Europeans in Van. It was a war-zone now, and no one was coming to the town or boating on the lake.

The shop was a palace of textiles: carpets, saddle-bags, kilims, from Iran, from Iraq, from India. Massoud was sitting like a magistrate behind his table, next to the fax and the cordless phone – rare in Van but comforts for a man who has travelled in the world. His sophisticated intellect and tender charm were as foreign to Van as his expensive aftershave was to the musty stink of the carpets in the shop. He was pleased to see us, which was good, because I did not want to bring him any trouble.

'Trouble?' he said with a thunderous laugh. 'Trouble? Who am I? I am Massoud.'

It had been a long time since I had last seen him here. 'Things are worse now,' he said. 'Really. It is dangerous for you.' Massoud talked only sparingly, his eyes always on the door. 'Not all can be trusted,' he said. 'This is a poor town, and many are informers. We must therefore take every care.' He was tall, thin and sleek, like a deer; his face always poised and alert, with intelligent, nervous eyes.

Why were we here, he asked. I had not told him before we set out. So I told him now. We wanted to visit the village of his ancestors, the village of the heroin traders.

'Yes, it is not so bad,' he said, smiling.

His boys were lounging around. Normally they would have been at the bus station waiting for the tourists to climb down from the coaches and press Massoud's business card in their hands. But now there was no point in their leaving the shop. The only other foreigners in the city were members of a Swiss delegation, posing as tourists, which had come to negotiate for the release of some hostages held by the PKK. Massoud said that everybody expected the release of the hostages within a few days.

Van was under a curfew. The army warned that after dusk it could not guarantee the safety of civilians. The soldiers patrolled the roads in eight-wheel German-made personnel carriers with bulky machine-gun turrets. The town was emptying: many of those who had stayed did not work. Only those who did could afford to leave. Most worked for the police. Everybody was informing on everybody else.

Massoud sat in his shop all day, listening to French classical music on his tape-recorder. Whenever an informer walked in, he would change the cassette to *arabesk*. He did nothing. 'But this is being a Kurd,' he said. 'It is why I come back to Van. It is not doing nothing. It is passing the day.'

Later on, a Swiss man and an Italian woman came into the shop to look at carpets and, when they discovered that Massoud could speak French as well as English, told him that they hoped for the release of the hostages very soon. But they were bitter. The man had narrow, cruel eyes. 'These bastard police. They are confining us to our hotel. To make sure we do not talk to the guerrillas.' There had been some talk that these 'hostages' were nothing of the kind. They were people who wanted, for one reason or another, to meet the PKK. The 'kidnappings', it was widely rumoured in Van, were arranged some weeks in advance. European liberals often see the PKK as romantic freedom fighters, and sympathize with them.

Some Kurds were optimistic about the future of this war; that they would win something, even if it was no more than equality with the Turks. But Massoud was not one of those. Two weeks before we arrived, soldiers arrested a man for having a Kurdish cassette in his possession – just a music cassette, which was perfectly legal under the new concessions. But the soldiers tend to ignore the laws, said Massoud. 'People are very hopeless.'

There had been a ceasefire a few weeks before, and it was trumpeted all over the newspapers, even the Kurdish ones. It seemed like a breakthrough and Massoud said that the 'people smiled'. They were pleased because they thought that rents might go back up again, and some were openly talking about returning to the villages. But the ceasefire broke down quickly and the Turkish armoured cars were back on the streets.

The war had not, however, done much to damage either the heroin trade or the feudal society that supported it. In the south of Turkish Kurdistan the old tribes have been virtually extinguished. The pressures of the war had broken them. But in the northern regions it was different. The drugs trade generated great wealth for the old lords and paid for their power. The state was forced to work with the tribes, and so they confirmed their influence.

The tribes were generally pro-government: the military administration allowed them to bear arms and paid good money to unemployed retainers to work as village guards – the local Home Guard. They earned more than the prison governor in Tokat. The government, in return for this loyalty, turned a blind eye to the drugs trade. The result was lawlessness.

Massoud's father was a lord. A medium-sized lord who owned a handful of villages and around fifty miles of land. 'The lords are respected,' said Massoud. 'If my father came in I would stand up and I would not smoke.' His father does not often go to see his land. Recently a Turkish general had been blown up along one of the roads that ran through it. 'There are many people in the city when they should be in the fields harvesting,' said Massoud. 'But people are frightened to go outside. It is dangerous.'

Constant vigilance must be tiring. And not far away a nightmare was waiting: columns of soldiers, and burning villages. Massoud worked hard to keep the nightmare at bay, because he is a coward and he is the first to admit it.

These two seemed fairly run-of-the-mill. They had such deep creases around their eyes that their eyeballs looked as if they were set in crêpe paper. The sidekick told us that he had been in Van for just two months. They were talking because Massoud said that we were tourists.

'Are you waiting with the group for the tourists to come free?' the more senior one asked.

'No,' we replied.

'I did not think I had seen you with them,' he said. 'Those people, they are against this country. I do not believe that they are tourists; they were here to meet the terrorists. And we should have taken them to prison when they arrived.' He had his orders, however. He had to follow the Swiss party around Van. Massoud ordered them some food. It was best to keep in with all of them, even the lowly, dispensable ones.

'You all think we are ignorant fools,' the senior policeman added. He spun his glass tea-cup, like a top, on its saucer and it fell, dribbling, on to the floor. 'How would you like it if I went to Britain and worked against your state? Would your police allow it?' He picked up the cup. 'The new strength of Turkey means that people want to destroy it. Look at Suleyman – from history – the Conqueror. We are a strong people and we can defend ourselves.'

'Ah yes,' said Massoud.

'People should behave well towards one another and not always think of their own profit.'

'The war seems to be getting worse,' I said.

'Yes, there are secret international plots,' the policeman replied. 'It is all an attempt to make a big Armenia.' The Interior Minister himself had said in public that he believed the PKK to be an Armenian conspiracy. 'And these Kurds, excuse me, Massoud, but they are ignorant. I mean, take the condoms. They use them over and over again. They need the Turks to teach them civilization.'

He was tired, he explained. He had been up until 3 a.m. watching the Swiss party in their hotel. 'They speak Italian on the phone and we don't understand it, nobody in the hotel understands it. So what are we supposed to tell the bosses? Well, we have to tell them something. It is pretty obvious – even if you can't get all the words – that they are with the PKK. I mean . . . they are from the Green and Socialist parties.'

Once they had left the shop, Keith and I went to see old Van castle, at the foot of the old Armenian city, overlooking the lake. It is a massive and isolated rock, a mile long, which lies on the surface of the surrounding water-meadow, like a sleeping dragon. It is nearly 3,000 years since the first citadel with its ashlar fortifications was completed, staring out to the north across the sea. How many human lives have been terminated within its sight?

The meadow marshes were lined with trees: golden-orange and olive-green, fields of dandelions, and long grasses clumped in fresh-water streams. The dead Armenians were buried beneath this plain, or that was what the locals believed. Above the general silence a penetrating peacefulness was broken by shooting – cracking, snapping like a whip. Duck shooting.

At the entrance to the castle, in a small grove of trees clustered around a brook, were some security men. One approached us and said, 'It is dangerous to be here at such a late hour. You must be careful for your safety.' He said it with sincerity, but he let us up the worn old steps that run to the top of the fortress. There was still time. There was a warm breeze, and there were dogs barking on the plain below, and flocks of geese squawking. It was rich land. The poplar trees, tall and feathery-green at this distance, bent and swayed in the wind. I remembered that one of the policemen in the carpet shop – the more senior one – had said, 'The fighting will stop, you know, and it will be for nothing.'

The sidekick, who had not said much, looked nervously at us.

'Are you frightened in Van?' I asked him.

'My wife is coming to Van soon and she will not like it,' he replied quietly. 'You know that we are the targets and that many of the Kurds would like to kill us.'

Shortly after they left the shop, Massoud had pulled an old loose-leaf file from a drawer and shown it to us – it was stashed full of letters from foreign tourists he had slept with. There must have been hundreds of letters. There were letters from German housewives 'relaxing from their housework' and airmail correspondence from a middle-aged French professor – dozens of them, almost daily. He had stopped replying.

Massoud proudly held up a string of condoms he found inside another drawer. Then he knelt down by the senior policeman's chair and felt the carpet. He was examining the tea stain. 'You see this kilim,' he said – it was a big, colourful square, worn in the middle – 'I was born on this carpet.'

The following morning we found a place for breakfast near the hotel, which served tumblers full of warm milk, white cheese with herbs, and eggs. Keith was quiet that morning, a Turkish newspaper rolled under his arm. He was always quite smartly dressed. But he was growing depressed with the south-east. 'I really had no idea. None at all. That all this could be going on. "Peace at Home, Peace in the World",' he said, quoting Ataturk. He unfurled his newspaper and read it again. There was a front-page story claiming that after a recent raid on a PKK camp, the government had found that some of the women guerrillas were on the pill.

A man passed by, swinging on wooden crutches. He had one good leg, the stump of the other was wrapped tightly in his trousers, secured with a safety pin. The wind blew his cap off his head on to the road. He looked at us, through us, and leaned forward to pick it up. It was a difficult manoeuvre: and at one time he looked as though he was about to collapse on the road, but his long arms reached the cap in a swoop and he retrieved it. Keith said, 'We should have helped him.' But we did not, and we were ashamed. Why didn't we get up? The wind picked up a little and caught at a page of the open newspaper, lifting it off the table and throwing it on to the road. It was the gossip page: pictures of Istanbul socialites at some diplomatic function. Keith left it to blow to the other side of the road. By now the sun was streaking across the table, and the air was heating up.

There was still no news of the hostages.

After breakfast we went to the heroin village. Massoud had given us directions. He said, 'Look, so long as you don't mention drugs, you'll be fine. Don't mention drugs.' Our driver was one of Massoud's tribe.

Before the fighting reached this pitch, displaced nomads from the war zone used to camp out along the road to the east of Van. Now their broad, flat tents, colourfully tassled, had gone. Every few hundred metres there was an electricity pylon marching across the landscape, and more often, a Turkish army checkpoint. Twin symbols of progress for the Kurdish farmers, who lived between the two, in small mud hamlets.

Our driver was full of bravado, in his car, playing Kurdish music. 'If they catch us, then they will beat us,' he said. I will call him Ali, because I cannot use his real name. But Ali was frightened. 'You know, the PKK came to a village a few days ago, and they found some village guards. But they did not kill them. They do not kill civilians. They are good people. But you mustn't tell anybody I told you this. The Turks don't like the Kurds. They hate us.'

The cassette was playing music by the Kurdish singer Shivan, who lives in exile in Germany. It went: 'This land is ours; it is ours.'

Past long columns of armoured vehicles, past shattered villages – levelled almost, and uninhabited, the mortars having generally missed the road – we drove through the land of Massoud's father. Ali was respectful. 'He is a big lord.' It was grazing land, not worth much, and it was strange to think that somebody owned this wilderness. There was a tractor on one hill baling up hay.

He stopped the car to show us a bomb crater in the road. 'This is where the head of the Turkish intelligence was killed with ten guards. You know this bloody man said once he would make this place a graveyard for the Kurds? So he died, and we are dancing for it. "I'll bury the Kurds of the east," he said – I can't believe a man would say that.'

It was here that Massoud's land stopped. Now we could see the village, in a valley masked by dead brown hills. Behind it, and in front, were giant mountains tearing straight into the sky, and beneath them rich pasture and fast-flowing rivers. At a distance, it looked like a filthy rag spread out at the feet of the Kurdish highlands. 'It's not beautiful but it's rich,' said Ali. 'Everybody is a smuggler here. There are drugs everywhere.'

The landscape became more severe the closer we came to the

Iranian border, the edges sharper. The hills were purple, not brown – the colour of blackcurrant – and the rock escarpments pink, like roses.

The Kurdish drugs trade had boomed since the Iranian authorities imposed a mandatory death sentence for drug smuggling. They relocated to Kurdistan. The Turkish tribes take the raw opium and refine it. They buy the huge quantities of distilled water they need from Syria and they tell Customs that it is for local photographic shops.

This village has a reputation which extends far beyond the borders of Kurdistan. It has been discussed in London and Washington and in most of the capitals of Europe. It is one of the main clearing-houses for Afghan opium exported through Iran. There are few other villages which can match it; one is Yuksekova, where the tribes are also strong.

Outside the village they were cutting hay with scythes, and there were boys on donkeys. The boys were wearing denim jackets and silk shirts: the first hint of prosperity. There was a checkpoint at the entrance to the town, but the soldiers did not carry their guns and when they approached the car and saw that there were European passengers, they did not ask for passports.

The main street was full of cars: there were Mercedes, new ones, with Istanbul and Ankara plates. Some of the biggest hotels in Istanbul and Ankara are owned by residents of this village; there was not much to invest in here. It looked at first much like any Kurdish town: dirty, most of the houses made of mud. But when you looked more closely, some of the mud cottages had double-glazing and new corrugated-metal roofs; in the market there were imported European products: electric blankets from Holland, thermos flasks from Germany.

The lord of this village is also the mayor, although politics played very little part in his election. Technically, he was the representative of the ruling party, the conservative True Path. We stopped for a bowl of lentil soup in one of the restaurants and the cashier told us that he was a 'man of sugar', continuing, 'He is rich – fabulously rich, so rich that there is nobody who is richer than him. And yet he gives much of his money to the poor. He owns half of this place and many of the villages around it. And he pays his men when they are ill. Of course it is modern now. The lord does not expect tribute from his villagers; sheep or vegetables every year, or the pick of the young girls.' He laughed. What a thought.

The restaurant was smart and clean, with new chairs and metal tables. After the soup, we went to the mayor's office and were told that he had gone to Yuksekova to attend a funeral. On the wall of his outer office there were some shocking pictures of dead children, their arms wrenched off and their faces without skin. The poster warned: 'PKK MURDERERS'. The council office was a scrap-heap: concrete and breeze-block.

The lord's chief-of-staff made us sit down and drink tea and eat chocolates. He assumed we had come to trade. But we were anxious to show that we were only tourists. I had brought my camera along. Nobody else would be stupid enough. The men were dressed loudly, like gangsters in shiny black shoes and purple and green double-breasted suits, good-quality shirts and silk ties. Even the male telephone receptionist was dressed like this. We could see no women.

I asked one of the men how the village came to be so well off.

'Well, yes, it is,' he said. 'I mean, it is comfortable.'

'Why are you here?' another man asked.

'Well, we would like to meet the lord, who is famous throughout Turkey,' Keith said. Men were coming into the room carrying machine-guns, but they were not threatening us. They laid them down and took tea off the boy who was carrying the tray. He was a hunchback, and could not speak.

The chief-of-staff thought that the lord would not be coming back that day. He advised that we try at his house before leaving, because he might not yet have left for the funeral.

Just as we arrived, a Mercedes pulled out of the drive, and the lord had gone. This was all very disappointing. We walked back towards the town and decided to follow him to Yuksekova. Ali, the driver, had been told by Massoud – correctly – that we were tourists. But he kept on asking why tourists should want to go first to this village and then Yuksekova. He decided that we were dealers. And he started to tell us his story. 'I have been to prison for trying to take drugs out of the village,' he said. The first shock. 'I saved up some money by selling 300 sheep – and then I bought some heroin – about 600 million lire it cost and then I sold it in Istanbul . . . but I sold it to a policeman. I had only just started.' He served one year of his five-year sentence.

'Now I cannot do it because I have no money.' The herd was his inheritance. Now he had nothing. 'I would if I could, of course. Everybody knows it is the only way to make a decent living. Many of my friends have sold their sheep, and some have been very successful indeed.' But not Ali. 'God does not look kindly upon me.' He looked at Keith. 'I only need a little. If you give me the money, I will give you half the profit.'

I looked at him: his eyes were small and dark, his skin had the texture of marshmallow, soft and fatty and wet; small rivulets of sweat glistened in the crevices by the side of his nose. He scraped his palm across his forehead in a confused gesture of discomfort and insecurity. He said again, 'I can arrange drugs for you, if you would like that – but please don't tell because I can go to prison just for saying that.' It was a difficult moment. Keith nodded, sort of – it was more as if he was leaning his head to one side – and smiled. He did not say anything, but Ali understood. He said the best way was to buy Afghani powder in Iran and then sell it in Istanbul.

'If Massoud found out that I was thinking of it again, I would be beaten. If the PKK found out – and they don't like drugs because they say it keeps the old tribes alive – they would arrest me, and after three times, they would kill me. But we have to do business somehow. We have to.' He was warned by the PKK not to do it again. 'But with this, I told them, you can buy hotels.'

It was a controlled trade. The drug barons in Kurdistan and their relatives across the border in Iran ensure a firm discipline. They discourage freelancers because they can compromise the bigger operations. Occasionally, they will give them up to the local police so that they appear efficient.

'There was a recent case, a drug shipment from Iran to Istanbul worth 18 billion lire. The Iranians sent it to Istanbul and the guys in Istanbul didn't pay up, so the Iranians asked the lord to send to Istanbul to get the character who hadn't paid. He was forced to pay, and as a result all the heads of the lord's tribe were given a Mercedes as a present. Four of them.'

Yuksekova is the closest Turkey offers to Dodge City. It is very close to the Iraqi and Iranian borders. The clans do war here quite frequently. No one of them has possession. The main street was full of people but all the European cars had gone. The town, unlike the village, which has government protection, is in a free-fire zone. First the PKK will come, and then the army. The army were here, according to Ali, two weeks before. They shot the place up and killed four or five people at random – picked off the street in broad daylight by soldiers in armoured personnel carriers. The soldiers were taking revenge for some PKK attack on a nearby barracks building. The incident had not been reported in the national press.

The windows of most of the shops had been shot out or were riddled with bullet holes. Some shopkeepers had already cleaned up, and installed new panes of glass. The glaziers' fingerprints were still smudged around the edges. Boys on ladders on both sides of the street were painting letters on the new windows. But other signs hung limply above shop doors – there was an *Aygaz* sign which had been wildly contorted in some crossfire, twisted and bent. The billiard hall was full of holes.

'This used to be a beautiful town,' said Ali as he squeezed between the carts and the potholes. 'But everybody has left.' Beautiful? Even now, when the sun was so high in the sky and the heat so intense, there were puddles of dirty stinking water on the mud of the main street: a leaking sewer or, maybe, a water main. Little rivers of fluid rolled down the pavement. There had been no rain in days.

When you looked at the people, you realized that this was a border town with no distinct nationality. There were Kurds from Iraq in the old-fashioned smocks of the *peshmerga* guerrillas, and Shi'ite traders, in turbans, from Iran. Ali pointed to another bunch: 'From Afghanistan,' he said. They were climbing into a minibus for the journey home. 'Modest, religious men,' he said. The few restaurants that remained open printed their menus in Farsi as well as Turkish.

Next to one of them was the office of the town's newspaper: the *Voice of Yuksekova*. It was four sheets long and was printed by hand. The publisher made his living printing business cards. He worked in one room, with the printing press at the back, curtained off by a plastic sheet. His fingers were full of ink and he smudged them once or twice across his face while he talked. Keith and I wanted to know if the Turkish army had really just walked down the high street a fortnight before and shot at passers-by.

He was direct. 'The Turkish army declared a curfew at about 10 p.m. and then shot the place to pieces. As a journalist,' and he gave us his card, 'I sought some comment from the local governor over this atrocity. He, however, insisted that nothing had happened – despite, I might add, the evidence of his own eyes.' He said that it was an official interview, and he produced a miniature tape-recorder from his desk to show that he had recorded it.

'So then I had a call from the governor not to write about the incident. He said it was the PKK that was responsible. But I defied that order and did write about it.' The rest of the Turkish press did not, however, follow his courageous lead; the atrocity remains unofficial and undeclared. How many others were there? The publisher said: 'I think a man comes to the point of having had enough.'

It was early afternoon by now. We had to leave to be sure of getting to Van before the curfew. As we left, I noticed that several dead animals were lying by the side of the main road. There seemed no explanation: nobody had dropped chemical weapons, but it was as if there had been a virulent plague – cats, dogs and sheep were just dead by the roadside. No blood. Ali said that the sheep had been thrown off the back of lorries that were smuggling stock across the Iranian border, but he could not explain the other animals. 'Maybe there was a crime against God,' he said. But he didn't pursue the thought.

*

The next day we called back at the village.

We waited in the outer office. It was hot, and there were many flies. The telephone receptionist was sitting in a cubicle across the hall. I watched him. He was motionless in front of two phones and a fax. The muscles of his face were quite still; his eyes did not move. He twitched when a fly settled on his eyelid. It was so quiet. A lorry passed, rattling the window-panes, loaded, strangely, with footballs in net bags. There were no telephones ringing, no typewriters chattering. Nothing. After a while, we asked the receptionist to call the mayor and find out if he would be coming to the office today. He said that the lord was having breakfast. You could feel the heat clawing at your cheeks and your forehead, pricking the skin, pulling it taut around your face. You started to notice your own flesh because it was crawling across the bones of your scalp.

And then there was movement. Some henchmen started to appear, clunking their heels up and down the corridor. A typewriter started to tinkle, like a cash register, in the distance. People started to talk. We were offered tea. A boy shouted down the stairs.

One or two officials were standing beside us waiting for the mayor to arrive. 'He is on his way,' one said. In the meantime, they talked about the price of Mercedes.

'There are many in the village,' I said.

'Well,' said one man. 'This is the best heroin . . .' Immediately he had said the word, he coughed. We tried not to be surprised by it.

The receptionist wandered into the room. 'You know why the village is so rich? It is because of watermelons. They come from Iran and they are sweeter. Everybody loves them.'

The mayor's assistant arrived. He told us that the lord was a very popular mayor. Ali had told us earlier that one of his cousins had challenged him in the elections the previous year and that he had been banished from the village under threat of death.

The assistant had stopped talking and was holding his head

erect, listening. Then his body relaxed, and he ushered us into the main office. It had rich wood-panelled walls, glass shelves and a large mahogany desk. The room reeked of cologne: it assaulted your senses, stung your eyes. The Turkish flag hung limp from a chrome pole in the corner.

The assistant had heard something: the stamping of feet. In a rush, falling over each other, the mayor's entourage spilled into the office. The gunmen came first, carrying a couple of machine-guns, and then several grey-haired men in dusty suits, and finally the mayor in a pristine white suit, and open-necked pink shirt. He had a pair of clean white loafers on his feet. He was dressed like a night-club crooner.

The lord had a broad grin, and was laughing with some of his retainers. He invited the older men to sit on the low sofa at the back of his office. He offered us two chairs in front of his desk. 'Welcome!' he said after a moment. 'So, my friends, welcome to our small town. You are from England . . . which is a great country.' He spoke very quickly, merging words into each other. He fluffed the handkerchief in his breast-pocket while he talked. 'Do you speak Kurdish? May God be praised for Kurdish. And English . . . which is a great language. I will order cola for you, a cool drink. You will prefer cola to tea, I think. So you will have cola—' Keith put his hand forward to mean, tea. 'Good, then it is cola.' He pressed a buzzer above his desk. 'All the people in the village love me.'

One of the men at the back said, 'Of course!'

'There are twelve tribes in this region. We came from Iraq 3,000 years ago. Things have not changed in 500 years. It is still the same family in charge . . .' He paused while the boy brought cola to our chairs. Then he lifted the lid off an onyx box crammed with Marlboro cigarettes. 'Please smoke one of these,' he said to me. 'I will be offended if you do not.'

'Do you smoke?' I asked him.

'Do I smoke? Do I smoke?' He looked at the others in the room. 'I do not smoke because it is a bad habit and against God. I ban smoking, drinking and gambling in the town. There is no smoking in any restaurants.'

He had huge fingers, and he fumbled for a moment to get a grip on one of the cigarettes. Then he passed it to me and insisted I smoke it.

'Mayor, you say that the tribes are as strong as they were 500 years ago, but I thought modern Turkey didn't much like the tribes. The old ways?' Keith asked.

'There is a perfect harmony between the tribes and the Turkish government,' he replied. He threw his hands up into the air, and everybody laughed.

Keith went on, 'Why is the village so rich?'

'There are two divisions: one is rich and the other is normal and deals with livestock and the government officials. There is trade here,' he flexed his fingers, 'animal, sheep, vegetable and fruit. Watermelons.'

One of the men at the back had opened a window and heat was rolling through the office in waves. The lord's evenly tanned face was beginning to gleam with sweat; in the small gap between his nostrils and the strip of black moustache, moisture was gathering into droplets. He stood up and looked out of the window. He was a tall man and he dominated this room.

'This war. I am a Kurd but I am also a Turk. My mother tongue is Kurdish, but I am a Turk. We have a proverb: he who denies his essence is a carrier of shame, is ignoble. The Turkish and the Kurdish nations are fingernail and finger and have been together for hundreds of years. There must be peace.'

This man was a prince, a potentate who ruled 30,000. He may be an ally of the Turks but he was not part of their country. He could not be. Ataturk hated the tribes; they are the antithesis of democracy, of any ideology. I was surprised he was so frank about his feudalism. 'You see, the Turkish state respects human rights, and so they have no effect on me – they respect my right to be a lord.'

The men at the back clapped at this point. One said, 'Yes!'

He was not 500 years old. He had changed with the times. His money was of little use in the village, so he travelled a good deal to the western cities and spent it. 'This is the situation. I am rich. I work with trade. I find the village rather small and I decide to invest in Istanbul. I throw my belly with beautiful girls in Istanbul discos.' The old men tittered, and he smiled at them. 'There are those who say people leave here because the state oppresses them. They are lying. People move from Kurdistan to the west because there is no entertainment and amusements here. You know my favourite place?' He glanced around the room. 'My favourite place is the Bird Paradise at Mugla.' He paused. 'But we come back because here is the tradition of the tribe. My villagers are mine; their lives are mine. And they love me.'

One of the old men at the back leaned forward to speak. He had no voice box; he used a microphone pressed against his throat to croak out words. 'He is in accord with the state – occasionally there are slight misunderstandings. But no effect – they are like finger and fingernail . . .' His sentence dribbled off into a ghastly ripple of hoarse laughter.

'I help the state with social insurance,' said the lord. 'This is our tradition. One of our villagers might need an operation in Van. I give him two million lire and a car. I say, "Get well" and then he repays me, or I say it doesn't matter. You see that man' – he pointed – 'he had throat cancer and we sent him to Ankara and he had an operation, and here we sit together in the same room.'

The writ of the Turkish government did not run here.

I asked him about condoms, because these are a symbol of Turkish impotence. The government has a stated policy of introducing condoms to the villagers of the south-east, to control the birth rate. The European Community has told Turkey that it will remain ineligible for membership as long as it has such a large and growing population.

He hated the idea. 'People have a political aim with the condom. I have several children. The state can't say, "Don't have more children." People have as many as they can afford. No such thing as you can't have children. I am rich and I can look after twenty children. What do we say to the shepherds?' He laughed like a boy. 'You cannot buy such things here, I have forbidden it. Even if it was sold, people would be ashamed and they wouldn't buy them. It's a sin . . . no, it's not a sin. As for abortion that's a sin.' Everybody was laughing, some had tears in their eyes. The lord wiped his forehead with his handkerchief.

The telephone rang. It was the provincial police chief on the other end, calling about guns. A number of people had been involved in an incident. The army had arrested one man and wanted the police chief not to press charges.

The lord was shouting: 'The shooting was the result of a provocation . . . no, that is not what I think. I am telling you that . . . you idiot . . . provocation, yes . . . are you arguing with me . . . IDIOT! Look, I can come and explain it to you myself . . . Now, my friend, this is a small incident, and we need to resolve it or it will blow up . . . yes, yes, let us talk like friends. My nephew would not kill a goat, let alone a man. It was an accident. The other boys insulted him. They called him *jash* . . . yes, they called him a donkey. They are bad people, and they were drunk when they provoked him. He tells me that there is another witness and he will bring him to me today or tomorrow. There is no gun because he didn't use it, and besides, you will never find it even if you hold him for twenty years . . . to be honest, you tell me that people have died in the street, but I am not even sure anybody has been killed.'

He put the receiver down, and smiled. He saw that I had stopped smoking, and forced another Marlboro on me. I could see fat bundles of cash peeking out of his inside jacket pockets. The boy he was trying to save from prison, we learned from Ali later, was a relative.

'I am a member of the True Path Party – you know, this is the party which rules Turkey. I have always liked President Demirel. We know him. We go to his house whenever we like, just as I go to my own house.' He claimed also to have known the late President Turgut Ozal. 'I knew him personally. Ozal was a leader of world proportions.' If he was telling the truth, this made him a very powerful man indeed.

There was another telephone call. 'Three hundred dogs,' he said. 'I know but you are talking about *three hundred dogs* . . . what harm have they done to you? They cause trouble to the garbage? . . .No!' He put the phone down. He turned to us: 'For three years I have refused to put down the stray dogs. It is against my principles.'

The telephone rang again: 'Dogs, dogs, can you talk of nothing else?' he shouted. 'You will kill a dog and then you will eat it. Speak to me when you have finished this meal.' And he put the receiver down with a bang. Then he said, 'So far, the PKK has killed none of my men, but we have killed many of them. If we gave them the chance they would, but we do not. They have been to our villages and they put down mines. One villager lost his feet. These *are* dogs. And I would shoot them myself.'

A man came through the door. He had come to present the lord with a petition for assistance. He approached the desk.

'Stand up straight,' the lord said. 'We do not keep our men as slaves.' The man wanted help with his eyesight. He had been injured by a landmine. He wished to go to a hospital in the west, but was finding it difficult to get permission from the military governor to leave the region.

He left the office. The lord picked up the phone. 'My dear governor, you are well? One of my men needs some help in going to Ankara . . . yes, you know the one . . . I am so pleased. I thought as much: an administrative problem. Dear governor, do you have any orders for me today? . . . No? . . . I am grateful.'

Then a boy with a wispy young beard came in. He wanted to go to Ankara to see his father who was ill. The lord told him to leave the room while he considered the request. He talked in Kurdish to some of the other men at the back of the room. Then he turned to us, and said in Turkish, 'This boy's father is not ill. The boy wants to run away. So I will not let him leave. Instead I will send an imam to see him, so that he can improve his soul.'

He stood up, dressed down his jacket, and motioned us towards the door. 'Now we eat.'

We walked through the outer office, down the dark stairs and into the street. There was a large entourage. Several men on the outside jogged along with AK-47s prone lazily across their hips. This was an alarming moment – the man most wanted by the PKK walking down the high street of the village, which was crowded with people. He walked in the middle of the street; all traffic was stopped and people stepped aside. He smiled at some and shook hands with others. Some clapped at him. But these were frightened people. You could see them scurry around corners. A car full of armed men followed behind us.

We finally came to a narrow, dingy restaurant, which was the lord's favourite. The owner showed us to an upstairs room, to a table already laid.

'How many wives do you have?' he asked in all innocence.

'One,' came the reply.

'This is the sad thing about your country, just to have one wife. I have two – one is married by the imam and the other by the state. I love them both equally. Some here have four wives. But it is what you can afford. My wives live in different houses; I have no desire to have four houses for them.' He looked at us, wedging a piece of bread into his mouth, and then at the others around the table. 'They find this strange!' And he laughed.

The waiter had brought huge amounts of food to the formica-topped table, and the lord had a loaded plate. Like a child, he had tucked his napkin into his collar. 'You must come hunting with me for wolves, foxes or rabbit. There were boars but we have shot them all now so there are none left.'

The table overlooked the heaving market. He looked down through the greasy glass window. 'This is beautiful,' he said.

He was a peasant in his heart.

16

The First Ark

In Van, Noah had come to be synonymous with prostitution. It surprised me that there were any prostitutes at all here. This was still a conservative town – there were no women in the restaurants. Massoud frequently complained that there were few opportunities for recreational sex. He was the first to tell us of the Hotel Noah. One of his girlfriends was in the shop at the time. 'What is the Hotel Noah?' I asked her, and she smiled weakly, as if I was making some comment on her virtue. 'No, I don't think I would want to stay there,' she said.

We asked the two secret policemen. They told us it was closed, but later we went to find it. Across the high street, past the road excavators, and into the lobby of the Hotel Noah. It was dingy and thick with dust: even the vertical surfaces were grey and clogged with filth. It was dark: a sallow yellow light from a faltering bulb hanging shadeless from the ceiling. On the walls were large photographs, treated like wallpaper, of harbours in western Turkey: gleaming white yachts and brilliant light, with reds and yellows, clean striking colours, and blue water the colour of ink. Above one of them was a dead mongoose hanging from a nail. A Minnesota University sweat-shirt was mounted on a board like a trophy above the reception desk.

Some old men, the same shade of dusk as the rest of the room, were sitting in the foyer. They wore skull caps on the back of their heads and seemed religious men. Despite the dirt, there was nothing decadent about the place.

We were told that the whores at the Noah were from Russia, but there was no sign of them. 'Every night they are arrested, and the hotel is closed, and then in the morning it reopens and the women come back to trade,' said Massoud.

'Why are you here at this time?' asked one of the old men. 'Are you foreign? From Istanbul?'

'Yes,' said Keith. 'Foreign.'

'Why is this place called the Noah?' I asked.

'This is the name of the owner, Noah.'

'Noah's a common name,' said a man who had suddenly appeared behind the reception desk. 'It is neither Turkish, nor Kurdish but all are called it. It is a kind of universal thing which we all understand. Noah is a prophet.'

The European hostages held by the Kurdish guerrillas had been released. There was talk of it all over town: one of Massoud's boys told us as we left the hotel. Apparently they had been taken for questioning by the local police as soon as they were freed, on suspicion of colluding with the guerrillas. Massoud said there was an Englishman among the hostages.

Keith remembered the name. 'I've met him,' he said.

'Who?' I asked.

'The Englishman. He came to dinner once in Ankara after attending a service at the Embassy Chapel. He wasn't English. He was from New Zealand, a former accountant who had given up his job to find Noah's Ark. Can't believe he was involved with the terrorists. They must just have found him up Ararat.'

He explained that the man had tried to climb the mountain before. The first time the accountant–evangelist had set out to find the Ark, he had encountered a Kurd selling gold relics halfway up Ararat. Despite the illegality, the man bought the trinkets and decided to melt them down to finance another, longer expedition. He told the guests at the Embassy dinner that he was going to bring the Ark to the people 'so that they might share the love of God'. 'He said that he had tried to talk to the locals about Jesus and he said he planned to return to the mountain to tell the local PKK that the Lord wanted them to put down their arms,' Keith remembered.

Ararat was in the middle of the fiercest war zone. Most days the fighting claimed around a hundred lives. Ararat. The Ark.

People have come in search of it for thousands of years. Astronauts, preachers and female missionaries; charlatans, thieves and gold-diggers. Mostly, however, they were born-again evangelists, and mainly American. Nobody has ever found it. Bits of wood; the odd shady outline beneath some glacier. That is all they have discovered, but the hunt goes on. It is the only miracle in the Christian Bible which should be possible to prove. The boat was not destroyed. There must be some part of it left. That is the attraction: confirming that God does not make up stories. Keith, a former evangelist himself, could understand the need. 'Everything would fall into place,' he said while we sat in Massoud's shop. Massoud was listening to us, quietly, and then he said that somebody had found it.

'Found what?' Keith asked.

'The Ark,' Massoud said.

'You must be joking,' Keith replied.

'No. The Ark. The old one,' Massoud explained. 'Not much to get excited about when there are no tourists to go and see it.'

Neither of us had heard of this new Ark. We decided to visit.

There had been fighting the night before. The soldiers at the checkpoint were exhausted, their jackets open, unwashed. We told them that we were looking for evidence of Noah's Ark. It was the only acceptable explanation you could give, as a foreigner speaking to a frightened soldier, for your presence in the war zone. They waved us through.

The previous night the Turks had won an international sporting competition: a Greco-Roman wrestling tournament. It is not often that the Turks hear their national anthem on a sporting podium. Everybody, including Ali the driver, was talking about it that morning. It must have been particularly satisfying to have beaten the Greeks. Ali said to the soldier, 'Good about the fight last night!' And the conscript looked at him and smiled.

Beyond the checkpoint much of the landscape was smouldering; there were several fires – ten at least – on the skyline. Keith and I were counting the smoke trails. They were villages burning. Ali swerved to avoid dozens of sparrows flying out of the sun towards the windscreen, and nearly went off the road.

Otherwise it was calm. Sheep and cattle grazed by the roadside. Further along dispossessed villagers were sitting in small herds by the tarmac. Some had tents but they all looked miserable. There were one or two demolished villages close to the road. Some of the walls had been prised off by the Turkish artillery. You could see the kitchen in one stone house: pots and pans hanging from the wall. The occupants had had to leave quickly.

Ararat towered in the distance, an awesome sight. Streaks of snow flashed from the summit. It had a handsome symmetry. I wanted to look at it, and I wanted to remember looking at it. History: this mountain was as familiar to the Assyrians as it was to the modern Turkish army.

And the Ark. You could imagine the plains beneath the mountain filled with water. They were remarkably flat. Was the flood the world's first genocide? Ararat has seen others since. Perhaps this is the real purpose of the Ark: a metaphor for genocide.

The shells of seven Iranian coaches lay along the road. Nobody had bothered to remove them and they were rusting. The engines had been cannibalized for parts. There were jack-knifed oil tankers as well. Ali said, 'Allah Korusun' – God Protect Us.

Dogubeyazit was the last town before the mountain. It was long and straggling, built around the road that leads into Iran a few miles further on. Along the main street there was a market: tea-bags from Iran and aspirin from Russia. It was Sunday, and families were promenading up and down, past the vegetable barrows. Despite the filth and the noise, there was a sense of purity about Dogubeyazit: thin, clean air. It was a magical town, full of possibilities.

Keith and I looked for a guide to show us the new Ark. We found the tourist office – a small door beside a shop. But it was locked, and nobody was about. The pharmacy across the street, we were told, was owned by the father of the boy who worked in the tourist shop. But the pharmacy was also closed. We were directed towards an open truck which was unloading furniture on to the pavement a few yards away. The removal men told us that the boy had disappeared several days before. A policeman told us where to go for a guide.

A few miles outside the town was the Issah Pasa Palace, dug into the side of a cliff. Below the palace, before you could see its spindly red and yellow minaret, was a tea garden for visitors with white plastic chairs and red tables. It was empty, the furniture in disarray and the grass patchy. A yellow sign opposite said: 'Welcome to Noah's Ark Country'. The derelict palace had a special serenity: it was a rare surviving symbol of a distinct Kurdish history in south-eastern Turkey. It was not an Ottoman ruin but had been built by some Kurdish baron centuries ago. The authorities were restoring it: there were bags of concrete and sand scattered across the broken inner courtyard.

Ahmet, a tall man with a fat, bristling moustache, was lolling outside the gates of the palace. He was the Ark guide and we were his first business for months. He offered to drive us in his car to what he said was the 'place of the Ark'.

'Really the Ark?' asked Keith. 'Come on, we're not stupid.'

Ahmet replied quite flatly, 'There are many books at this place which will explain it to you – and there is a man at the top who has the plans.'

The place of this new Ark was, he said, frequently the scene of vicious fighting. 'Are you sure you want to go? There was fighting in the area during the night.'

'Will we be safe with you?' I asked.

'Yes, you will be safe.'

In the car Ahmet explained, 'They wanted to bring it down the mountain, but the Turkish government refused. Now it is in the hands of the PKK.' He shouted above the engine noise, 'Don't worry about being kidnapped! The PKK don't kidnap tourists – why should they? They are already well known in Europe as it is. They want the tourists to come and see the Ark because that brings us money; it brings money to our people. There have been no tourists this year – two or three, that's all. Tourists used to come and climb Ararat – each day five or six thousand people came. It had a big effect on our town. Now nobody has work. There were thirty hotels in Dogubeyazit, and now they are all closed.'

Ahmet's father worked at the Kurdish palace for thirty-five years. He was the caretaker. 'At that time people said the Ark was actually on Ararat.' The car zipped along, the old engine roaring. 'There was an astronaut called Irwin. He came and I used to take him to the fish lake and the thermal bath, which was good money. Irwin looked on the summit of the mountain but he couldn't find anything. Then the two Americans came: Fasold and Wyatt. And they found it.'

This was the archaeological find of the century and I had never heard of them. 'Were they Christians?' I shouted at Ahmet.

'We get them but I can't remember which is which. They didn't make propaganda in the town. Nobody has tried it with me.'

Ahmet worked for fifteen years as the ticket-seller at the palace, and now he managed the tea garden. He talked about Irwin. 'This man, this man was crazy – he was both political and religious, a fanatic. The guy Wyatt is also religious but a good guy. Irwin had other aims with the Ark, political ones. We didn't know it – maybe he was an Armenian. He always used to go around the military areas. One day about four years ago he was caught in Erzurum and he was arrested for a short period. Everybody who has been here has an aim. They don't tell us; they don't tell us whether they are true or false. They come, just like you, like ordinary tourists.'

Ahmet explained that he was a good Muslim. He did so because one of the complications of the new Ark is that Muslims do not believe it is on Ararat. The Koran states that it is on Cudi, a mountain some distance to the south. Ahmet had a problem because he actually believed that this new Ark was *the* Ark. 'I used not to believe it but so many people have come and given so much effort and they've spent so much money on it. If there wasn't such a thing why would they put in so many resources?'

The little car shook its way towards the foothills of Ararat, which rose steeply off the flat plain that encircled Dogubeyazit. 'We do believe that there was a flood here,' he added a few moments later. 'Of course it seems very dry now. But there are fossil stones round about which indicate that there must have been water at some point.'

Ahmet was surprised that we had not heard of the Ark's discovery. 'It hasn't been properly advertised. There are some who confuse things and claim to have found other ones; but this is the right one. I'm sure of that.' Before we reached the Ark, he stopped the car to show us the meteor. In the 1920s a rock fell from the sky and created a big hole. We looked into the hole: it was certainly big. There were some trees and bushes growing at the bottom. The rope ladder that would let you down inside was broken. The meteor was covered by a blanket of earth. Ahmet told us that scientists once came to try and protect it. 'They could not do it, so they went away again. But the fact that they came shows the importance of the meteor.' The sign above the hole claimed that it was the second-largest meteor crater in the world. The largest, it said, was in Alaska.

We returned to the car. Ahmet shouted, 'The men who found the Ark, they first came in 1985. They come every year. They have big electric instruments. They haven't built a church. But on Ararat itself there are churches.'

We were now driving away from the mountain. 'Isn't the Ark on the mountain?' I asked.

'No,' Ahmet said. So many disappointed Christians. This Ark was near the village of Uzengi, which means stirrup. The old Kurdish name for it was Masha, which means crowded. Most of the people had left by now, Ahmet said.

Schoolboy conscripts were putting up razor-wire fencing at the bottom of the mountain road that spiralled gently up to the Ark. At the top was a circular building in the style of a motorway restaurant. It was unusual because it looked brand-new, with smart large panes of glass around its circumference. The panes were dusty and unwashed, however, and the place had been abandoned. It stood on its own, on a small peak of rock, surveying the foothills of Ararat. The village itself was further up the hill, hidden behind a stone ridge.

Ahmet stopped outside this strange café-building. He walked to the edge of its small car park and pointed down into the valley. There were some ridges in the earth, covered with a thin membrane of green grass. They looked as if they marked the site of walls around an ancient tumulus, elliptical rather than circular in shape.

'The boat is three to five metres below those ridges,' Ahmet said. 'Turkey has refused to give permission to bring it out of the earth. But some research is permitted. There is an agreement with the Turkish government but I don't know exactly what it is.' The wind beat between us, flapping through the leaves of the acacia trees that had been planted around the restaurant. 'There is wood beneath the ridges,' he shouted. It did not look much like a boat: the ridges were uneven, broken in places. If it was a ship, it was not a large one.

Inside the café-folly there was an old man, Hasan, dressed in badly frayed green trousers and a brown cap who slept in a room by the door. He had a house in the village, he explained, but he stayed here, because he was paid to guard the Ark. 'This building?' he said. 'No, it is not a café. It is a museum.' There was nothing inside it at all: the floor was exposed concrete; there were no chairs. There was only his sheepskin blanket and a small gas burner for making tea. The authorities had taken everything away, even the carpets. They were concerned about the fighting. But the museum would come back when there was peace.

He was protective of the Ark. 'There are books which prove that this is a Holy Place.' He went into his room and brought back two. One was entitled *Discovered: Noah's Ark*. It was written by Ron Wyatt and published by the World Bible Society of Tennessee.

'The Turkish government officially recognizes Ron Wyatt as the archaeologist who discovered Noah's Ark,' it said on the dust-jacket. 'The government of Turkey has built a visitors' centre on the site, accessible by a four-lane highway. This centre is now open to the public.' Four-lane highway? 'The Ark of

Noah was discovered in the village of the Eight in the mountains of Ararat after a twelve-year search.' It added that during this search Wyatt was 'jailed as a spy, shot at by terrorists, beaten, robbed and persecuted'.

The other book, by David Fasold, was called *The Ark of Noah*. The blurb read: 'Heading one of the last teams allowed excavation rights in Turkey, he deduced the Ark landed not on Mt Ararat, as had been popularly thought, but on Mt Mattiser Dagi (the Doomsday Mountain), some seventeen miles south.'

Who discovered the Ark – Wyatt or Fasold? Neither credits the other. But they were both describing the same set of ridges and the same experiments. The style of their books was very different: Wyatt's a paperback and full of sensation; Fasold's a hardback and more serious-looking. Fasold wrote in his introduction: 'In the attempt to retrace our ancestors' footsteps to the door of the Ark itself, however attractive such a mission might appear, I have failed to interest the academic community at large in participating.' He said that his investigation had been met with 'ridicule and scorn'. Is this what Wyatt meant by 'persecuted'?

The old man, who had made tea, found some letters from Fasold. His book did not identify who had paid for the research. Was Fasold a missionary, like Wyatt? He signed himself: 'Ark-ologist'. His letterhead read: 'The Deluge Myth – exploring the tangible remains of the Ark and the cataclysmic event in the history of Man.' Mr Fasold was originally a sea captain and thus a 'professional colleague and ideological descendant of Noah'. A Christian? It was difficult to tell.

The old man said that Fasold was not coming to work the site this year, as in previous years, because of the fighting. He prized the books although he could not read them. He had clearly enjoyed the American's company and was proudest of the fact that Mr Fasold had dedicated his book to him. He told us that in 1985 he had been a farmer. That was when the Americans first came.

'Did they try and convert you?' Keith asked.

He stood like an old soldier. 'Praise God! I'm a Muslim.'

'Oh yes, I didn't mean . . .'

'But this is a holy place,' the old man continued, 'whether or not there is a boat on the hill. When I was a child, it used to shine like a candle, like electricity, the area around the ridges of the Ark. People said it was a treasure. And then the Americans came, a guy took a photo from the air and said that this was the Ark. He gave the news to America and then Mr Fasold and Mr Wyatt came to see it. They told us again that Noah's Ark was here. They took me by the arm and told me that I should help them. They had special instruments and they took measurements and they brought a scientist from Saudi Arabia – he came with the Koran – and they measured it. It was 164 metres long and 42 metres across. In 1989 they spent $6 million on their research and they paid me 100,000 lire a day.' The old man paused. The tea was hot and he was slurping it around his gums. He had no teeth.

'They took sonar soundings and found pieces of wood and metal below. They were so pleased with what they found that they sacrificed two sheep and gave them to us villagers.' He sat down on the floor. 'This village used to be the sea. They found very clean sand, black and white. It shone like gold and you did not need to clean this sand. In the old days the hillside used to shine in the night. But when the Americans came, it . . . stopped shining. We used to graze sheep there but they told us, "You can't put sheep there – don't make it a toilet – this is a very, very special place." Before the Americans came, we knew that there was a boat somewhere around here, because people would come and ask us if we had seen it. But we did not know that it was Noah's. We used to believe that there was a boat on the hill. The villagers would say, "The sheep have gone to the boat." The Americans say that the boat slid down the mountain after the water drained away. Thanks to God it has appeared! And now we have had the Germans with their television cameras. Look,' he said, pointing to a poster on the wall of his room by the door. It was a painting of Babar the Elephant. 'This was given to me by the Germans. When the Americans came they brought Bibles with them . . .'

He went into his room to fetch something. There was a dog yawning outside on the patio. 'They finished the work and left some fluorescent flags and some foil tape – they said they would be back this year to continue their measurements. But I am keeping it safely until they do come back. They asked me to.'

The discovery of the Ark was certainly a miracle for the village. 'The village has changed – the villagers have had this road made; the state likes the village now and they bring water to us. A bit of state benefit comes to us. Before the Ark there was not much water, and when the Ark was found then electricity was found and they made the beautiful road outside.' He pointed to the track leading up the hill past the centre. 'Now they place a lot of importance on this village. We had gas lamps before electricity. When they found the Ark in 1985, then the whole village lit up with electricity and they brought a TV transmitter,' he pointed at an aerial on a nearby hill, 'and they brought telephones as well. There are ninety houses, with 750 people, and there is a school.'

But only the visitors' centre had a metal roof. The centre cost the Turks 120 million lire to build. 'More than any other building in any of the villages roundabouts,' he said with gravity. 'But I will not let people come and sleep here. They try, but I stop them. I have my own little bedroom and I must remain here because I am an official and I give information to people.' His children were still shepherds. 'This is a poor country.'

Hasan was full of life: his eyes glowed and he was smiling. He was a very happy man. 'Lots of missionaries come to ask me questions. They bring cameras and they are very pleased and they take photographs, you see, and measurements – everybody is taking measurements – and they send us thank-you letters. But they do not try and make us Christians. They just say that it is a very special thing.'

The Turks have expressly banned the Americans – or the villagers – from removing any part of the wood or metal found in the earth from the site. Hasan was carried away by now. 'Of course we have none in the village, but the Americans come and take pieces away. It was made forbidden – even the governor sent a directive to me saying that when foreigners come they must not take anything away, and I didn't say anything. Mr Wyatt took bits of earth, some stones, and pieces of wood and iron. They filled out forms and were allowed to come, but not to take things away . . . like thieves.' He narrowed his eyes.

Ahmet said that we should leave. He was concerned about the curfew. Hasan stood by the door, smiling. 'You must give me a tip. And please come back and bring your friends.'

Ahmet insisted that we drove back over the hills. He said it was a short-cut, but I was uneasy. I did not want to become the PKK's next hostage. The villages beyond the Ark were desperate places. The earth was dry and barren. Dusty men pulled ox-carts along rocky tracks. The hills were bare and smooth, eroded of their top-soil.

'You know that Noah is supposed to have drunk wine when he came out of the Ark, and become drunk?' I said to Ahmet. 'Do they grow vines here?'

'In the time of our grandfathers there used to be trees on these hills, but there were no vines,' he replied. 'I should tell you this as well because you are my friends. But I never saw the Ark shine before the Americans came. I'd never even heard of a boat that was here before. I don't think the old man had either. I think the Americans told him to say that.' In the distance, you could hear a muezzin start calling people to prayer. 'I don't trust these people.'

We arrived back at the palace. Ahmet said, 'The palace was built by Isak Pasa. The guide-books say that he was an Ottoman, but he was a Kurd. Why did they build such a centre by the Ark? It should have been here.' We walked inside the courtyard and met a stone-mason. 'Tell them,' Ahmet said to him. 'Tell them that this is a Kurdish palace.'

17

The Road to Midyat

This war had a strange geography: it had no front nor any edges. It travelled along the roads. You might drive down a road and there it was: a tank raising its cannon, ready to fire. A mile further on there might be children playing in a field. It was beyond terrorism. The violence was continuous. It was like a jelly; the whole region quivered with it.

It was early in the day. First light spread over the endless expanse of the blue lake. It came in ribbons of colour: blue, gold and red streamers glancing off the soft water. Along the edge of the lake there was a band of deciduous forest and spiky conifers with swollen, hard fruit – harsh grey-greens; primeval colours. Elsewhere meadows touched the water: dashes of white and yellow, of flowers and flowering shrubs.

We drove past the resort cafés on the waterfront outside Van, with the chairs pushed up against the tables to keep them free from dew, and the parasols closed. We came to Tatvan, a substantial lakeside town. At the start of the settlement a foul-smelling sludge was being slowly pushed into the water through a thick, corroded pipe. Where the pipe touched the water, there was a ring of orange light. Once the lake is dead, none of the tourists will return.

We carried on towards the border with Iraq and Syria. Just outside Tatvan we came across a group of tanks clustered in tight formation across a hillside. Keith had bought a newspaper. It reported that three people had been arrested in one of the villages we had just passed for murdering the famous left-wing journalist Ugur Mumcu in a carefully plotted assassination in Ankara. Separately, the police had detained a Kurdish MP.

Bitlis was next: an ancient Kurdish town with old squat stone houses, dug into the hillside; the window arches were intricately sculpted with filigree metal screens across them. It had well-preserved cobble streets and an air of distinction, or do I mean dignity?

After Bitlis the ascent into the highlands of Kurdistan began. These great mountains stretched in every direction: sharp and angular. The road climbed the steep escarpments between them, glowing pink in the morning sun.

We returned to the plains on our approach to Batman. There were fields for miles and miles but there was nobody to be seen, just giant black machines, rocking up and down, sucking oil out of the rocks. In between were some tobacco fields. Some of the villagers had built wooden frames on which they draped the leaves to dry before rolling. They had not benefited much from the discovery of oil on their ancestral land.

Inevitably, petrol stations in Batman were out of fuel. There were few cars on the road in any case. We stopped once for petrol, but the attendant shook his head lazily. The station was on the main road, on the outskirts of the town. The next building was some distance away. Behind it was an expanse of scrubby savannah, dry and hostile.

The petrol station was also out of food and drink. It was a large garage – with a restaurant and a few shops. None of them were open. Unaccountably, however, four men, including the chef, were sitting on a step on the forecourt. Everywhere else was deserted. The men, when we walked closer, seemed exhausted and dazed. They had a small plastic urn of tea which they said was finished. They were waiting in case some customers showed up. We were customers. No food, no drink, they said. Sorry. Why didn't they all go home? They had no answer. One said he had never known things so bad. 'We are burning in a fire now,' he said, dragging on a cigarette. We drove on.

At the next checkpoint a young conscript told us that his unit had lost five men and there had been four recent fights with the PKK. These young soldiers were no match for the much better trained and equipped PKK. This man had torn trousers – you could see the flesh of each buttock through the seat of his uniform – and worn boots. He was exhausted; and he spoke with a cool recklessness about the way in which his senior officers had lied about their success against the PKK. 'The government said that sixty PKK were killed in the last fight, but I only saw eight or nine. Life for me is very difficult. I am from İzmir and I don't mind the Kurds; but I only have four months left to do and then I can return.' He was offered a pear by another driver waiting for his papers to be cleared at the checkpoint. He took it. 'I have hope,' he said. 'The terrorists are fighting for nothing because they have no country. They are fighting for nothing so in the end they must stop fighting. Is that right?'

We continued along the Tigris to Midyat, past villages of sagging mud bungalows. The floodplain of the Tigris was broad and wide. It was hot beside it, and many farmers had put their metal-framed beds on to the roof of their shacks to sleep. Armoured vehicles, bristling with heavy machine-guns, patrolled up and down the road. At Hasankeyf the tobacco was already in flower – little white clusters on vast blankets of green. There were few trees this far south. It was harsher, stony land, and dry.

Finally we arrived in Midyat. This was where we would find directions to the monastery of Mar Gabriel. It was four years since I had last been there and I had forgotten the way. Midyat was a Christian town in the midst of the Muslim Kurds, with a community of Syrian Orthodox. They were here first, of course. They were members of the first Christian church founded by St Peter at Antioch, and they continue to speak the language of Christ: Aramaic. Now their numbers are dwindling.

In Turkey, Midyat is famous for its silver jewellery. It is the Christians who are the finest local smiths. We went into one shop to ask for directions to the monastery. A boy in his teens, who was polishing a bracelet, told us which road to take.

There is nothing on the road to the monastery: no villages, no people. We were told to take a small track that branched off to the left, and we bumped along the stony driveway until we encountered smiling women with sacks on their backs, and men on tractors moving boulders to build a wall. And then on the crest of a hill, not visible from the road, was Mar Gabriel. It merged into the landscape, with its stone walls the same beige as the surrounding country. A new building of brighter orange brick stood out: this was the nuns' quarters.

At the entrance to the monastery there were tall, iron gates. We left Ali there, telling him that he should wait in Midyat for two days and then pick us up. He was angry because he wanted to come inside with us, and turned the car noisily and drove away in a puff of dust. Once through the gates, a long avenue lined with trees in tended beds led to the walls of the monastery. It was blindingly hot. By the time we reached the great doors we were sweating and thirsty.

18

The Monks

The door was ajar. We walked through it and up the sandstone stairs, blinding in this light, towards the Archbishop's quarters. To the right were the school buildings where the local Syriani children were taught to speak their language, and beneath them the church. Outside the door of the Archbishop's rooms, on the veranda, stood Issa. Picture a fisherman confident of calm seas.

I recalled the gentle atmosphere here. Issa remembered me, but only dimly. He stood talking with a guest, taking tea. He was not a monk: he had a wife and family. But he was a theologian and a teacher permanently employed at Mar Gabriel. He was cool when we arrived. He did not ask us anything; he did not say anything. He just looked at us, and continued to talk to his guest. His eyes were hard. With his open-necked shirt and pressed slacks, he looked like a well-to-do trader.

Issa was assessing the threat we presented to the monastery. The Turks are quietly trying to oppress the Syriani out of existence, to make their lives as intolerable as they can, and they will seize on any chance to brand this ancient community a threat to the stability of the state. As Christians, they are always under suspicion. Issa was alert to the danger of strangers. He was the watchman. He knew the world better than the others and he protected them.

We sat for a while with him on the wall of the veranda, just introducing ourselves, trying to win his confidence. He said little, and he did not smile. He had a fine head of ash hair and strong, handsome features. Would he rather have been a monk? He seemed bitter about something.

The sun had dipped a little, and a cool breeze snaked across the balcony. Then the Archbishop emerged from his rooms, swinging the tassels of his red smock, with a broad grin. Archbishop Timotheus Samuel Actas was an entertainer. He was tall and well-built – his smock was taut around his belly. He had a full beard which he stroked while he talked. He walked with the gait of an old soldier, abruptly changing course with angular precision. He was never still: stomping, getting up, sitting down. His mood was equally erratic: hot and cold, laughing and then cynical. Under his smock he wore a pair of thick red socks stuffed inside a pair of black leather moccasins. Football socks. 'Football is the only thing,' he said, by the door to his quarters, while he tied his shoelaces. 'But I have hurt my finger.' He came towards us without any greeting or acknowledgement and sat down next to us on a chair, lifting his smock up so that he could cross his legs, revealing a smart suit underneath. He scratched his ear, then tied a knot in his tassles, and asked for tea.

We were talking about Noah's Ark with Issa. Like the Muslims, the Syriani maintain that the Ark is on Cudi, not Ararat. The Archbishop said, 'The Catholics know nothing of this land. Don't you see, the Ark is not on Ararat . . .' He seemed, in a way, rather mad. His conversation stopped and started. The meaning of what he said was often obscure. He might appear angry when he was offering praise; or sad when happy.

Issa was a scholar. 'The name of Cudi itself comes from Noah's Ark, and the word "Kurd" derives from Cudi. Cardho – this means the people of Noah. That was the original Aramaic name for the mountain. That is the origin of the word Kurd. In other words, the Kurds are the people of Noah.'

He insisted that there was considerable proof that the Ark had indeed finished its journey on the Cudi mountain, which is south of the monastery, and not on Ararat. When Noah stepped from the Ark, he founded a village which was called the Eight. There was such a village – it was called Temseth – close to Cudi. Temseth was Syriani, Issa added. But now it was Kurdish.

The Archbishop snorted his disapproval, then carefully inserted an index finger up his nose and excavated.

Issa seemed more relaxed now. He smiled for the first time. He said that priests were allowed to marry once; but monks could not. He had trained in Lebanon and then returned to Midyat, where he was born. He was a deacon.

Mar Gabriel is the only working Syriani monastery left in Turkey. The Muslims have destroyed a number of the church's centres: Dar Ul Zafaran in nearby Mardin was closed because the local authorities claimed the monks were brainwashing children in the church school. Most of the clergy have fled to Europe and North America. The local villagers have gone as well. Their oppression has been cruel and efficient. The Archbishop's seat at Mar Gabriel has survived because it has powerful friends in the West. The British Ambassador always made an annual visit, to remind the Turks of their own secular constitution which guarantees religious freedom.

But the war was making the position of those Syriani who remained difficult: the army suspected them of assisting the PKK; the Kurds distrusted them as Christian fifth-columnists. There were still twenty churches in the region open when we arrived. That means that the doors could be opened. The number of Syriani villagers, by then, numbered no more than 2,000.

In the school of Mar Gabriel the local children were taught Aramaic. Some lived permanently on the premises. Their parents hoped that a decent education would give them a headstart in life. All of them had to go to the local Turkish school as well and they were made to study the Koran. The monks are allowed to teach the children Aramaic informally, but it is illegal for them to publish literature in the language.

We moved into the Archbishop's waiting-room, a simple reception room with pew benches on either side. There were tiles on the floor and a large concave ceiling. The Archbishop sat on a pew, his legs curled beneath his smock, leaning forward rather like a bird preparing to fly. He was looking out of the window. There was a monk beside him wearing a black skull cap with thirteen crosses picked out in white around the edge, denoting Christ and the apostles.

'Many of our priests are farmers,' said Issa.

'Many theologians are dry statues,' said the Archbishop. 'A sign of the times.' And then he fell quiet again, staring into the textureless blue sky. He seemed very bored. Issa ignored him.

I was curious about the impact of the war. Did the soldiers harass the monks? Or the PKK?

'The PKK respects the monastery and keeps away,' he said. Nothing about the army. 'Ah yes, when they need us they come, then they stone us,' he added.

An old green telephone on the small coffee table by the window rang. It was a startling sound inside these cool stone walls. There was a small padlock on the dial. The Archbishop took a key from his trouser pocket. A diplomat from the Dutch Embassy was calling. 'A letter, yes . . .' he said. 'Yes, I remember. Of course I remember . . . I applied for visas, yes . . . we planned to leave the area. Your government promised us asylum . . . we would have closed the churches. Abandoned the place . . . do we still want to leave?' He looked around. Issa was surprised. Clearly he did not know of the Archbishop's plan. 'We have decided to stay.' You could hear the diplomat at the other end asking him why he had changed his mind: had the situation improved? The Archbishop held the receiver up, so that the whole room could hear him, and then, with the man still talking, he hung up.

There was silence. Then he shuffled his smock and said, 'I wanted to know we have visas just in case.' They were that close to giving up. It was a shock. 'If we left, we would never come back. In fact I was due to attend a meeting in Istanbul but did not because I was worried at what they might do to the church.' He became intensely serious. 'The army is burning villages and hundreds of people are leaving. In January five Syriani were killed in one incident, and then two others later. We are being drawn in.'

There was an Englishman living in the monastery, studying Aramaic, a trainee Anglican priest called Andrew. He came into the room just as the others were leaving. It was nearly time for evensong and they wanted to make ready. Andrew said that the situation for the monks was grave. 'A ransom was paid yesterday,' he said. 'A local teacher was released by the PKK after seven months. The Syrians are seen as rich and so they become targets for kidnap. Within three years they will all have gone except those who want to die in the villages.'

The Archbishop came back into the room and said, 'Why are we not allowed to publish, when the Kurds are free? And our children, who are forced to learn the Koran in their schools? We will all have gone soon, and they will have won.'

A Syrian family from Damascus had arrived. They came into the reception room and kissed the hand of the Archbishop, who did not stand up but remained curled up in the corner of one of the pews. The man was carrying a package, a loosely wrapped bundle, tied with a ribbon bow. They meant to give it to an old friend, a local villager. They had come a long way to give him this present. After their introduction, they asked the Archbishop how they could find the man.

'He left long ago,' he said, looking out of the window. 'I am sorry.'

The villager had left for Germany with his family. The couple sat down. The man turned to Keith: 'Are you also Syrians?'

'No,' Keith replied in Arabic.

The man, who was smartly dressed in a suit and polished shoes, complained about the journey. His wife said that they would go home. They had hoped to spend a holiday with their old friends.

A boy came round with dishes of sliced watermelon, a delicate shade of rosy pink and molten with water, and cake. We picked at these without a thought. Keith was the first to break the silence, turning to talk to one of the monks about the spelling of Aramaic. The Archbishop stirred and laughed. 'You are the race of Sheikh Zubeyir . . .'

The Syrians laughed. A layman called Johannes put his head round the door to inquire about the joke, and he laughed too.

He was visiting his son, who was a pupil at the school. His son was called Ohan. 'That is his name in our language,' he said. 'But on his identity card it says Orhan because he must have a Turkish name. That is the law.'

Outside on the balcony, sitting on a metal chair, was a local villager who helped with odd jobs at the monastery. This man had family in Germany. He said that he wanted to go there but he did not have enough money. 'The Turks have sweet tongues but they stick it into you,' he said. He hated them. 'In 1914 my grandfather was killed by the Turks.' He was talking quietly. 'No, it's not good but it's normal. In the time of the Armenians those who were opposed to the state rose up and then Ataturk decreed that the Armenians, Syriani and Greeks should be shot. I am reluctant to say this but I will say it and please don't tell anybody. We are not allowed to talk. I am unhappy to say these things.

'Before 1914 an English plane landed in our village – all of us were Christians. There was no police station. When the pilot landed everybody ran and said, "Oh English! Oh English!" We took the plane back to Iraq. After that the government got news of this and became very angry and took a lot of money from us. I say this but I am very frightened. It's very hard to live.'

He said his village was paying protection money to the PKK. He was terrified. It had grown dark and he was just a silhouette on the terrace. 'Please don't say I told you this. The army will burn us.' He was smoking and he gave me a cigarette; in the light of the match I could see that they were Chesterfields.

Inside, the Archbishop called out. He had found some letters about the Ark and he wanted us to see them. There was one from something called the Ancient World Foundation Looking For the Ark. 'I find these people amusing,' he said. That was a crushing word: amusing. The letter came from PO Box 3118, Pinedale, California 93650. Looking through the window, the world outside was black. Not shady like an urban night. Black. I thought of Pinedale, California. Urban planning and leisure parks, amenities and drive-in cinemas.

The Archbishop said: 'I am full of doubt. I sometimes doubt

that men have humanity.' He despised the New World evangelists. He threw the letter at me:

'Greeting to you, my esteemed Christian brother. And thank you for your prompt letter of reply. In the Providence of Almighty God our Saviour Jesus I hope to discover at Mount Cudi a significant evidence of our father Noah that will not only validate the historicity of Genesis 1: 11 but also serve as a signal of the approaching second coming of our Lord within the lifetimes of men now alive. This enterprise is not only an effort for biblical archaeology but also with the covert intent to strengthen the church of the East and convert the Turks. You will be interested to know that in Germany the Turkish Christian community has increased in the last ten years over 2,000% . . .'

'What they will find up Cudi,' the Archbishop said, 'is the PKK.' If the Turks had found that letter they would have closed the monastery – covert intent? Convert the Turks? Keith and I were horrified.

The letter, which was long, said that the archaeologists intended to come in the summer – a 'tiger team', as they were described – to look over the mountain. 'These crazy Americans,' said the Archbishop. They proposed to bring underground radar, a cavern-balloon system, metal detectors and satellite photos. 'I would also like to hire some of your non-smoking young men as porters for our team's equipment.' His church had marvellous music, he wrote, and he suggested that the local people might enjoy the 'interaction'. It was signed: Charles D Willis MD, neuropsychiatrist.

We woke at 5.30. The sky was the colour of stone, so that you could not make out the steps down to the church. The boys were in white cassocks with red and gold cloth bands tied across their bodies in the shape of the cross. They gathered in clusters around two podiums on either side of the altar. One of the brothers stood between them: he was wearing a red and silver cape; a weighty man of religion. The Archbishop sat on a chair by the altar, fidgeting.

The boys sang a moaning, imprecise chorus of the Psalms

which was lighter and more fragile than a lament. They were singing in Syriac, a strain of Aramaic. The youngest children lolled, with their hands in their pockets while they chanted. The notes floated into the great white concave space of the ceiling. The church was large, and simple: a cave of shadows. It was much the same as it was when it was built in AD 397. Ceremonies are always beautiful. They are the moments when history pricks through into the present.

The boys flanked the brother as he consecrated the bread, waving incense and holding candles. The smoke trails made the place seem larger: huge, bleached, with flaking plaster and carpets hung on the wall showing some of the saints, etched in silver thread. Above the altar there was no crucifix, but there was the symbol of a cross. Later, the Archbishop said he did not know why there was no crucifix: 'Everybody is different.'

The nuns went up for the bread last, hidden under long black shawls. They sat in alcoves at the back of the church, behind the men. Andrew, the English trainee priest stood with the children around the podium, reading rather than singing the text of the psalms. It was a difficult language: he had been here for some time and he still did not know the hymns. He must have been envious of the children's unthinking familiarity with this music.

Then it stopped. The boys and the monks started filing out of the church, kissing the silver-slabbed Bible, and we went for breakfast: olives, tomatoes and bread in the canteen on the floor below the Archbishop's rooms. He seemed in a good mood and was serving all the boys. Then we returned to the reception room. Issa was giving some lessons to a young pupil. He stopped when we came in. 'Look,' he said. 'I will find the reference to the Ark.' He flicked through a copy of the Peshitta, the Assyrian Bible.

'Now it is written that on the seventeenth day of the month, the Ark stopped on the mountains of Cardo,' he read. 'Genesis Chapter 9 Verse 4. The Ark had three floors: one for people; one for birds; and one for animals. In Arabic, Cardo is Cudi.' That was the original Bible. The first Bible. The Jews translated it into Hebrew. Their version was then translated into Greek and Latin. Those versions are the ones on which modern editions are based. Where did Ararat come from? A mistake in the translation? A whole civilization brought up with the wrong mountain?

The Archbishop was reclining on a bench. 'Bad translation. That is the history of the world. A bad translation.' He paused, then asked, 'Now, what do you think about birth control? You see, I really don't know. I really don't know. So yes, yes, what do you think? Nobody listens to the Church any more. But they should not do it. I mean, use these contraceptives. And women priests. Shame on them!' He raised his hand when I tried to answer, and shook his head. 'You see, we are a monophysite faith. You know what this means? It means that Jesus was fully God and fully man at the same time.'

Issa had gone off to get some old texts relating to Noah. 'We are the guardians of all the local history,' he said. 'The Kurds cannot read or write. They do not know – only we do.'

Andrew came in. He was leaving for Syria that morning to continue his studies. The Archbishop fished a roll of notes out of his pocket and gave them to him. 'Look, your Anglican church once bought us a tractor. Take it and go.' He would be gone for ten days. 'Maybe we will have gone when he gets back,' the Archbishop said, smiling.

Issa returned with a stack of Bibles. There in the Arabic translation: Ararat. The English edition: Ararat. They did not have the Hebrew version. The Archbishop was growing angrier and angrier. He had other papers from the library: the story of St Eugene, hand-written on a piece of old manuscript. Eugene brought monasticism to Turkey from Egypt. His monastery was founded near Nusaybin. He visited Cudi and he baptized all the villagers.

The Archbishop was still looking at the Bibles. 'They thought it was the highest mountain in eastern Turkey, so they said Ararat, but they were wrong. Translators! We are the oldest Christians in the world.' He was full of puff, like a bird of exotic plumage.

Issa took no notice of him and went on reading from the

manuscript. 'St Jacob thought to go to where the Ark landed on the mountains of Cardo to pray there. When he arrived at the skirts, the angel of the Lord led him to the Ark, then he prayed and passed several days there. He was asking in his prayer that the Lord should show him relics and give him a board. He found a plank and he took it with great happiness. Then he thought to build a church where the Ark landed. He took part of the plank and he made a cross of the plank.' He then built a large monastery on the mountain. The ruins of that monastery are said to be near the village of Hasana, two or three hours from Mar Gabriel. The PKK was said to have set up a camp nearby.

The monastery had a serious academic purpose. Brother Saliba, who was sitting in a corner of the room, was in charge. He was younger than the other monks and was preparing a new edition of the *Peshitta*, a great undertaking for a young scholar. He offered to teach Keith the Aramaic alphabet, and the two of them sat, sucking on sweet melon and reciting the grammar, while the Archbishop stared out of his window.

I walked outside. It was a cool morning. Behind the Archbishop's quarters were the gardens. Every kind of vegetable was grown here: watermelons, lying like footballs on the soil, salad greens, onions, potatoes, all in formal, precise arrangements. The melons were laid in hexagonal shapes, as if the gardeners were setting – or solving – some mathematical puzzle. The gardeners were the nuns, who were toiling away, plucking at the ground like crows in thick black cotton skirts. The earth was red: it had been brought many miles to this stony hill. Is this what the Archbishop was looking at through the window? Remembering how he had brought this garden to life? The hills all around were bearded with gorse. Nothing grew on them. Below the garden were the ruined stone walls of gardens from much earlier generations: rubbled now, evidence of the trauma through which this community had lived in history.

Saliba had offered to show Keith and me around. I met them walking back through the gardens. He took us to the crypt.

There were marble graves of holy men: dead archbishops were buried upright, sitting upon their thrones, Saliba told us. Just inside the entrance to the crypt there was the tomb of an Egyptian merchant. Saliba said, 'He was a great merchant who had a friend in the monastery. He loaned 1,000 gold dinars to the monks and then he came back and his friend had died. The merchant said, "Where is my money?" The monk who died had a student. The merchant beat the student: "Where is my money?" It was in the time of the holy St Gabriel and he was Archbishop then. He said, "Did you hit the boy?" and the merchant said, "Where is my money?" The Archbishop said, "Let's ask Johannes." This was the name of the dead man. So Gabriel came here and he spoke into the grave of the monk, asking, "Are you a clean monk? What happened to the 1,000 dinars?" Then there was a voice from the grave: "The gold is where we left it."

'The merchant didn't believe this. So they opened the grave and they could see the lips were moving; and after that the merchant became a Christian and he stayed in the monastery. "I'm not going to go from the place where the living can speak to the dead," he said. He was very rich and he had 800 retainers with him. He sent the gold and the soldiers back to Egypt but he kept his servants. This Egyptian took the name Johanna. It was in the seventh or eighth century.' His retainers were buried in a tomb in the garden.

Twelve thousand people were buried in this crypt. Two saints, Gabriel and Samuel, were buried under the floor. Samuel was the founder of the monastery. Saliba led us out across the courtyard which was now white under the eye of the sun. He took us into the church. 'There was a woman called Sifne who had two sons and they went from Urfa to Istanbul and one of them learned architecture. He came back here and they built this church. Our law states that the monastery has to be completely isolated. So they built it out here in the wilderness.' The bell was ringing now for evensong. The sun cast a pale yellow light through the cloisters, a warm glow.

Afterwards the boys ran around the quadrangle next to their

dormitories. The guest rooms were opposite. Below were the showers. Some had come from abroad to live here and learn Aramaic, but most were local. Generally, it gives them a chance. Some have graduated from here and become engineers, doctors and journalists. Saliba was strangely proud when he told us this.

The Archbishop and Issa walked out of the church and through the front gate into the tree-lined avenue that leads to the outside world. It was dusk, and birds sang across the parched landscape.

I said to the Archbishop, 'I think this is beautiful.'

He replied, 'It would be beautiful if it were in England.' The sun was setting across the vegetable gardens and Johannes plucked us two baby cucumbers, which were crisp and succulent.

The Archbishop kicked the ground as he walked. His head was bowed. He looked out across Kurdistan: a vast tundra of rocky hills. The desolation, which must have been the attraction to the first monks, remained intact. But the Archbishop was exasperated, muttering about how everybody had left. The nuns ferried armfuls of maize into the monastery to prepare the food. The gates were of sandstone, and the portals had a simple motif: the links of a heavy chain running up each side. These were delicate, simple symbols.

A local Syriani was standing with us – his family lived near the Cudi mountain. 'Do you know that even in the sixth century, when this was a young church, there were more than 400 monks here? It was a big university.' He waved to a lay workman who was making his way home. 'Very few come looking for the Ark in these parts now. That letter he showed you is the first for a long time.' Now it was sunset and we all walked back inside the monastery. He locked and padlocked the gates. Big, heavy iron keys. He learned his English from the visitors who used to come to the monastery.

Once inside, he said, 'I know Andrew told you about the teacher who was kidnapped and ransomed. He was wrong about one thing. It was not the PKK. It was the government. This is all about making the Syriani leave. We are rich and the others want our land.' He had a good watch on his wrist, cased in silver. He was not a poor man. He knew the risks he was taking.

We returned to the reception room. The sky had closed in. The Archbishop produced the letter again. I noticed the letter-head: 'Gospel Projects in Granite'. It quoted a verse from the New Testament: 'He did not spare the ancient world, but preserved Noah, a herald of righteousness with seven other persons, when he brought a flood upon the world of the ungodly.'

It was time for dinner. We ate a humble, nutritious meal in the canteen, a simple room with solid tables and benches. The monks sat at the high table and the boys served them. They had meat on Saturday, but today it was a stodgy bubble and squeak. Afterwards the Archbishop went to his rooms to watch the evening news on the only television in the monastery. He thoroughly enjoyed the news. Every night he watched and scoffed at the politicians, howled at the stupidity of the rhetoric, sighed at the escalating violence in the south-east. He invited us to watch it with him, and at the end, he laughed. 'The prime minister said her party was best and everybody should be happy. That was the news. Now it is time to sleep. So goodnight!'

As we left his rooms, I mentioned to him that we hoped to visit Cudi. 'I was told that there is a priest in one of the villages,' I said.

'Yes,' he replied, 'there are many priests there. PKK priests.'

Ali was waiting for us beyond the gates. He stood silently by his taxi while we slung our bags into the boot. He looked at us but said nothing.

'He wants to see the monastery,' Keith said. 'The Archbishop won't mind, I'm sure.'

Ali did not understand what Keith had said because it was in English. But he clearly had an inkling. 'I feel that at least I deserve the opportunity to meet the Christians,' he said.

We took him inside and showed him the church. The Arch-bishop followed us on our way back towards the car. As we approached the monastery doors, he shouted, 'You should be paying that driver a good deal more than you pay him now. I hope you pay his hotel bills.' He said that in Turkish so that the driver could hear what he said, and he smiled. He walked outside with us and sat on the wall opposite, plucking fruit off a tree and peeling the skin back. 'Yes,' he said. 'I hope you are paying him for his hotels.' Inside the fruit, there were thousands of tiny seedlings. He poured them into his hand and then threw them high into the wind.

We knew by now that it was the Archbishop who had planted the vegetable garden on the other side. He had reclaimed the land and brought soil to make it fertile. Before he came to the monastery, it was dying. One or two old monks lived in broken-down quarters but most of the monastery was uninhabited and uninhabitable. The Archbishop is proud of the gardens and the trees. He brought the monastery back to life. He raised the money to restore the buildings and build a new roof for the church and new quarters for the nuns. He re-established the reputation of Mar Gabriel as a centre for Aramaic scholarship. Without him this monastery would have been abandoned long ago. It was a monument to his life.

19

The Devil Worshippers

The sun was behind us when we left the monastery. We continued along the road to the south for a mile or two, and then, to our left, we saw the village. The Archbishop had said, 'They are godless people.' But they were persecuted as much as the Christians. He had some sympathy for them. 'You should not go.' He was serious. 'The army will be watching you. They will think you are their friends and they will shoot you. They are suspected.'

This was Kiwak, the village of the Yezidi, survivors of an obscure medieval cult, which worships the fallen angel, Lucifer. Muslims frighten their children with stories of the Yezidi: how they defile their women, execute ritual murders, eat their children. I was told once that they 'dance in darkness at the New Year and then have sex indiscriminately' and, by another man, that they 'shoot dead anybody who uses the word Satan in their presence'. He claimed that their women did not have underwear.

The Yezidi were once a substantial Church. They numbered as many as a million, spread throughout the Middle East with satellite congregations across the Indian Ocean and into the Far East. They believe, like Christians, that Satan was the fallen angel. But they also believe that he was restored to grace and forgiven by God, and that he can intercede with God on behalf of sinners. Satan was unique among the angels – he had wisdom. He knew both good and evil. He became God's chief lieutenant. They worship the rising and setting of the sun, and the moon, in his honour. Their icon is a peacock, which symbolizes Satan. The Muslims call them Devil worshippers but this is not true.

The Yezidis believe that there is no Devil. They deny the existence of Hell.

The Church – the only Kurdish religion – today has its headquarters near Dohuk in northern Iraq. The shrine of Sheikh Adi, a twelfth-century mystic who is the prophet of their faith, is there, guarded by one of the east's only surviving eunuchs. It is there, too, that the sacred books, the Black Book and the Book of Cilve, are kept, and the Kavval, the itinerant preachers who travel around the communities, trained. There are still around 150,000 worshippers of the Peacock Angel in the Middle East. There used to be a large population in south-eastern Turkey but it is now almost extinct. The language is banned; visiting preachers are no longer able to visit the villages. The Yezidi are the victims of deliberate institutional prejudice.

Four years ago, when I last visited Kiwak, there were only a few people living in the village, which is modestly sized, neither rich nor poor, with finely proportioned, sturdy stone houses built into the sides of a steep crescent hillside. There were only five families, a handful of old men, and one or two teenagers working the ploughs across the rough soil, all anxious to leave the area and find proper work. All anxious to leave Turkey. The others had, by one means or another, been able to emigrate to Germany.

One young man I met showed me his identity card – there was an 'X' in the box marked religion. He wanted to study political science at university, but no Turkish university will admit a Yezidi. 'For being a Kurd and a Yezidi I am an outcast,' he said. 'What can I do? To survive in Turkey I have to deny that I am either.'

We sat in the house of one of the older men who laughed at all the gossip among the Muslims. He said his people did have a few traditions, but none of them involved sex or murder. For example, they did not eat lettuce or haricot beans, or the cock, out of respect to the Peacock Angel. They did not wear blue. They did not marry non-Yezidi. Until recently, he said, they wore white robes and did not trim their moustaches. 'We decided that we had enough problems as it was, without drawing more attention to ourselves.' So they started to cut their whiskers.

They were being harassed because they were Yezidi, but one furrowed brow after another revealed that nobody in this village had any clear idea about the doctrine of their religion. Nobody could remember the last time one of the preachers had come. They just did what they thought was right. Shortly before we left, a few of the old men walked in a brisk, informal procession towards the cemetery on the edge of the village. They passed through the tiny gate and started to kiss the strange conical tombs. Hands clasped, they turned towards the setting sun and chanted: 'Peacock Angel! Peacock Angel!'

I could remember the old man sitting cross-legged on the floor describing a representation of the Peacock Angel that was kept in Iraq. 'It is tall,' he said, 'and made of gold in all kinds of colours, with gemstones pressed all around its edges. I have not seen it myself, but my father's father did see it.' He laughed, and so did the other villagers.

That house was now rubble: the Turkish artillery had blown off its roof and ripped out its walls. It was up a small slope from the road: through the demolished wall, you could see the sitting-room and the kitchen. Small items of clothing were blowing through the hole. Indecency. The Turks had raped the place, it was deserted. I suppose I had expected that.

Above the village there was a Turkish radar station – maybe there were people watching us. There was debris everywhere, in tidy piles inside houses, on roofs, on the road: some clothes, clogged with filth, lay by the side of the track, an indication of how long it had been since Kiwak was abandoned and looted. Or perhaps the villagers had escaped with their possessions. Whatever, there was a feeling that something monstrous had happened here, as if there had been an atrocity.

Ali was nervous: doors had been forced open and windows smashed. There was a bit of army webbing here, and a torn curtain there. There were bullet-holes in strange places: in clusters on the back walls of houses. Firing squads? Flies were picking over the small piles of rubble near these walls. Ali was worried about the radar station. We could see people milling about up there. We were very easy targets.

He agreed to stop briefly by the graveyard. It was an exceptional place, with its pointed tombs. There were two of these, simple shrines. On one it said: 'The shrine was erected in honour of the founder of the Yezidi religion, who visited here, Memir Muaviye'. And on another: 'Made in 1966 in the year of King Sehsemsedin'. It was very poor Turkish, barely intelligible. Keith said, 'Something bad has happened here. I just don't know why they do it, the bloody Turks. And what an ancient culture, just destroyed, just like that.'

The cone graves were enclosed by stone walls covered by a carefully woven mat of small sticks and twigs. The grass on the ground was parched and yellow, and the place was a mess: more abandoned clothes, cans and saucepans lay discarded beside the graves. By the gate entrance there was a broken torch which seemed to have been trodden underfoot by a heavy pair of boots. In the middle of the cemetery there was a fig tree.

'The difference is that they don't have the British government interested,' said Keith, who was looking at some of the humbler graves with small square headstones. Ali was scrutinizing one of the shrines. He said, 'I cannot understand why there is nobody here – this place is big and beautiful.'

Then we left. We stopped at the first village we passed. Did anybody know what had happened at Kiwak? A boy standing by a barrow of fruit told Ali in Kurdish, 'The army attacked it. But I think most of the villagers had been able to leave. I don't know exactly.' The boy looked into the car and pointed at Keith. 'He should be careful. He should tighten his seat-belt. It will save his life.' Keith asked him if there were any other Yezidi in the area, and he gave us directions to another village.

It was an hour or so away and much poorer than Kiwak, on the side of a rolling hill, up a long and treacherous dirt road near Midyat. We stopped at a petrol station to check directions. The pump attendant said he thought all the villagers had left.

It was empty out there: apart from a few trees beside the track, there was no other shelter as far as the eye could see: the land baked under the sun. The soil was only good for growing watermelons. A tractor passed us, with a couple of boys on it. One of them had a plastic bag on the back of his head. The clothes they wore were torn, no more than rags.

We drove as far as we could into the village, where the track stopped. We asked two old women, straining under enormous loads of firewood, if this was the village of the Yezidi, and they looked at us with great suspicion. Their worn faces, coloured with henna which had cracked like plaster, crinkled with alarm. But then Keith said, 'Melek Tavus', Peacock Angel, and they smiled and put down their burdens. They came to the car, put their heads through the windows and kissed our hands. 'Thank you, thank you,' they kept repeating in very broken Turkish. 'Please will you take us away.' Their eyes were full of tears.

We asked if we could see the headman of the village, and they pointed us towards a mud house further down the hill, which had a roof of matted twigs. Still they were saying, 'Thank you.' The headman was not at home but others came to greet us: old men and women. Young people were notable by their absence. There were children's bicycles outside one or two of the houses, but no sign or sound of children, indeed there was no sound at all as we walked through the village.

Those who had come to the headman's house seemed subdued and led us inside without saying a word. They sat with us on the floor and waited for us to speak. Finally an old man, the headman, came in and asked us what we would like to drink. 'We can drink coffee if you like,' he said. His Turkish was very slight and intoned with a penetrating whistle because he had few teeth and none at the front of his mouth. There was a small plastic bag hanging on a hook on the wall at the back of the room, and in this bag there were four of five dusty sachets of Nescafé and a small tin of powdered milk. The labels were in German. The women were not used to making this drink, and they used one sachet between three of four cups, so that it was the water you could taste, syrupy and polluted. They brought us some metal plates with clusters of unwashed grapes. Then Keith asked them in slow, simple Turkish how long the Yezidi had been in this village.

'Three thousand years,' replied one man with matted red hair protruding beneath his cap. 'There were eight villages, but now we are the only ones left. And the young have all left. It is just us now.'

Another man interrupted him. 'It is very hard for us here, they put a lot of pressure on us. The soldiers come and they insult us.'

Keith leaned across to me, across a worn cushion on the floor and said, 'God, this is deprivation.' He meant that specifically: it was not just poverty, it was deprivation. These people lived a wretched existence: there was virtually no water and infrequent electricity. Even in the poorest villages, the locals had a fridge between them, but not here. There was no school or doctor. They lived like refugees. The place smelt like a refugee camp: the rising stench of shit, animals and sweet-wood fires. Anatolian villages are famous for their cleanliness: hygiene is a sign of self-regard. But here it was filthy, everything was unclean: the cups and the plates, the floor, the clothes. The blue wash on the walls of the living-room was splotched with mould. How different this was to Kiwak as it used to be: spruce and pukka.

The room suddenly exploded into conversation. There were a dozen elderly people and, at the back, a young girl. It was not possible to make out a single voice with any clarity. I was not sure what language they were speaking. It was a kind of pidgin Turkish. They had been so isolated for so long.

'What is a Yezidi?' Keith asked.

'Our faith is in Iraq,' the red-haired man replied, shouting at the rest of the room to be quiet. 'Sheikh Ismail is in Iraq.' It was not Ismail, he meant, but Adi. 'In the morning and in the evening we worship the sun. There is no special place, we just stop where we are and raise our hands to the light. That's the way of our religion. The Peacock Angel.'

An old woman sitting in the room, who had henna painted on to her face so that she looked rusty, shouted at the man, 'Pah!

We don't understand anything in our religion. But we don't worship Satan. The Muslims say we do but we have no idea of this.'

The room erupted into noise again. The red-haired man, whose name was Issa, shouted again for silence. 'The Peacock Angel is the one who takes life and gives life.'

'Ah yes,' rebuked the old woman, 'but he does not give us any money. We get our money from Germany' – she turned to us – 'otherwise we would die. The people here pick watermelons and try to sell them in Midyat.'

'When I was a child,' the red-haired man replied, 'there was no school but the teachers would come from Iraq. Now we have no teachers, so how can we know anything?' He glared at her. 'You know, we believe in God, and we live in the Great Republic of Turkey, but still we know nothing. Three years ago a *hoca* from Iraq came with a passport and he stayed for a week and then he went.'

This caused a lot of dispute. 'No,' said the old woman. 'There has been no one for fifty years.'

Issa's children had gone to Germany. 'So they are able to send you money?' said Keith.

Issa looked at him. 'I don't know where they are. I write but I don't know how to write. There are telephone numbers, but there is no telephone here. And we do not know if they are right.'

There had been a change in atmosphere in the last few moments: another man had come into the room and was pointing at us and whispering to the others. All eyes were trained on us, critically. The man went up to Issa and spoke quietly into his ear.

'I have to say that there has been no Yezidi religion in this village for maybe five or ten years,' Issa said. 'People have stopped praying to the sun. They used to stand up and face the sun, but this has stopped now. When somebody dies we wash them and then we bury them.'

The young girl in the corner was helping to serve the grapes. 'Why has she not gone with the others?' I asked Issa.

'She has not been to school yet. We need her to work here.'

They were growing suspicious of us. 'We love the Turks,' said one man. Everybody followed him and said, 'Yes, yes.'

On the wall was a calendar which featured a large portrait of Ataturk. It was more than a decade out of date: 1982. I asked Issa if I might see his identity card and this provoked a flurry of concerned glances. It had an 'X' by religion.

'This is unfair, isn't it?' I said.

'We do have religion – we just don't have anyone who will look after us. There are 150 villages in Iraq that are Yezidi and nobody is treated like us.'

Keith asked again how they practised their religion, and Issa was frightened to talk about it. 'We follow it but do not do anything else. We think about God when we look at the sun. God protects us. God is in us.'

The old woman said that they had planned to abandon the village and move to Midyat. But they could not leave because the town would not have them. Issa was angry. 'The village guards are against us; the people in the shops in Midyat hate us. The army comes here and does a lot of things and they make life difficult.' But it was the Kurdish village guards who frightened them most: they had guns, and no law. 'They come and they beat people and they steal and they curse. It is they who have no religion. They come and they take things from us – we had a tape-recorder but this was taken.'

Issa invited us to see the graveyard. We walked down the hill with him. There was a stream that ran through the middle of the village, but it was dry. It was growing late, and the sun was dark red, misshapen like a blister, casting long septic yellow streaks across the village. 'This is dangerous,' Issa confided. Each night these hills swarmed with Turkish commandos. 'They will shoot you if they see you.' The cemetery was very simple; straight rocks marked each grave. There were no conical shrines.

We returned to the car with Issa. He said he did not want to leave for Europe. 'We must do what we can here. None of us will leave here. Our children have gone and they do not want us. But it is good they have gone.'

A man driving two mules past the car stopped to talk to us.

He was much younger than the rest, in his thirties. He spoke German and good Turkish. A dirty toddler, the first we had seen, was hanging on to one of his ankles.

We asked him, 'So what is the truth?'

'The religion survives. The old people are frightened to talk of it. The older men may be worried to tell you much because they may believe that you are agents of the fundamentalists. The villagers continue to observe the annual nine-day fast in the eleventh month.' He said he lived for a while in Germany but his eight children were not allowed to travel with him, so he came back. He had some wealth, he said. He opened his mouth to reveal four gold teeth.

'For nine years the *hoca* has not been to the village, so we have stopped regular prayer – how can he come here when we are being raided every day? Let me tell you another truth: about the end of our culture. I cannot send my children to school because if they go to Midyat they will be killed.' He sliced his hand across his throat. 'Why? Because they are Yezidi.'

'Do you know your religion?' Keith asks.

'Of course. We can know it but it is forbidden to write it.'

'And what about the Kurds?'

'Before the system of the village guards, we Kurds were all friends. Now this village is totally apart from Midyat. You can see that there are no signs on the road; that there is no police station; and there are few trees.' He lifted the little boy on to his shoulders and smiled. 'There is no shelter here from the sun.'

By now it was growing dangerously dark, close to the hour when the Turks and the Kurds renewed their war. We drove back to Midyat. The army convoys were already on the move, and the soldiers were resuming their places in the machine-gun nests.

20

The Last Ark

Midyat was closing down. It was an hour before the curfew. We went straight to the jeweller's shop, and asked the Syriani boy there, who was smoking Marlboro cigarettes with his friends, to take us to his priest. We hoped he would be able to help us find accommodation. The boys said that there were no hotels open in Midyat. Nobody stayed the night. Ali had found a hotel to stay in while we were in the monastery but he said it was suitable only for animals.

The boy led us into the old quarter of the town, which was a maze of small, well-built stone houses with high walls, clustered around a number of churches. It seemed prosperous: the small pillared steeples had survived centuries of intolerance and looked like tiny sentry boxes on the skyline. The minarets were in the other direction: there was no mixing. Children were peeping out of the doors, but otherwise the street was deserted. The sandstone made it warm, but the emptiness was unnerving.

We arrived in the courtyard in front of the main church which was like a jewel, and entirely unexpected: a proud cathedral with simple whitewashed walls. A group of men sat in the courtyard. They noted our arrival with obvious concern. One stood up. His face was drawn and he rolled up his sleeves.

'Hello!' we said.

'Why are you here?' he replied.

'We had hoped to see the priest,' I explained.

The man said nothing. His hostility was shocking mainly because it was so surprising. By now some of the other men had stood up too and were standing behind us.

'Who are you?' I asked.

'I am the deacon.'

'Well, we have just been with the Archbishop. He was a very kind host.'

'You should have stayed with him. Why did you not stay with him?'

We walked into the church.

'Surely we are allowed to see the church?'

He said nothing.

'What is the problem here? We are not your enemies.'

The church was beautiful: gold chandeliers, an altar lined with velvet. The candelabra were of silver, and the frescoes layered with gold. A small red light hung over the altar. It was a well-loved place. We sat down on a long pew at the back.

The deacon was agitated. 'The BBC came here and they came with the police. There were police and police in here.' He wore a chain with a tiny portrait of the Virgin Mary mounted on a gold charm around his neck. 'They were being followed. The police said we were making propaganda. They nearly closed the church. Please will you leave.'

Was there anyone following us? We could not be certain.

The deacon then told us that the church was 103 years old and dedicated to St Bartholomew. He said there was only one priest left in Midyat, and only this church was still open. All the other priests had fled to Europe.

At the back of the church was a notice: 'Love Those Who Hate You'. The deacon paced around the pews, and then the priest arrived wearing a black suit and tie; and a small black Homburg on his head. He was unshaven. We walked out into the yard towards him. He looked at the deacon who stood with his arms tightly folded across his chest by the entrance to the church, and walked away from us.

'Can you ask him if he would talk to us?' I said to the deacon.

'Why did you not ask all your questions in the monastery? We cannot answer questions. You know why? You know why? Because a man's life is worth no more than a bird's. A small thing can cost a life.' He looked at Ali, who was standing at the entrance to the courtyard. 'Your driver knows very well,' he said. 'We can help someone to show you things, but not someone to answer.'

We left, but where would we stay? It was evening now, and we had to keep off the street. This was downtown Midyat: a famous battleground. Ali drove us to his hotel which was bug-ridden and humming with sweet water mosquitoes. He said that he had even been bitten in the hand.

The place was on the first floor above a kebab shop. There were two eager boys, no more than ten, behind the reception desk. We were the only guests. The sheets in our room had been slept in several times since they were last washed. It was, however, a religious hotel. Behind reception some posters announced: 'The Government Belongs to God'; 'What have you done for God today?'

Since we could not leave, we asked the boys to buy us some beer. It was OK, they said. The owner was not coming tonight. They brought some newspapers as well. The government was embroiled in yet another corruption scandal. So too was the Opposition. Eighty-two Kurds had died in fighting the day before in the region of Ararat.

One of the boys stood behind us while we read the papers. 'There is fighting here every day,' he said. He laughed. 'I am going home now, so anyone can come and burn down the hotel.' Just the three of us were left now. It was very quiet outside, nothing was moving. Once or twice we heard a rumble in the distance – a convoy, we thought. Ali was asleep by the time we had finished the beer. He was perfect grazing for mosquitoes: he had not pulled a sheet across his belly.

We did not get much sleep. There was fighting nearby. In the small hours I woke to see Keith perched on a window-sill, drawing open the curtains, watching another armoured convoy pass through. Later, a minibus stopped outside the hotel and a dozen Kurds climbed out, carrying machine-guns. Ali was awake, and all three of us peered silently out of the window. You could see the stern, drawn faces of the Kurds in the orange light of the street-lamps. But there was no shooting. I started to itch. The mosquitoes had been busy: there were small white swellings on my hands, my feet, and my head.

The next morning we started out for Cudi. 'Please, you should be discreet when you go to Hasana,' the Archbishop had told us at the monastery. 'Do not let anyone know of your intention. I am concerned for the safety of the villagers.'

We passed through the provinces of Siirt and Sirnak where some of the bloodiest of the fighting had occurred. Siirt was the site of one of the worst atrocities of the war. Hundreds of corpses had allegedly been dumped in the town's refuse tip. It was said that these were the bodies of Kurdish civilians who had been detained by the army and killed during their interrogation. The rubbish dump was called the Butcher's River by locals. The local authorities excavated a small amount of debris and found six bodies. The digging was then stopped on the orders of the regional governor.

Mass graves had been reported at Sirnak as well. A local MP had called for an investigation into allegations that as many as forty people were buried in waste ground near the local military headquarters. On the hills outside Sirnak wisps of smoke were rising where villages were burning.

We reached Cizre, on the banks of the Tigris, the last town before the Syrian border. Here the river was broad, and the floodplains stretched for miles. Through the mist in the distance the mountains, still capped in snow, were a deep crimson in this early light.

Cizre was a trucking town, full of tyre and mechanic shops. The place stank of oil and the pavements were thick with grease. This was the first stopover in Turkey along the Silk Road. All the lorries passed through. But that day the road was almost deserted. The war had stopped the traffic. There had been killings: executions in the high street; assassinations on the roads leading into town; car bombs. We drove around looking for somewhere to have breakfast. The grand hotel on the main square was virtually empty. It had been closed temporarily, the manager said, because of the fighting. The windows were still full of bullet-holes. They had stuck packing-tape across them to keep the draughts out.

We drove on towards the mountains, and as the day became hotter and the mist started to clear, the wisps of smoke rising from the foothills of Cudi became thick, dirty brown columns. The plains were planted with cotton. It was in flower: delicate pink blossoms. Noah would not have known cotton. The Ottomans imported it into the Middle East from China.

We followed a track across the plain towards one of the pillars of smoke. It was a little way up the mountain. Keith and I both worried that the army had already reached Hasana. The track was bad, bomb-rutted. Ali drove carefully between the deep tank treads. Everybody was quiet, concentrating. We passed some villages. There were Kurds dressed in traditional boiler-suits, and long-haired goats pecked in the mud for food. The huts were made of sticks and mud. The men did not smile at us. They looked at us with deep bitterness. This was not a game, they seemed to say.

Hasana was further down the track, over a small hill. When we arrived, it seemed like a dream: jumbled solid stone houses huddled around a small labyrinth of paths. There was a stone canal for fresh water. Cocks strutted between the houses. There were fruit trees and vines. People smiled at the car. They were clearly pleased to see us. It was a wonder and quite unexpected. We had only twenty minutes. To drive back to a town that was safe for Europeans would take six hours and we had to be there by dusk.

We were taken by the villagers to the priest's house, which was at the other end of the village. It was a small house, carved out of the rockside, with pretty little curtains on the small, uneven window-frames, and brightly painted furniture – green wardrobes and red tables. There was a small veranda from which you could see deep into the mountains, into rich green of the trees and shrubs. This was a cottage from mythology.

The priest was out, we were told. But we were invited to wait, and did so, full of excitement and joy. That is what I felt most: joy. This place provoked delight; delight that it was here at all, and that it flourished. Ali was surprised that there was no signpost for the village and that there were no soldiers or policemen here. There was nobody official here at all. I thought that the village had been abandoned to its fate. It was no-man's-land.

It was all the more shocking, then, to come across a young Aryan man on the veranda. With his blond hair and blue eyes he was obviously European: I guessed German, but he said he was Austrian. Beyond this he said nothing. Human rights activist? Journalist? Who cares. He was lying low, waiting to make his way up the mountain to make contact with the PKK. Perhaps he would be the next 'hostage'. He had a rucksack and climbing boots. What an idiot! What an idiot to put this village in such danger. If the army discovered him, it would burn the village. He backed away from us.

Another young man, a Syriani, came into the room. He said in English that he was a tourist guide but had come to visit his family in the village. We told him that we were interested in the Noah's Ark up the hill.

He looked at us and said, 'The search for the Ark is very difficult. It is very dangerous. The PKK are living in the Ark.'

'Are they really living *in* the Ark?' I asked.

'Yes. In the Ark.'

'So there really is an Ark up there?'

'Yes.'

'Have you seen it?'

'No, but it is there. We have come across some pieces of wood. There is a monument to the king of Assyria in the foothills – Nebuchadnezzar – showing that this was once a great mountain, and part of a great civilization.'

The villagers were neither pro-PKK nor pro-army; they took no sides. But both sides put them under pressure. The PKK sometimes came to the village for food and forage. The soldiers, explained the young man, were too frightened to come into Hasana as they used to. The barrack block at the entrance to the village had been destroyed by the PKK in recent fighting. In the distance you could hear rifle fire, but the man said that there had been no attack on the village for the last few weeks.

They had refused to be village guards for the government; they had refused to give succour to the PKK. They tried to walk down the middle of the conflict.

Hasana is one of the oldest Christian settlements in the Middle East. It was Syriani until, in the nineteenth century, European missionaries started to arrive. Protestants and Catholics descended to convert the already Christian villagers. Our young guide said, 'They were full of cowardice to prey on the Syriani . . .' A passing goatsherd interrupted him: 'Quiet, boy! We are grateful that we are Catholics.'

The missionaries brought prayer books, and they built churches. In Hasana there were three churches: the Syrian, the Protestant and the Catholic. The Protestant and the Catholic congregations had long since lost their priests; only the Syrian remained, and now all villagers prayed in his church, regardless of doctrinal allegiances. Of the thirty-two families in the village, twelve were Protestant and two were Catholic. But they were closely knit and they all spoke the same language: Assyrian.

The Protestant church was built in 1873: there was a clean courtyard outside and inside wooden pews, on a sloping stone floor, and a painting of the Last Supper on the wall. The walls were clean, with a thin green wash. The pews were all at odds; it had been some years since they had last seated a congregation.

One of the villagers opened the door from time to time with a great iron key, to check that the children had not been playing inside. Few of the village children attended school. They were afraid to go to the school in the local town because of threats from local Muslims. They were regarded as rebels. There was no classroom in the village and the hospital closed two years ago. Turkey really had abandoned Hasana.

Inside the Church the altar – a table covered with a green cloth – was laid. The Bible on the top was open at the page announcing that the Ark landed on Ararat.

Keith talked to a number of villagers gathered in the church courtyard about the Ark. They were divided in their views.

'Some say the Ark is on Cudi, and others in Ararat,' said one shepherd.

'I know nothing about the Ark,' said another. 'I've been up there a lot but never to the place of Noah's Ark. I don't know anything about pieces of wood.' All the others assembled shooed him away, smiling as he went.

'An Australian archaeologist went up there,' explained another man. 'He said that it was there, and the old people, they say it is there. I've heard it down the years, you see.' His brother had been the Protestant village priest, but he had gone to Holland. 'My brother told me that according to the gospel it can't be here – it must be on Ararat because Ararat is the higher mountain. But I'm afraid this is not true, and he is mistaken.'

Another of the Protestants said, 'You know, I can't remember when I became a Protestant – my grandfather I think was the first. But my first language is Syriani and I think of myself as an Assyrian. Having said that, no one in the village has seen either a piece of the Ark or the whole of it.'

Many foreign visitors came to Hasana, they told us, to search for the Ark. 'But we don't go up the mountain because we only have the time to think about our economic problems,' said one man. 'We rely on the vegetables and the pomegranates. We make our own clothes but we cannot sell our food or our clothes any more. We can sell a suit but nobody buys any more.' Not everybody suffered in the same way, however: I noticed a fairly new remote-control television in the priest's cottage.

'Has the priest been to see the Ark?' I asked.

'No.' And all the villagers laughed. 'The only people who see the Ark now are the people who go to the PKK. But you see, they are not looking for it,' said the young guide.

Another young man arrived. 'Now look,' he addressed the whole crowd, 'there are some who believe the Ark is on Cudi, but it is on Ararat. You see, it has to be on a high place. I went up there recently and I didn't see anything – it's flat, there's a flat top – and I didn't see any wood. I was up there a while. We should ask the PKK if they have seen anything.'

We reached the Syrian church, which was small and had a low ceiling. A piece of velvet was strung across the altar, like a curtain. The young guide said that he was desperate to go to Europe, and that he would go. 'We find it so hard to get by because the Kurds are in charge of this area. We are frightened. If we fall out, they would destroy us.'

I asked him, 'You know this Austrian in the priest's house . . . why is he here?'

'I think he is here to meet the PKK. There is nothing we can do to stop him.'

'It is very sad.'

'Yes, and dangerous . . . I know the dangers. They will kill us. The Christians have no choice, believe me.' He had a young, immature face.

We had no more time: the villagers wanted to give us fruit; they plucked peaches and apricots and grapes and insisted that we take them. Just as we stepped into the car, the young guide said, 'You know, the Australian archaeologist did prove that the Ark was on Cudi . . .' The crowd of villagers waved.

We passed the bombed-out school house as we left. As we descended, we took in the view: the Tigris curling across the floodplain, like a ribbon. At this distance everything was brown; by now – mid-morning – the sun was burning everything into a dull, uniform, dirt-brown. Behind us Hasana was flanked by green; and the further we drove, the taller the column of smoke rising behind grew. We had forgotten to ask the villagers about the smoke. Was this the Ark going up in flames? Ali said it could have been the PKK or the army – they both burned villages. He had been depressed by his experience in Hasana. 'I feel badly that the PKK would endanger the lives of the people in that village. They are good people and they will die. Do you know something? I have never met a Christian like these ones before.' He did not say anything for a long time after that.

Several weeks later, browsing through a newspaper in London, I noticed this small report on the foreign pages. It filled me with great sadness. So much has happened in Turkey, so many good things. But all that seemed suddenly to have no weight.

The report, a dispatch from Reuters in Ankara, was dated 3 December 1993 and read as follows:

> Turkish authorities drove 200 Christians from a village in south-eastern Turkey. Residents said state-paid village guards detained and tortured seven Christian shepherds, using molten plastic to brand one of their victims with a cross. They said 32 Syriac Christian families, the entire 200-strong population of Hasana village, in Mardin province, were forced to leave their homes. The authorities thought they were Armenian sympathizers or Kurdish PKK guerrillas.

We are back to burning. Turkey is setting light to itself.